BOLLYWOOD BADDIES

BOLLYWOOD BADDIES

*Villains, Vamps, and Henchmen
in Hindi Cinema*

Tapan K. Ghosh

SAGE   www.sagepublications.com
Los Angeles • London • New Delhi • Singapore • Washington DC

First published in 2013 by

 SAGE Publications India Pvt Ltd
B1/I-1 Mohan Cooperative Industrial Area
Mathura Road, New Delhi 110 044, India
www.sagepub.in

SAGE Publications Inc
2455 Teller Road
Thousand Oaks, California 91320, USA

SAGE Publications Ltd
1 Oliver's Yard, 55 City Road
London EC1Y 1SP, United Kingdom

SAGE Publications Asia-Pacific Pte Ltd
33 Pekin Street
#02-01 Far East Square
Singapore 048763

Published by Vivek Mehra for SAGE Publications India Pvt Ltd, typeset in 10.5/12pt Adobe Caslon Pro by Diligent Typesetter, Delhi, and printed at Saurabh Printers Pvt. Ltd., New Delhi.

Library of Congress Cataloging-in-Publication Data

Ghosh, Tapan Kumar, (Professor)
  Bollywood baddies: villains, vamps, and henchmen in Hindi cinema/Tapan K. Ghosh.
      pages cm
  Includes bibliographical references.
  1. Villains in motion pictures. 2. Femmes fatales in motion pictures. 3. Motion pictures—India—History—20th century. I. Title.
PN1995.9.V47G56   791.43'652—dc23   2013   2012049738

ISBN: 978-81-321-1097-2 (PB)

The SAGE Team: Shambhu Sahu, Shreya Chakraborti, Rajib Chatterjee, and Rajinder Kaur

To those who have played baddies over the decades

Thank you for choosing a SAGE product! If you have any comment, observation or feedback, I would like to personally hear from you. Please write to me at contactceo@sagepub.in

—Vivek Mehra, Managing Director and CEO,
SAGE Publications India Pvt Ltd, New Delhi

Bulk Sales

SAGE India offers special discounts for purchase of books in bulk. We also make available special imprints and excerpts from our books on demand.

For orders and enquiries, write to us at

Marketing Department
SAGE Publications India Pvt Ltd
B1/I-1, Mohan Cooperative Industrial Area
Mathura Road, Post Bag 7
New Delhi 110044, India
E-mail us at marketing@sagepub.in

Get to know more about SAGE, be invited to SAGE events, get on our mailing list. Write today to marketing@sagepub.in

This book is also available as an e-book.

Contents

Foreword

I am delighted to know that a full-length study on Bollywood villains has been attempted here, analyzing the frames in detail in which many of my worthy colleagues and myself appeared and mouthed the familiar lines over a long span of time. It is also a pleasure to see that even the henchmen who have added to the villains' empire and the vamps who contributed to the pride of villains have also been carefully studied in this book.

In this connection I remember *Kati Patang*, where I played Kailash, the bad guy. Kailash was a member of the society, a man rather common but with dimensions; unlike some fictional characters, like Mogambo, for example. Even down the seventies I was once again the bad corrupt boss in *Kala Patthar*, taking advantage by following a divide-and-rule policy among workers. Gradually, the villains turned out to be so fascinating that the heroes started playing negative roles, possibly trying to understand how someone becomes a bad guy. This has been a noticeable feature in the development of villains in Bollywood cinema, something that has been looked into in this book, making many other insightful observations.

I have been privileged to continue till now, and in this context I remember some of my colleagues who have departed from the scene. I was a college-mate of Amrish Puri, who was four years my senior. I love to think how these people would have been glad to see and read a book like this that has been dedicated to the baddies. In *Dostana*, Amrish Puri was my henchman, and it was great to share the stage with him. This too has been examined in this study.

"The web of our life is of a mingled yarn, good and ill together," wrote Shakespeare. True, beyond doubt. Human life justifies the experience, and Bollywood films have always shown this. Written in a witty and friendly style, this book recognizes this unique contribution made by Bollywood cinema.

I recommend the book for the viewers and readers of all kinds, and wish it a success.

Prem Chopra

Preface

*L*ong back, sometime during the nineties, the idea to write a story on the villains in Bollywood cinema first took its origin in my mind—rather nebulously, to be honest. I wrote to Shyam Benegal, seeking his advice on the subject. I had the privilege of getting introduced to him at Dubrajpur, a town in West Bengal, where the distinguished director (also a man of exemplary candor and cordiality) was shooting his film *Arohan* (1983). Mr Benegal encouraged me and spoke, among other things, on the traditional battle between the good and the bad that worked as a basic source of inspiration behind the Bollywood-entertainment parlor through the decades. In the early eighties, I was working on a film based on caste issues, and had sent the prologue and synopsis of the proposed film to Shyam Benegal. He felt it would make "a good film," provided the idea was dramatized through a "well-organized script without over-simplifying the issues."

However, the proposed film didn't take off due to this author's pressing academic engagement and other reasons. Possibly as compensation, I made a documentary—*Under the Sky*—in 1991, immediately after finishing my four-year term as a jury member on the Central Board of Film Certification. Events were happening pretty fast in the country. Political rivalries took precedence over national problems. The sociopolitical scenario was shadowed by a pall of gloom, like the early dawns in *Parinda* (1989), a Vidhu Vinod Chopra film. The film shows smuggling rivalry on a gruesome scale. Kabutar Khana, a well-known crossroads near Mumbai's Dadar railway station, unfailingly bawled out by bus conductors and used by pedestrians more than a hundred times a day, becomes a center of activity in *Parinda*. Prices of commodities soar as checkmating of politicians increases. A hungry boy watches the pigeons eating grains inside the sprawling net-wire at *kabutarkhana* that shows a murder later in the film.

The suffocating dawns of *Parinda* suggested that days feared the strangling menace of nights, making the sun look pale and overpowered by a waning moon. Something in the rule of nature had gone wrong because of a complete reversal of values on earth.

This was, then, the situation. Deepa Gahlot, writing in 2001, says that "corrupt politicians, sadistic cops, remorseless rapists, gangsters, hitmen, extortionists—these villains proliferated in the 1990s, both in real life and in films."[1]

Mere citations cannot suggest the range of indebtedness to previous writers in the field. Articles occasionally wrote about Bollywood baddies and vamps in their own ways. At least, the subject has been on air since the turn of the century. This gave credence to what this author was thinking in the early nineties. The present story of villains, henchmen, and vamps, along with some minor characters—the role of the editor, for example, in *Mr. India* (1987)—had to be a straightforward account for the sake of popular readership, especially those who contributed over the decades to this unbelievable phenomenon of mega entertainment even in the context of world cinema. In that sense, this book can be considered to be as much a tribute to the villains as it is to these viewers, who unfailingly lined up for purchasing tickets from the booking counter in theater halls all over the country. They came out with their stomachs full, whistling the popular numbers, or singing the tunes, some still shaken by the awful baddies they had seen a while before. It has been a real bonanza, dear readers. This is why the notes provided at the end look a bit emaciated compared to some other books on cinema. The room on the table is filled up with delicious items made with the help of countless visuals, each studied from a different perspective.

The subject, therefore, was considered important, and enough to capture popular imagination and readership, providing a two-and-a-half or full three-hour entertainment. Can the viewers of *Kismet* (1955), *Do Bigha Zamin* (1953), *Mother India* (1957), *Jaal* (1986), *China Town* (1974), *An Evening in Paris* (1967), *Sholay* (1975), *Karma* (1986), *Karan Arjun* (1995), *Om Shanti Om* (2007), *Agneepath* (2012), and so on be hooked again like they were in the theater halls in the form of written words in their drawing rooms, on trains, or on planes? After all, the great Bimal Roy, Mehboob Khan, S. Ali Raza, Sachin Bhowmik, Hrishikesh Mukherjee, Salim–Javed, and others of their ilk did it first on paper with written words. Any visual, after all, has its genesis in the mind. What if the films were taken into account from beginning to end, recreating the spectacle visually and imaginatively? The author got to the task, a daunting one, no doubt. While writing, it was found that the previous directorial effort on paper, however tentative and short-lived, yielded results, providing insights into the visuals; details, in particular. Not all grapes are sour.

How is Pran walking into the frame in *Madhumati* (1958), or how does he return to his fold in Raj Kapoor's *Jis Desh Mein Ganga Behti Hai* (1960)? What is M. B. Shetty doing on the deck of the ship in *Night in London* (1967)? What is the ever-boisterous Tun Tun doing in Kishore Sahu's *Dil Apna Aur Preet Parai* (1960) or down the valley in *Bluff Master* (1963)? What does Sharat Saxena's funny way of crawling up to his trusted hunter mean in *Mr. India*? Who is the bitterly anguished schoolteacher in *Nishant* (1975) aiming at when he throws a stone in the air? How does the wicked subedar in *Mirch Masala* (1987) chase Son Bai or what does the priest in the crowd assembled at the masala factory say? Why does Anupam Kher, another versatile actor of Bollywood cinema, adjust his spectacles in *Karma*? These and such others turned out to be the questions for the sake of pure entertainment, for understanding the villain's mode of operation and yes, for enlightenment too. This scintillating Bollywood show, remember, has a subtext in it—a film within a film—shooting off a layer of suggestions. This is why the actors essaying villains in Hindi cinema have been given a separate treatment in this book. If Hamlet, in Shakespeare's famous play, felt that the world was "out of joint," and that he'd catch the conscience of the murderous king by staging a play within the play, enacting the events, then it might also be profitable to look at Bollywood baddies from a fresh perspective to catch the conscience of our heroes, who have always hogged the headlines of newspapers in this land of hero worship. This could remind one of how the country, still plagued by scam and corruption, was progressing under political leadership in the seventies, eighties, and nineties. This generation of movie-goers may not know much about the social–political scenario of the past and many actors and actresses of bygone days.

Needless to say, this kind of a viewer's approach to Bollywood baddies began not to prove anything. The films are already there, along with brilliant fringe works. But, during work, a whole lot of possibilities emerged, making one aware that these things do indeed add to the entertainment package. This is possibly another glitzy aspect of Bollywood cinema, maybe cinema in general. Kancha's father in *Agneepath* (2012), for example, is shoved off down the stairs. He's an addition to this film's awesome show, like the other additions. But, this one adds to Kancha's uncompromising and over-the-top villainy shown in the film. Mithun fans might have been irked to hear before the release of the film that the character of Krishnan Iyer MA of the 1990 film was done away with in the new version. The end product, however, shows that the filmmaker was justified. We have discussed this in the book.

It was rewarding, for example, to note that the villains were a bit unjustifiably intimidated by the rebirth impasse of heroes and heroines right through the fifties till the present century. Look alikes, giving them at least 30 confused seconds before they have the faintest idea about what's going on, have kept the villains tantalizingly wary. But, they soon spring into action, solving the puzzle. This is in addition to the fact that the villains are on many occasions challenged by criminal heroes, some sentenced for life-term imprisonment. Finally, the villains are thrashed, biting the dust, according to the trend of the decade; though the heroes, facing a grim challenge, hardly ever snuff it. The fierce battle, raising uproar in the elements as it does in *Agneepath* (2012), leave everyone stunned, and they remain glued to their seats till the end or till the titles slide up on the screen.

Villains are the unsung heroes of Bollywood cinema, just in case the notion of heroism is extended to imply everything that is both moral and immoral, virtue and vice spun together. What virtuous action, after all, was taken by the hero in *Agneepath* (2012) in wiping off Mazhar Lala, Rauf Lala's elder son, and later Shantaram? Of course, he had his agenda. Everyone has. The web of our life is like that of a mingled yarn, good and ill together—so wrote the Elizabethan bard.

Right through the seventies and the decades that followed, the heroes became restless and wary in choosing their paths. The problem of making a choice mounted as the decades rolled on and as the overall scenario in the country went downhill. It wasn't a special feature of the mid-nineties alone. This should set us thinking differently about the so-called disappearance of the baddies in the last decade of the previous century.

This, along with others, forms the subject of this narrative. Divided into three parts, this story of baddies, their henchmen, and the vamps have been scripted to provide entertainment, just as Bollywood films have done over the decades.

Can we "write good angel on the devil's horn?" That's possibly a good question to ask, philosophically and aesthetically, because it lies at the root of human experience on earth.

It's time now to raise the curtain.

Note

1. Deepa Gahlot, "Villains and Vamps," in *Bollywood Popular Indian Cinema*, ed. L. M. Joshi (Piccadilly, London: Dakini Books Ltd, 2001), 252–97, 211–12.

Acknowledgments

I am deeply indebted to my predecessors who have written on Bollywood baddies and vamps in the form of articles over the decades. Some of these have been recorded in the notes and references at the end of the chapters. Those not mentioned have also encouraged me, working as a source of inspiration in my mind.

I do recognize the interest shown by Prem Chopra for looking into the pages of this book at his residence and writing a foreword that clearly shows how he looks at this study of villains, vamps, and henchmen.

I admire the prompt help of Sri Swapan Nath of Chitrangan, Sonarpur, Kolkata, in handing over to me the VCDs and the odd DVDs of both old and new films, many of which I initially thought might not be available. To my surprise they were, and some were borrowed on rent by the local film buffs. Chitrangan has an enviable collection, and among other reasons, I felt proud to be a Sonarpur-ean in the far south of Kolkata. Long live, Swapan!

But, no word of acknowledgment is enough to express my debt to Shambhu Sahu, Assistant Commissioning Editor, SAGE Publications, for keeping me continually egged on to the task and giving his valued opinions on some areas of this narrative. Thank you, Shambhu!

I'm grateful to Shreya Chakraborti, Editor, SAGE Publications, for bearing with me in making the last minute changes, and yet bringing everything to perfection. What a team she handles! They all speak highly of the SAGE management, encouraging an author to work more frequently with this publishing house. A great experience!

Finally, I recognize the help of Foara Ghosh, my daughter, in playing better with the trickeries and worries issued occasionally by my PC. She says I am by nature apoplectic. Maybe, threatened as I have been by the Bollywood baddies!

Mitali, my wife, untiringly supplied me with the odd cups of tea from morning till night. I'm sorry for not being able to remember the numbers.

Part I

KNOWING the BADDIES

1

Who Are These Villains?

"*Mogambo khush hua...*"

Everyone remembers this grandiose and legendary refrain of Mogambo in Shekhar Kapoor's *Mr. India*, as if it was heard yesterday, blurted by a terrorist baddie out to destroy Hindustan. Toward the end of the film, Mr India, alias Arun Verma, breaks into Mogambo's den, much like Vijay had done years back in the film *Zanjeer* (1973). Arun says, "*Mogambo aaj main tumse Mr. India ban kar nahin, balki ek aam hindustani ke roop mein ladunga ... isliye ke tumhaare liye ek hindustani hi kaafi hai*" ("Mogambo, I'll fight with you today not as Mr. India, but as an ordinary man, since a common Indian is enough to take you on").

Mogambo is delighted, like he always is, especially in moments of crisis. Like weapons, he has an enviable cache of rhetoric. So, he retorts differently this time: "*Toh phir main iss aam aadmi ko keede ki tarah masal doonga.*" "*Keede ki tarah*"—as outrageous as the "*khush hua*" refrain. Only, this sounds more bold and assertive, concealing the unavoidable comical touch of the previous refrain. Both are spoken by a menacing villain hiding in his technological paradise in the changed scenario of the mid-eighties.

If one tracks back to include the viewers in the dark theater, one watches the audience in the light bouncing off the screen. Everyone is glued to their seat. Even as they hear the rhetorical battle, the audience fidget anxiously; some scrabbling about for the half-finished packet of peanuts as the violent duel is likely to last for quite some time. After all, it is a battle to save Hindustan from the evil Mogambo. The result is well known and anticipated, much to the pleasure of the audience, but posing an obvious disadvantage for the villain. In many other similar instances where the villain uses the heroine as a shield—in *Karan Arjun*, for example—the truculent hero becomes calm when the terror-stricken girl, now free from danger, runs to him and finds herself happily bound to his bosom. Music and dance follow to signal the happy end. All's well that ends well. In *Mr. India*, Arun, Seema, the children, and Calendar, all are saved while Mogambo dies, entrapped miserably in his den.

This could be the end of any Bollywood commercial, and the grand show goes on repeating itself like the cycle of seasons, with minor deviations here and there. Still, it cannot be denied that everyone feels relieved after the show, having received his money's worth. This is a reality that no amount of intellectual spoon bending can deny. Yet, few of us have tried to understand what makes one enjoy the show again and again, like a schoolboy gaping at a sprite, doing impossible feats.

What has not been noticed in this scenario is the unique position of the villain—his ungrudging contribution to the grandiloquent finale, the sacrifice he makes, and the humiliation he endures for ensuring the so-called "poetic justice." Yet, the villain is not to be discounted in anyway; he too has a major share in the narrative, having a towering presence on the screen and a whole battery of tricks up his sleeve. If the romantic pair captivates the hearts of millions with songs penned, tuned, and choreographed beautifully against scintillating valleys and streams, within the country and abroad, the villain engages our attention with his intimidating presence and peals of laughter. The audience gets involved in the story and is kept on tenterhooks about the possible end, though with a little foreknowledge. Therefore, the villain contributes substantially to the commercial prospect of the story. His presence adds to the charisma of the hero and his flamboyant activities, though the villain has to accept in the bargain a moribund fate for himself. The question here is not one of probability or any lack of credibility for we have responded to the "formula" with unerring promptness over the years, feeling a bit peckish, like a child that enjoys every bite of the nut offered to him.

The villains presented in Bollywood cinema both prior to Independence and after offer a valuable case study for identifying the social, economic, and political faces of India as the country progressed over the decades. If the country stuttered in the thirties and forties, the villains did much the same. Running in tandem with the nation that tried to articulate her voice since the Independence, the villains gradually broke their shackles, and looked far more aggressive and authentic as the decades rolled on. Bollywood films have from the beginning shown an awareness of what was happening within the country. This probably explains its overwhelming popularity among the masses. The present narrative tells the story of the use of villains by Bollywood filmmakers in different decades, keeping in view the changes brought in by the sociocultural scenario. This in itself is engrossing, and the kaleidoscopic presentation has the features of *drama* in it, an intense exhibition of spectacular and thrilling actions that have kept the audience enthralled over the years.

During the fifties, sixties, and early seventies, politics was not an epiphenomenon. The state was not considered an agent of the ruling class. Author Rajni Kothari speaks not only about the "distortions in the policies and in the functioning of the system since 1965," but also relates them to the "mistakes committed during the period before 1965."[1] The bourgeois as well as the landed gentry were fragmented even in the fifties. Still, people believed that the state was going to be a provider, ensuring liberation from social inequity. This faith in the state was gradually lost, and there has been since then a massive erosion of the idea. This book takes the feature into account and relates it to the changes it brought in the operation of villains in the seventies and the eighties. Within the fifties, down the decade in particular, there was a feeling of discontent about the implementation of the policies of Nehru's socialist agenda. The sixties witnessed changes in social hierarchy, making it difficult for people to accept traditional values. This was also the time of the uprising of backward classes. The opposition parties in politics were gaining strength, questioning the Congress hegemony which was reeling with discontent. This led to the division of the Congress party down the sixties, and again, later also. This has been discussed in the relevant section of this book, showing how the villains during the sixties started operating from cities, a feature that signaled emphatically the villain's location shifting from the rural to the urban.

For now, it's necessary to identify the villain. Who is he, and where does he reign? The simple answer is that the presence of the villain is ubiquitous. Still, most often he operates from within the mind—the deep turbid well, where things are deposited. That's why the essence of villainy is unpredictable. Gradually and imperceptibly, the deposits within us assume strength and thump on us in the most unlikely moments, like they did when Macbeth, Shakespeare's villain–hero, met the witches on the heath. Thus, the bad forces started working when Macbeth was ready for it. Bollywood uses the concept of the antihero in the famous "Dev noir" films of the early sixties. Shah Rukh Khan takes it over in the nineties, as if completing a cycle. This has been discussed in the relevant chapter of this book.

So, if we acknowledge the good forces, we must also the evil ones, a rule that forms an integral part of the strategy of creation. Thus, villains and villainy lie at the root of human nature, forcing us to guard ourselves against their sly imperceptible attack, like we often are to viral diseases. One redeeming feature of the troubled scenario is that our instinctive knowledge of the good and the bad helps us in identifying the sinister forces around us. A little while after this we have discussed the rich tradition of our mythology—the two great epics, in particular—and related them to some specific scenes of the films. Bollywood has always fallen back on this tradition, and the audience-response to it so far has been outstanding.

Let us explain how, since childhood, we become endowed with an intuitive awareness of the good and the bad, irrespective of the country and its culture. While reading or watching the popular story of "Snow White and the Seven Dwarfs," *no one* needs to be told that the stepmother is *wicked*, hatching schemes to ruin the peace of the little girl. Yet, the knowledge dawns on the viewer, allowing him to empathize with the miserable victim as she passes through her ordeal. In the story of *Thakurmar Jhuli* (*Grandma's Bag of Stories*), a collection of fairy tales, once very popular in Bengal, one hardly needs to be told that the stepmother, who sends the girl to the old woman weaving her loom at the center of the moon, is wicked, as stepmothers usually are. Bollywood films have used this popular ire against the stepmother in the film *Beta* (1992). Aruna Irani plays the deceitful mother, killing her stepson with feigned kindness. Suryakumari plays the avenging lover Raj Rani in *Uran Khatola* (1955), thwarting the love interest of Dilip Kumar and Nimmi. The role of the villain in such cases passes from the male to the female. This justifies a separate chapter on "Villains as Vamps" in this book. In the story of Prahlada, an *asura*, but a devotee of

Vishnu, Prahlada goes through a series of tortures inflicted on him by his wicked father, a hater of Vishnu. Curiously, one establishes empathy with the son, though both are *asuras*. Prahlada is good; his father is bad. One may recall that *Bhakta Prahlada* was the first sound film in Telegu and was released in 1931, the year when *Alam Ara*, reckoned to be the first Indian talkie, was released on March 14 at the Majestic Theater in Bombay. We'll come back later to this film.

So, the villain is one whom we want to see punished in a story. Still, he should be there, brandishing his sword and challenging the hero. If the villain is not there, the story fails to hold our attention, and loses much of its charm. The presence of the villain in a story brings out the qualities of the well-meaning charismatic hero, his inner strength, and self-belief to go through the ordeals put before him. If the villain is weak and effeminate, indulging in thoughtless carousals and luxuries, the image of the hero gets tarnished. Any easy encounter between the villain and the hero turns out to be a mere bagatelle. The heroine who looks for the exploits of the hero, whom she adores, may have second thoughts before spending the rest of her life with a gullible fellow. That would be disastrous.

The stronger the villain, the more charismatic becomes the image of the hero. It wouldn't be blasphemous to say that the hero receives a considerable mantle of the villain when the latter falls down, releasing some parts of his vigor. One cannot be sure if the invisible translucent process has anything to do with the duel when the two are engaged with physical confrontations.

The larger-than-life image of many villains during the seventies and eighties of Bollywood cinema has stunned viewers. As a continuation of this phenomenon, the *gazal* singer in the film *Sarfarosh* (1999) impresses even when he perishes. Satan and the fallen angels in Milton's *Paradise Lost* have captivated the imagination of critics and readers. Bollywood cinema, following this pristine tradition, has shown many powerful villains on the screen.

While understanding the villain or empathizing with anyone in a story, the viewer/reader experiences a kind of self-projection necessary in the enjoyment of every art form. Some sort of projection into characters, villains as well as heroes, enviable and pitiable alike, guides the readers as they go on sucking the pleasure. The reader or viewer begins with a hypothesis of his own, something he can later empathize

7

with. When he sees his expectation ignored, at least not the way he'd anticipated, he proceeds no further and closes the book with a thud or turns off the television, flipping to some other channels. In films, especially the commercial ones, such expectations play a vital role. Even a sudden turn in the narrative or the development of a character, especially that of the protagonist or the villain, has to be in accordance with the inherent narrative plan and should be bound by the laws of probability. One might add verisimilitude, something in total conformity with the viewers' experience without breaking it. Storytelling by a writer might be difficult. Within the film-reality, it is more so. The viewer inside the theater cannot go back to pages.

Therefore, we should be able to empathize with the feelings of both the villain and the hero, though no one wishes to see the villain triumph. Also, we do not want to identify ourselves with an act of stupidity, or cowardice. We empathize with Margayya in R. K. Narayan's *The Financial Expert*, knowing he hasn't been behaving at all like an expert on the subject. Still, we love Margayya, and share his feelings, because he's essentially a dreamer, struggling against poverty. We know many such characters in real-life situations. Bollywood villains, similarly, are rooted in society, earning the recognition of viewers over the decades. The duel between the hero and villain has been seen as a replica of the battle between the good and bad, shown in our mythologies and the Puranas.

While arguing about certain imaginative empathy with the villains, we should remember that, like the hero, the villain too has to fight against his fate, society, family, friends-turned-foes, even intransigent siblings who, unknowingly or even knowingly, as the case maybe, conspire against him. This is in addition to the hero (often more than one) the villain has to tackle. When the villain believes that he has licked his adversary, another, a look-alike, takes his place, as it happens in the film *Kalicharan* (1976). The struggle, thereafter, resumes, like it happened in the Ramayana when both Rama and Lakshmana were bound to death by serpents, or when Lakshmana got back his life due to the heroic feat of Hanumana. This is an example when the villain's efforts are frustrated by fate. In *Parvarish* (1977), Amjad, looking forward to the help of his police inspector son, is anguished to see him working against him in the company of his surrogate father, Shammi Kapoor. Later, the villain is denied the affection of his son. The villain-father's anguish is brilliantly conveyed by Amjad in the final sequence of the film. In *Gangster* (1994), Ajit is threatened and bewildered by the activities of his son. In *Sarkar* (2005), a Ram Gopal Varma film, the father, an underworld don, is challenged by his own son.

The other instance of unprecedented working of fate, cruel and unkind, is found in the rebirth fiasco, as it happens in *Madhumati* (1958), *Karan Arjun*, and in a recent film. The poor villain in all such instances finds no respite. He is dragged on every time from oblivion and has to surrender to his fate. Society also conspires against villains. Suddenly, everyone becomes united against him, as it happens in Shyam Benegal's film *Nishant* and in *Karan Arjun*. The villagers, united, play the trick against Durjan Singh (Amrish Puri) by joining hands with the reborn heroes. In *Mirch Masala*, the women beat the subedar and throw red *mirchi* in his eyes. Often, society operates through law. In *Shaan* (1980), the villain is overpowered by Rakesh and Jagmohan, both friends-turned foes.

Dear readers, now pause for a while to think of the grim plight of these villains, and try to empathize with them, at least for a while.

The audience, for whom films are made, needs change from everyday monotony. That explains at least one major apparatus of appreciation resorted to by the audience in popular art forms. As soon as the villains bounce onto the screen and spring into action, the audience locates themselves in his environment. That ensures empathy, playing a major role in not only commercial films but in the esoteric also. One major reward of making this study on the villains of Bollywood cinema has been to realize that Bollywood makers never belied the expectation of their viewers. They dared not, because they had to make money.

It is a well-known fact that people have thronged round the movie theater more than once to watch films like *Mother India*, *Zanjeer* (1973), *Sholay* (1975), *Mr. India*—to name only a few among many. This writer knows a government employee who, initially unwilling to disclose, grew reminiscent over a cup of tea and confessed that he'd watched *Sholay* a dozen times when he was young. How could he remember? Well, he stayed in a mess, and along with his friends took pride in writing the numbers of his viewing on the inside door of his room, scratching the figures till they reached the magic number 12. Why 12? Because, it reminded him of the 12 zodiac signs.

And, what a saga of entertainment it has been over the decades! Bollywood filmmakers know how to hook their audience. When things look settled apparently, everything turns gloomy all of a sudden. In all cases, it's always the villain who occupies the center stage, causing fresh hazards to the hero and his relatives. Think of the submarine sequence in the film *Parvarish* that deals with the lost and found theme, or the film *Don* (1978). When it looks like the villain is going to be vanquished, the hero's mother, sister, or the heroine is seized by someone among the villain's henchmen with a knife or pistol. Awestruck, the hero surrenders his weapon to save his relations from being butchered or shot dead. In *Don*, the criminal, disguised as a police officer, arrives at the graveyard in the last moment. This leads to what might be called an intense practice session of catching, a diary in this case, as if a cricket match is going to start. The scene is handled with such brilliant timing (immaculate editing, in this case) that even Jonty Rhodes or Yuvraj Singh, great catchers of the game, would start doubting their abilities. Bollywood is startlingly good in creating such chicken-and-egg situations within the narrative, making them look real and convincing. It has all along been a fantastic show.

There was a time when Bollywood commercials were looked upon with distrust, as if they were serious aberrations from civilized norms. This didn't stay for long. With the proliferation of culture and film studies in the academia and increasing popularity of Bollywood films among the masses, the skeptics soon caved in. Books started pouring in on Bollywood films, and many felt that Bollywood cinema deserved better attention. The villains, however, still stayed out of focus, languishing in the darkness of disapproval. Probably, we have a tendency to cringe at the sight of the darker forces of our psyche. That makes the present study relevant.

Pre-Independence baddies

The villains in pre-Independence cinema showed their chicaneries and duplicitous minds, though they were largely subdued in their activities. *Alam Ara*, the first Indian talkie, shows the rivalry over the throne of Kumarpur between the two fighting queens. The motif of seduction is there, and the vengeance of Dilbahar wrecks the stability of the family of the army chief Adil. The film moves on to narrate the upbringing of Adil's daughter Alam Ara by the nomads. Later, helped by the nomads, Ara raids the palace to release Adil, imprisoned by Dilbahar. The seduction scene involving Adil and Dilbahar is memorable; the final raid has been shot convincingly. The film, based on Joseph David's Parsi play, popular in those days, was remade in 1956 and 1973, showing that the theme of rivalry for a throne still enjoyed the patronage of filmmakers.

In the forties, films portrayed the moneylender, "the blood-sucking Soukar"[2] as he was called by the *Amrita Bazar Patrika* of June 12, 1884. The country, during colonial rule, staggered under the land revenue system of the government. This continued till the fifties when the moneylender villain started looking more aggressive and menacing, basking in the country's Independence. The hapless peasant in the pre-independent era borrowed to pay his dues to the government. The *Kesari* of February 18, 1902 said that the British rule had killed indigenous industries, and "about forty-five crores of rupees were every year drained away to England."[3] For the peasant, the choice lay between starvation and surrender to the moneylender. Mehboob Khan uses the moneylender as villain in *Aurat* (1940) in the character of Sukhi Lala, who later becomes more crude and lecherous in *Mother India*, widely known as a post-independent classic, creating history along with Satyajit Ray's *Pather Panchali* (1955). The villain as moneylender has since then been a skulking, heinous personality, an icon, negatively inclined. Yakub, who later appeared in many such roles, plays Sukhilala in *Aurat*. The moneylender as a screen villain has been discussed in greater detail later in this book.

Lala Murlidhar made an interesting observation on the moneylender as villain at the 1899 session of the National Congress. Lala said, "The moneylender is a curious formation of man and beast. Those who believe in the transmigration of souls will readily agree with me in believing that he has the claws of a lion, the brain of a fox, and the heart of a goat."[4] This statement has a familiar resonance with what Lala Sukhiram does in *Mother India* (1957). The villain as moneylender had a grotesque macabre feature about him, veering occasionally to the comic. The leaders in pre-independent era felt that the moneylender couldn't be fully abolished from the system, because he was an economic necessity in rural India. The moneylender, they felt, should be corrected and controlled, and not suppressed. Feudal values operated through the fifties and sixties, even later also in disguised forms. Shyam Benegal's *Ankur* (1974)—discussed in this book—continues the theme during the early seventies. The landlords of both *Ankur* and *Nishant* contrast the larger-than-life image of Gabbar Singh in the most important decade of villains in Bollywood cinema.

Still, the villains in pre-Independence cinema didn't always operate as moneylenders. They were yet to assume any definite identity, probably because the sociopolitical scenario didn't allow it. They made nebulous plans, indulging in abductions and stayed obscure, without intimidating in a very serious way. Often, they were psychotic patients. During the thirties and forties, the national angst was laced with the blueprint of political idealism, human values, and protest against oppression. Young people, encouraged by their parents and adults, responded to Gandhi's call, left their careers, and joined the movement. That created a stir and positive ambience in the society. There were people who worked as the agents of the British, and this could possibly be used in the films to foment the popular hatred against villains. But, pre-Independence Hindi cinema remained shy in using this. The filmmakers didn't want to show anything that might upset the dream and encourage negative values.

So, if Mehboob Khan made *Aurat*, based on a menacing moneylender, A. R. Kardar made *Pagal* and *Pooja* (1940), both dealing with the shattering consequences of feudal sexual codes. *Pagal*, for example, shows the psychotic doctor Vasant, a sexually obsessed maniac, played by Prithviraj Kapoor. It is needless to say that a character suffering from mental disorder can hardly look convincing when it comes to disrupting a system. Kardar was drawn again and again to the subject of sexual abnormality. He might have considered it to be a depressing consequence of the feudal system prevalent during the time. Importantly, he wasn't doing this alone, for he might have been inspired by Moti B. Gidwani also, who operated in the late thirties. But, the theme of sexual abnormality was Kardar's forte.

The thirties made a number of films on caste issues, probably under the influence of Gandhi's agitation; while the nefarious consequences of agrarian feudalism was shown in the rural crime drama, *Kisan Kanya*, directed by Gidwani. This film was made in 1937 and was probably an ideal predecessor to Mehboob Khan's film. The role of the wicked landlord in Gidwani's film is played by Gani. Nissar plays the good peasant Ramu. Known as one of India's first color films, *Kisan Kanya* provides a commentary on the feudal system, ruled by the landlords and moneylenders. In a letter to Krishna Kripalani (September 29, 1939), Nehru speaks on the problem afflicting the country: "Violence and monopoly and concentration of wealth in a few hands are produced by the present economic structure. It is not large-scale industry that brings any injustice and violence but the misuse of large-scale industry by private capitalists and financiers."[5]

Films like *Kisan Kanya*, *Baghban* (1938), and *Samaj Ko Badal Dalo* (1947) provide examples of what Nehru identifies as the economic crisis of the time. In *Baghban*, made by A. R. Kardar, the role of Ranjit, a randy villain, seeking the hand of Durga, is played by K. N. Singh with remarkable assurance. K. N. Singh played villains in the fifties and sixties also. *C.I.D* (1956) and *An Evening in Paris* provide examples. *Kismet*, a memorable hit of the early fortiess, shows Ashok Kumar playing the antihero. Much of the action of this film takes place in the city. P. F. Pithawala plays the role of the greedy father, responsible for making his daughter disabled. Importantly, it's a film on lost and found theme that later became popular in Bollywood.

Mehboob Khan made *Ek Hi Raasta* in 1939, showing the abduction motif of the villain, played by Kanhaiyalal. This film, importantly, moves from village to city where the heroine Mala is abducted by Banke. The villain in this film prevents the hero and the heroine from getting united, a motif that is explored with greater resonance in the films of the sixties; for example in *Jis Desh Mein Ganga Behti Hai*, *Bluff Master*, and *Kashmir Ki Kali* (1964). In each case, it is Pran who uses his guile to thwart the love interest of Shammi Kapoor. Pran, along with the others of his ilk, has been given a separate treatment later in this book. Interestingly, the villains in the sixties nearly always returned to their folds. This might be because the judiciary and social institutions of the time tried to behave in a neutral way and took care of people behaving badly.

Muqabla (1942) shows the abduction motif of the villain. Spurred on by vengeance against the mother, the villain kidnaps one of her twin daughters. She's so reared up as to become a gangster moll. The villain, in this case, is guided by the desire of settling old scores. Thus, in pre-Independence era, the villains operated in many different ways,

13

making it difficult to trace any single pattern. The causes of menace differed due to the sociopolitical confusion of the time. The villains were skulking around, and waited to come out of their holes. They did later. *Dharti Ke Lal* hit the screen in 1946, showing the diabolical greed of a grain-dealing zamindar. Prices of grains soared as a consequence of the War. In spite of having a good harvest in the fields, the farmer loses his property to the crafty zamindar. K. N. Singh plays his role with ebullience, proving he'd come to the industry to stay put. As an actor, Singh shows gestures and smiles that are later used brilliantly by Pran at the start of his career, in *Madhumati*, for example.

The killing of the villain had to wait till the year of the Independence. *Samaj Ko Badal Dalo* (1947) shows a love motif that leads to the unusual event of the killing of Jayant, the villain, by Kishore, the hero. The sequence that shows the killing is full of drama and tension, built up with short, sharp exchanges of dialog. Probably, the title of the film that asked for bringing in a change in society made it necessary for the villain to be punished fatally.

Post-Independence baddies

The villains in Bollywood cinema were moneylenders, *sahukars*, and greedy zamindars up to the fifties. The sixties, apart from retaining the moneylender on some stray occasions, showed the villain jeopardizing the love interest of the hero. This is discussed in the chapter on villains before the seventies. Color was creeping into cinema in the sixties when the heroines were looked upon as objects of social desire. As a contrast to the all-virtuous heroine, vamps were introduced. The villains now needed molls for getting egged on to their task. As the country progressed, ritzy hotels sprang up in the major cities of the country. So, it wasn't surprising that the villains should now move to the city, and be warmed up by molls, lying in cozy hotel beds, making plans.

Industries develop, and a girl on the street complains that changes of coins are becoming scarce (Mala in *Zanjeer*). With *Zanjeer* (1973) begins the modern era of Bollywood villains. A moneylender as villain at this stage is likely to be an aberration. Pran, the old villain, helps the hero fulfill his mission. Ajit, the new villain, takes over, looking frightfully relaxed. He has lots of time at his disposal to intimidate his adversary and relaxes by the swimming pool, attended by "Mona darling." We have a chapter on *Sholay* and the seventies. Teza (played by Ajit) of *Zanjeer* fame makes way to Gabbar Singh. *Sholay* (1975), for the first time, locates the villain at the center of the narrative, probably because (said often) the villain now has to look awesome and larger than life to encounter the emergence of Amitabh Bachchan as a superstar. This would sound like a run-of-the-mill view when addressed from the villain's perspective, something that has hardly been done so far. Even philosophically speaking, concepts like god–man, man–god; or hero–villain, villain–hero, and many other such ways of describing the fundamental tenets of renaissance humanism take into account the distinctive importance of both facets of human nature, vying for higher status. Too much emphasis on the rise of a superstar disturbs the axis. The point is, did the villain have to look larger for the superstar or is it vice versa?

Watch, for example, the number of heroes taking on the villains in the seventies and eighties. The trend was set by *Sholay*: Veeru and Jai, both criminals, work on behalf of Thakur Baldev. They've no agenda of their own against Gabbar Singh and arrive at Ramgad village as Thakur's henchmen on the lure of money. Later, the interest switches over when they have a secret agenda of their own to join the mainstream society. They want to marry, and have children, like the so-called *bhadraloks*; members of civil society. But this is in no way related to their task of taking on Gabbar Singh. Gabbar, after all, hadn't wronged the heroes.

This seems to have an important bearing on the diminished stature of the heroes against the mighty villains of the seventies and eighties. In *Karma*, all three heroes, picked by the jailor (later known as *dada–thakur*), are social offenders, and sentenced to life imprisonment.

The question is, how far does this add to the image of the heroes? If addressed from the villains' point of view, this raises some interesting and fresh issues. This is exactly what we have done in this book. As a matter of fact, the villain grew so powerful in the seventies that the superstar did hardly have the time for romance. This probably left Amitabh Bachchan wary and frazzled toward the end of the decade, and Manmohan Desai was quick to exploit the entertaining talent of the superstar in *Amar Akbar Anthony* (1977), two years after *Sholay*, showing the wounds Gabbar Singh had left. This was repeated the next year also, in *Don*, where the hero, hotly pursued by his enemy, sings and dances to the famous number *khaike pan banaraswala*. Like in *Zanjeer*, in this film also, the hero is helped by Pran, and if it was Jaya Bachchan in the previous film, now it is Zeenat Aman, helping the hero. This presents an interesting scenario and provides the platform of an altogether different study. It's like looking at the number "6" from its opposite angle, something that David (Amitabh Bachchan), a lawbreaker in the film *Aakhri Raasta* (1985), asks his son (Bachchan in a double role) to do.

In the eighties, the nexus between the politicians and felons provided the platform for presenting the villains in more crude forms. The chapter on "eighties and after" relates the story to the eighties and the scenario beyond when, with the changing sociopolitical scenario, the villains operate as terrorists, politicians, and policemen. Terrorism now becomes a worldwide phenomenon, and the audience has no difficulty in identifying a Dr Dang (*Karma*), a Mogambo (*Mr. India*), or an Isaq Khan (*The Hero: Love Story of a Spy* [2003])—all seeking to destabilize the country. Mrs Gandhi was assassinated and there were two attempts on the life of Rajiv Gandhi before he was finally killed in 1991, a year after *Agneepath* was released. *Phool Bane Angaraay*, which shows Prem Chopra murdering his political rival, was also released in 1991.

The time was ripe for over-the-top villainy in films and real life. Later, society became so negative with regular incidents of rape, bribery, and violence that films couldn't always cope up with the real-life mayhem. Thus, the mantle of the villain passed on for the time being to the antihero, who took over the villain's job. With *Darr* and *Baazigar* (both released in 1993) a change in the concept of the villain took place, leaving the villain largely non-functional. Significantly, Sanjay Dutt, the blood-curdling bald-headed Kancha Cheena of *Agneepath* (2012), followed suit in 1993, playing the antihero in *Khalnayak*, the year that saw *Darr* hitting the theaters. The trend was set clearly.

Wishing for a pleasant trip round the scintillating valleys and hills abroad, filmmakers concentrated on making the so-called modern and multiplex cinema. The idea was probably to hook the interests of the NRI audience—a feature that almost totally discounted action films. Meanwhile, the screen Adam, much to the pleasure of the villains, had tasted the forbidden fruit and behaved like villains. Going out of focus for a wee while, the villains waited with hardened cheeks and clenched teeth to bounce back onto the screen.

The scene, down the mid-nineties, seems to be marked by a gradual phasing out of the villain. But, mind you, the villains didn't sit quiet, languishing in total oblivion. *Karan Arjun* has been mentioned before. Let's note that *Dushmani*, starring Anupam Kher in the awful role of a father-villain, was released in 1995, sending a reminder of Dr Dang of the previous decade. The interesting point is that this happened exactly when a young lad, a courageous and enterprising *dilwale*, got ready to take away his *dulhania*. A revenge thriller, *Dushmani* shows the rivalry between the Singh and Oberoi families in gruesome style. Javed Akhtar says that the dos and don'ts got muddled during this time. But, *Dushmani* was there with its strong intimidating message. There were other villains also around the time. True, such towering villains as Gabbar and Dang disappeared in a bleaker sociopolitical scenario. Sukhilala, for example, was a dangerous moneylender in the fifties. Can we now see him back in action? Even if he did, he'd have to be presented in the new format. We have argued this at the end of this narrative.

What made the heroes behave crazily, emulating the villains? The answer to this question lies precisely in the state of mayhem outlined above. Temporarily unable to believe in the existence of the good and the bad, the heroes started behaving in a queer fashion, something that suited the jittery articulation of Shah Rukh Khan, snatching the bottles of beer at the dead of night in a London store, owned by one of his own countrymen (*Dilwale Dulhania Le Jayenge* or more popularly, *DDLJ* [1995]). Later, he tries to make amends for his previous blunder. As years roll on, this same *dilwale* does everything to expose the tormentor of his previous life in *Om Shanti Om*. Receiving the Filmfare Award, actor Om in this film says that life cannot end unhappily, and likewise, films cannot as well, being a replica of life. If it does, then life as well as films on such stray occasions cannot be said to have really ended. There must be more frames left for a happy ending. This signals the coming back of the belief in the good and the bad. *Madhumati, Karan Arjun*, and *Om Shanti Om*, each based on the theme of reincarnation, make a cycle, offering a convincing and powerful slice of life.

Sapoot, released in 1996, shows both the antihero (Sunil Shetty) and strong villains like Kiran Kumar and Mukesh Rishi in action. So, films during the late nineties showed villainy along with the so-called confusion between the "dos and don'ts," felt by the antihero. The truth is that, far from wiping the villains, both features, working together, generated further pressure and fell on like a volcanic eruption in Prakash Raj's Gani Bhai and Jaykant Shikre in *Wanted* (2009) and *Singham* (2011), culminating finally in the latest Kancha Cheena in *Agneepath* (2012). Remember in this connection that Prakash Raj is also playing Teza in the remake of *Zanjeer*. There has recently been a revival of interest in stronger villains.

We thought it relevant to remember the major actors who essayed villains in Hindi cinema. Importantly, we cannot forget the villlains' henchmen also who have contributed to the Empire of Evil over the years—something that hasn't been properly recognized. Thereafter, the narrative moves on to look at a few memorable villain characters of Bollywood cinema. These people still possess the power to disturb our sleep at night when familiar objects look unfamiliar. We fear the villains and their acts of villainy, but this adds to the pleasure and popularity of the carnival. And, touché, the villain knows many tricks. If Pran shoots from inside his briefcase containing money in *An Evening in Paris*, then Prem Chopra does it from inside the hole of his pocket in *Dostana* (1980). Dr Dang in *Karma* hisses with a style of his own. Held to gunpoint, the villain adjusts his spectacles.

We have ended this narrative by tracing the growth and development of villains from the nineties to the present. The villains, we feel, now require a different look and dimension, responding to the dramatic changes in the social environment. Who can deny that the terrorist villain now pursues our psyche everywhere: at the classy hotel-lounge, parks, shopping malls, metro stations, and even remote towns. Dogs, led by security officials, sniff at garlands and swags at public meetings where ministers and political personalities are due to arrive. This is exactly the scenario that the villains over the past decades wanted to watch.

Thus far, we have understood only a tad of the villain. To know more about him, we should see him in action in the following pages. That promises a splendid journey. The uncanny beats within us, like a second heart.

Villains in mythologies

R. K. Narayan once succinctly commented:

> Almost every individual among the five hundred millions living in India
> is aware of the story of *Ramayana* in some measure or other. Everyone of
> whatever age, outlook, education, or station in life knows the essential parts
> of the epic and adores the main figures in it—Rama and Sita. Every child
> is told the story at bed-time.[6]

Elucidating his diagnosis of the popular Indian psyche, the writer
reminds that everyone knows the story and loves to listen to it again
and again.

This gives us a lead to understanding why Bollywood films which
show the trouncing of the villain over and over again has kept the
audience glued to their seats. The spectacle of the villain pummeled
and destroyed by the hero is associated by the psyche with Ravana being
crushed by Rama. The ugly and monstrous *rakshasa* abducted Sita,
and in spite of repeated warnings issued to him by his well-meaning
brothers, he wasn't prepared to hand Sita over to Rama, repenting
of his misdeeds. This association of the epic with the text of villains,
vanquished each time in Bollywood cinema, has resulted in overt or
covert statements, used by directors in their films for making money.
Even when there's no direct reference to the epics, the audience sees
the films in these terms. As a matter of fact, references to the epics
in the sequence and dialog are numerous in Bollywood cinema. The
result is that when the audience is not directly asked to recall the
incidents of the Ramayana or Mahabharata, they do it on their own,
led by an instinctual obligation of the mind. After all, almost every
one among the audience goes to sleep taking the story of Rama and
Ravana to his heart. Apart from the "Valmiki-Ramayana," Tulsidas'
Ramcharitmanas has played a singularly important role in shaping
people's inexhaustible faith in Rama and Hanumana. This child
grows up and joins the masses, standing in the queue on the first day
of the release of a film.

Thus, mythologies have played their role in helping one see in a
fixed image. He enjoys every bit of the fun when the smugglers are
beaten with the mighty Hanuman's mace in *Mr. India*. When gold
biscuits fall at regular intervals in *Nastik* to bless a simpleton, sitting

with folded hands before a vermilion-smeared image of the monkey-god, the audience feels simply overjoyed, some even hoping that they too might be lucky in a similar way at some point of their life. Still, someone bent on intellectual spoon-bending, likes to dismiss this reality as showing "a Painted Face."[7]

Vermilion-painted? One may recall that countless images of the monkey-god are seen covered head to feet with vermilion-paste throughout India. To grumble over that is like chiding the rainbow in the sky. Still, the million-dollar question that kept some people busy in a hairsplitting job was why the film-audience, putting up a painted face, betrayed an inability to distinguish myth from fact. Unfortunately, things didn't improve much after that since 1991, if one wishes to be exact about when this fruit of knowledge was delivered for the *ignorant* hoi polloi. The villains, by that time, had become infinitely stronger and were about to disappear for a while from the *painted* scene. A significant development, meanwhile, was taking place by the end of the nineties and the beginning of the present century. Students were choosing film studies as a curriculum of study in universities. Books on popular cinema started pouring in. This encouraged many to take a different look at Bollywood cinema.

Claude Lévi-Strauss, an eminent scholar, and often mentioned in serious books on film studies, speaks about "the mythical value" of myth, and the way "myths think in men, unbeknown to them." Strauss says it doesn't matter whether the mythology of the shaman corresponds to an objective reality. After all, "the sick woman" who wishes to be cured by a shaman "believes in the myth and belongs to a society which believes in it."[8] This was said in 1958. The English translation came out in 1968, then again in 1972. The famous scene in the film *Madhumati* that shows the shaman, curing the supposedly crazy man, is fraught with hilarious laughter and is graced by the presence of the inimitable Johny Walker. It is natural, therefore, that people should enjoy the battle between the hero and the villain. The triumph of the good over the bad, after all, follows a whole battery of myths and beliefs. In rural India, people still meet shamans, operating in various forms and capacities for curing diseases.

But hark! Let's listen to a dialog.

The protagonist, wounded deeply by the villain's henchmen, has been carried in a wheelchair inside a room on the pretext of treatment.

The villain, disguised in a doctor's uniform, tells the injured man that his three trusted men are in his custody. The protagonist, unperturbed, says: "Ay, have they, then, reached Lanka?" The villain (not an ordinary villain, mind you), unruffled, accepts with humility his identity with Ravana, and says, "*Ji, haa, saath saath Sita-mata bhi*" ("Ay, Sir, and mother Sita too with them").

In another shot, the audience sees the protagonist's wife abducted by the villain's men in a car, the modern counterpart of the chariot in the Ramayana on which Sita was abducted by Ravana. This association creates empathy and identification discussed in the previous chapter.

The scene is from the film *Karma*. In a previous sequence of the same film, Baiju, played by Jackie Shroff, sings a paean of praise for "Maryada Puroshottam Rama," trying to impress his girl. Kancha Cheena in *Agneepath* (2012) also shows his surprise when Vijay asks Mandwa from him. Incredulous, he reminds Vijay, not hiding his displeasure, that this is like asking Lanka from Ravana. This adequately proves the continuity of the tradition, an inexhaustible continuity, that associates the villain's identity with Lanka; the place, where, like Ravana, he is the ruling monarch. Significantly and deliberately, Kancha doesn't compare Vijay to Rama since today's Lanka is dominated by Ravanas.

Interestingly, Bollywood films have occasionally offered a critique of mere box-office stunts that exploit people's crazy adulation of gods and goddesses, shown as wrathful beings, and seeking revenge or showering blessings, according to their volatile desires. A second-rate film was thus made in 1975 (the year of *Sholay*'s release) by a man called Vijay Sharma, exploiting the "Santoshi ma" cult. Baiju in *Karma* ruefully mentions the event when he tells the heroine with a jokey tone of voice that *Jai Santoshi Ma* ran for 50 weeks in Bombay.

This should be taken seriously, since it differentiates between wild adulation (something to be remembered by the iconoclasts) and peoples' faith in sacred mythologies. Bollywood films have paired the villains with the heroes, both drawn from the social and political realities of the country, though the villains significantly have always enjoyed an edge in this scenario of verisimilitude. The huge success of *Sholay* gains relevance when one remembers the magnitude of battles among filmmakers for winning over their audience. In doing so, the makers of Bollywood cinema tried to revive the more baneful and value-oriented tradition of the country. The two epics we have are enough to fall back on. This doesn't mean that only the villains should refer to the epics, for there're other characters also, major and minor, and taken together, they make up the variegated scenario.

The practice of shamans has been used by Bollywood on numerous occasions. In *Ram Aur Shyam*, poor Ram, the good one, is opposed to his twin brother Shyam, a clever and smarter guy. See again. Ram is good and naïve but Shyam is clever. This association is maintained on many occasions. So, Ram has a bitter taste of the bizarre practice of the shaman on him, because he's mistaken for Shyam. During the clownish torture inflicted on Ram by the priest, he has to admit that he's Shyam. This makes for great fun.

Before this, Ram, dressed like a sage, reads out from Tulsidas to impress the villagers and earn money in a strange new place. On the other hand, Shyam, who has come to stay where Gajendra the villain (played by Pran) has been thumping around, looks upon himself as an incarnation of Rama for punishing the villain, that is, Ravana. For quite some time Gajendra, bewildered by the change in his brother-in-law's behavior, is duped by Shyam's appearance. Soon, the villain ferrets out the mystery. You cannot deceive the villain longer.

In *Madhumati* (1958), the funny sequence of the shaman's practice involving Johnny Walker and the bare-bodied angry priest is deeply absorbing. It relieves the tension of the story, like the Porter does in Shakespeare's popular play *Macbeth*. The imaginary ghost hovers around somewhere. He does indeed. But he is a real human being; the villain—operating from his palace. The audience, who knows about the disappearance of Madhu, the heroine, just as they know about the King's murder in *Macbeth*, has no difficulty in responding to the funny sequence of the film.

There is before this a scene in *Madhumati* that shows the hero and heroine, worshiping the tribal god, and seeking his blessing for their future union. The ominous end is suggested when the flower-offering is swept away by wind. Kalbhairav (very popular among people staying in hilly areas), the tribal god, refuses to accept the flower, a bad omen that leaves Madhu shaken. The villain, we know, is weaving his net from his palace, plotting to send the hero away from the place of action. The popular belief of people in the good and the bad has been superbly exploited by Bimal Roy, just as Shakespeare, the master wizard, had done it at the Globe Theatre on every noon. Caesar's wife, for example, dreams a bad dream before Caesar's murder.

Deewar (1975), released 17 years after *Madhumati*, continues to respect people's faith in tradition. Vijay, shot in the leg by his brother, who's a police inspector, cannot retrieve the lucky badge no. 786 he was given by Rahim Chacha, a worker of the dockyard. Vijay dies after this. In *Sawan* (1959), the good brother is still Ram, picked from the road by a good and well-meaning charioteer and later brought up by him. The other one joins the band of dacoits. An exception to the *Rama* and *Shyam* legend is made in the film *Ram Balram* where Ram (Dharmendra) helps Suleman Seth (played by Amzad Khan) and his gang. But, Balram (Amitabh Bachchan) becomes the police inspector. Balram in the Krishna avatar was the naïve one, contrasted with his sagacious brother. So, even here the traditional knowledge is not disturbed. Again, the brothers, mind you, act in connivance. Ram asks his surrogate father, the real villain, if he hasn't accumulated enough wealth by this time ("*Daulat kafi nahi huyi?*") to give up the wrong path.

Looking elsewhere in the world, it's seen that shamans were very common in Central Asian mythologies, entrusted with the job of communicating to the spirits reigning in hell and heaven. People, therefore, had to stay alert so that they could avoid the bad forces and tap the good ones.

It wouldn't be any exaggeration to say that mythologies have given us a lead to understand why the human mind, from the beginning, has been trained unwittingly to distinguish between the good and the bad and feel happy when good triumphs. An instinctive operation of this rule has guided humanity; irrespective of the boundaries of religion, culture, and creed. People have taken an active interest in stories that describe the hero's struggle against the obstacles he faces and his subsequent triumph over a dragon, an evil spirit, or a witch. When the name "villain" was unknown, the ugly monster was described as someone being wicked and bad. Often, the stories in myths of the world have similar resonances even though they sound remote apparently. It cannot be doubted that people throughout the world have loved to respond to traditional beliefs. Hasn't the Bible been a great influence on the Western psyche, including some Asian and African countries that have taken to Christianity? The stories of Fin and Cuchulainn in Irish mythology are well-known, and both have been used in the literature and films of Ireland. The story of Finn, for example, may remind the Indian reader of a similar story in the Mahabharata that describes the sleeping king Muchukund, who fought heroically for the gods when the throne of Indra, the god of rain and king of heaven, was in danger against the attacks of the *asura*s. In the Ramayana, Kumbhakarna, the mighty *rakshasa* and brother of the all-powerful Ravana, has been described as sleeping for six months every year. People have been great sleepers in mythologies, a feature that should have added to their prodigious strength.

The Siberian people, interestingly, are composed of several groups, possessing similar pantheons and myths. Before the arrival of the Russians, Siberia was home to the Samoyeds, the Tungus, Ostiaks, Voguls of the Finno-Ugrian race, and many others. The story of creation associated with the bursting of an egg is told in Siberian mythology. The egg-like universe is made up of three earths: upper, middle, and lower. The idea of a banyan tree, described in the 15th chapter of the Gita, is mentioned in Siberian mythology also. An axis-tree with an earth goddess at its roots in the lower earth (like what Sri Krishna describes as the *adhasakham*, the lower branches, in the Gita) rises up through the navel of the middle earth to the pole star. The Sun and the Moon sit at the top of the tree, while the souls of those unborn live in the branches. The Sun is worshipped as the giver of life, while the Moon brings the yet unborn to their human mothers. Mythologies, throughout the world, have spoken the same language, making the occasional variation. Popular arts have always used them. That is the point to be noted here.

In Chinese mythology, Pangu is said to have remained in the egg for 18,000 years, an idea that is strongly reminiscent of the Siberian mythology just mentioned. As the egg finally broke, the heavy elements called *yin* became earth. The lighter ones, called *yang*, became the sky. The birth of creation has always been a subject of interest in mythologies. One may look up Tibetan cosmogony for additional interest. Buddhism in Japan took several forms, but it was marked by a tendency to move to the esoteric, as it wanted to assimilate the old Shinto *kami* into their systems. The shamans, too, played a decisive role in earlier times, and they were still active when Buddhism was melded into the old system. Exorcizing demons, telling future events, along with the use of magical formulae for bringing in cures through rituals, were still very popular. The act of exorcism demanded that the demon and the evil spirit be driven out for restoring order and happiness within the human system. This is exactly what the priest was doing in *Madhumati*.

The story of the Seven Wise Men in Indo-Iranian series of tales describes the story of seduction of a prince by his stepmother—a feature that has been used again and again by Bollywood filmmakers. The role of the villain in such cases is taken over by the vamp. The notion of evil and good is ubiquitous, taking no account of gender issues. This has guided human thought ever since people started thinking about the world.

Echoing the Indian attitude of tolerance for every religion and creed, Bollywood has produced *Amar Akbar Anthony*. The industry has never been shy in using a slew of Muslim and Christian characters in its variegated narrative texture.

It might be interesting now to look at the *asura*s of the Puranas. They too had a role to play in the glorious scheme and worked hard in *samudra manthana*, the prodigious act of churning the ocean. The malicious scientist of *Krrish* (2006) lures innocent Rohit Mehra into joining him, pretending that their work is going to yield benefits for humanity. The terrorist-villain speaks in a fraudulent tongue to convince others, luring them to believe in his grandiloquent mission. Amrish Puri does this in the film *The Hero: Love Story of a Spy* (2003). Mogambo in *Mr. India* convinces his henchmen that the formula of invisibility would enable him to do wonders for them. The invisibility of Mr. India suggests that the formula does exist, and that some day the villain is going to have it.

The idea of the underworld that has played a decisive role in Bollywood cinema since the seventies, recognized as a major decade of villains, has a resonance with Indian mythologies. Bollywood cinema, reckoned to be born and thriving in a major Indian city of trade and commerce, has used this. Like other ideas, the bursting of creation, for example, noted in the above discussion, this idea too has been repeated in many mythologies of the world. The Siberian underworld lies somewhere below the domain of the Great Mother Goddess and is a place ruled by a king commanding the spirits of the underworld, those evidently bad. The dictionary provides two different entries for

25

"underworld": *(a)* the part of society that lives by organized crime, *(b)* in myths: a place under the earth, where the spirits of dead people live. Both meanings serve as tools in appreciating films and literatures of contemporary world: thrillers, for example, which go to the top and rank high on the *New York Times* best sellers' list, including the potboilers, produced in Hollywood.

Mumbai, being the origin and center of Bollywood cinema, has every now and then been intimidated by underworld activities right through the seventies, the period that saw the rise of Amitabh Bachchan as a superstar, taking action against the wrongdoers and criminals. Waging a gruesome war against the corrupt system, the hero often becomes a part of the underworld, wishing to demolish it in the end. It should be noted that, long before Amitabh Bachchan, Shammi Kapoor made his way into the underworld in the film *China Town*, using his look-alike image of a don, who was then in police custody. This often invests the hero with tragic dimensions, his face becoming smeared with the blood of those whose lives he's out to terminate. In *Deewar*, Amitabh's character was said to have been based on Hazi Mastan Mirza, an underworld don, who was put into prison during the Emergency. Bollywood has shown the sinister forces of the underworld convincingly, and the show has found encouraging patronage of viewers in terms of box-office return.

The underworld is described as *patal-loka* in our mythology. Bishnu sent the arrogant king Bali to *patal*, and Krishna asked Kaliya, the dangerous snake, to find shelter in the underworld, instead of killing innocent lives on the Yamuna river. As said before, the wicked *asura*s were great workers and they made *patal* look opulent and dazzling. Remember the lavish look of all such underground places in Bollywood films, in *Zanjeer*, *Shaan*, *Mr. India*, *Karma*, and so on. One cannot forget the marvel of scientific and technological excellence of Shakaal (*Shaan*) and Mogambo's den. The camp of Jabbar Singh, the villain in the film *Mera Gaon Mera Desh* (1971), is also reminiscent of the golden castle of Lanka, described in the *Ramayana*. In *C.I.D.*, Inspector Shekhar (played by Dev Anand) is helped by Kamini, the vamp (played by Waheeda Rehman), to reach the shimmering den of the villain; though previously, under instruction from the villain, she'd thrown the unconscious hero onto the Mumbai–Agra road. All these glossy associations of the underworld have kept human imagination alive and vibrant, eliciting a mixed response of fear and admiration. Bollywood has capitalized on this tradition.

The story of abduction has been very popular in Bollywood films both before and after Independence. In the film *Muqaddar Ka Sikandar* (1978), Kamna, the heroine, and the hero's sister are abducted by the villains in their cars on the day of wedding. This leads to a chase sequence on horse and motor bike. This happens so frequently in Bollywood films that any citation seems unnecessary. In all cases, cars become the modern equivalents of chariots mentioned in the epics. It is, therefore, of little surprise that *Ramayana*, made for television by Ramanand Sagar, should be an instant hit. Roads became empty on Sunday mornings. People scurried home after finishing a hasty bargain in the market. Some stopped bargaining altogether.

In the film *Gangster*, the "Vibhisana" motif becomes apparent in the role played by Rahul, the good-natured younger son of the villain Seth Chandulal, played by Ajit. Chandulal cannot believe that he is the begetter of Rahul. Ravana too is left gobsmacked to hear pious words from his brotherVibhisana, asking him to give Sita back to Rama and sign armistice. Is he a *rakshasa* like him? Ravana wonders, throwing a tantrum.

The stories of Vibhishana, Kumbhkarna, and Maricha have provided classic sources of inspiration for Bollywood filmmakers. The villain turns deaf and defiant to the advice aired by his well-meaning acolytes and relations. The advisers, in all cases, are kicked, killed, or banished with threats. Think of Baccha Jadav in the film *Gangaajal* (2003). Toward the end of *Ganga Jumna* also, Munimji, played by Kanhaiyalal, cannot tolerate the duplicity of the villainous zamindar. He decides to expose him before the police. The subject of hearing conscience from within by evil characters has been occasionally used in Bollywood cinema.

In *Mr. India*, the scene showing the hilarious beating of smugglers, especially Bob Christo, by the golden idol of Hanumana's mace, has been brilliantly devised. This has been enjoyed by children and adults alike, encouraging repeated viewings of the film. This author has watched the sequence at least a dozen times, and knows many who have loved watching it again and again. It was revealed on enquiry that the repeated beatings of the criminals by Bajrangbali (Hanumana is so called by millions of Indians) reminded the viewers of the wondrous activities of the monkey-god narrated in the Ramayana. The scene has been handled smartly, capturing popular psyche.

Both Kaikeyi and the humpbacked Manthara in the Ramayana have become examples of women doing monstrous acts of villainy. In the film *Rajkumar* (1964), starring Shammi Kapoor and Pran, the role of Kaikeyi in the Ramayana is narrated to provide a commentary on a similar motif shown in the film. Bad wives and stepmothers have always been associated by popular psyche with Kaikeyi and, consequently, they have become the vamps in Bollywood cinema.

Rama's courageous decision to go to the forest for fulfilling the promise of his father, and no less important, Sita's decision to follow Rama in his ordeal have been admired and cited in Bollywood films. In *Paying Guest* (1957), for example, the college debate watched by the hero, perched on the branch of a tree, centers round this popular subject. Is pure love without money possible in this world? That is the subject of the debate. Shanti, the heroine, argues that love for the sake of love is possible. She cites the example of Sita from the Ramayana: *"Sita kyun vanvaas gayi"* (Why did Sita go to the forest?) This view is applauded by all. We cannot, however, stay focused on the scene longer. The hero is soon pulled down by a constable, who considers it to be an offense to pry into the privacy of a girls' college.

The sacred relationship between Lakshmana, the faithful brother-in-law, and Sita-bhavi, becomes the subject of *Aanchal* (1979). Lakshmana's name has become merged in popular imagination with the example of ideal brotherhood and devotion to an elder brother. In *Aanchal*, the virtuous wife Shanti (played by Rakhee) is tested as if she is passing through fire, just as it happens in the Ramayana. She's threatened with divorce by her husband, the hero's elder brother, who suspects her of having an amoral relationship with his brother, Sambhu (Rajesh Khanna). Jagan (played by Prem Chopra), the villain, poisons the husband's mind, wishing to have Shanti to himself. The scene that shows Jagan approach Shanti, withering in anguish, is associated with the example of Ravana and his lascivious desire of having Sita by any means. When everything is resolved and Kishan, the husband, becomes repentant, they mention the relationship between Lakshmana and Sita from the Ramayana. The Ramayana motif of the film is also established by showing a performance of dance recital on the stage. It is watched with reverence by the villagers. Two strips of cloth are used on the stage to make the illusion of Rama and his monkey troops crossing the ocean to reach Lanka.

In the film *Do Raaste* (1969), the motif of Rama, Lakshmana, and Sita are used again to show the relationship of mutual respect and devotion among Nabyendu, the elder brother, his wife, and brother Satyen (played by Rajesh Khanna). After being beaten by the elder brother for a minor offense, Satyen says, *"Ram jaisa bhai aur Sita jaisi bhabhi"* ("a brother like Ram and a sister-in-law like Sita"). Therefore, he's ready to accept the beating and stay loyal to his elder brother. It wouldn't be an exaggeration to say that the sacred ties of family relationships in India have been held together by the examples of the Ramayana. Even Shyam Benegal's *Nishant*, catering to an esoteric audience, and one belonging to what once was called "parallel cinema," uses the Ramayana motif in the abduction of Susheela, the teacher's wife. The buffalo scene and the Ramayana events are recalled before the villagers decide to fight against the arrogance and injustice of the villains, as if they were going to wage a battle against Ravana. In *Karma*, the jailor moves round the scene of pogrom left by Dr Dang, as if he were inspecting the battlefield of Kurukshetra that stood a witness to the agonizing loss of thousands of relations.

Bollywood films have been rightly described as the most popular version of applied mythology in contemporary India. Iqbal Masud echoes the feeling when he says that mythology underlies even those films that deal with mundane contemporary issues. Masud believes that India lives and draws its breath from her mythologies, especially the Ramayana, Mahabharata, and the stories centering on the famous Krishna legend. If the villain is associated with a Ravana or a Kamsa, the malicious maternal uncle of Krishna, then the heroine too is seen in terms of the Hindu pantheon—Radha, Shakti, or Durga. In the film *Khoon Bhari Maang* (1988), Rekha plays the female avenging angel, settling her old scores. In the final sequence of the film, she is seen in terms of a Durga or Shakti, as if she has reincarnated herself, which indeed is nearly the case since she went through a plastic surgery for improving her damaged face.

In Bollywood films, reality is shown through the prism of imagination, running in tandem with the country's vibrant traditional beliefs. This is something that makes it different from the West. The daily problems of contemporary life and emerging moral, social, and political issues are seen through a process of translucence that remains centrally connected to primeval values derived from our epics and mythologies. It's difficult to dislodge this myth-oriented image by post-industrial modernity. This is not to mean that the country has never welcomed changes. It has, and the presentation of villains in Bollywood cinema has recorded the sociopolitical changes most faithfully without altering the basic foundation of the age-old tradition. Interestingly, this is not always the case with the heroes.

Sakuni of the Mahabharata fame has attracted the attention of viewers as a villain, who uses his guile and expertise in playing the game of dice. In *Nagin* (1954), Jeevan, playing the role of the villain, thwarts the union of the lovers. He throws the dice with elation, winning aggressively till Sanatan, the hero, appears on the scene, disguised as a fakir. Playing cards as a gamble is used in *Shri 420* (1955) also. The tramp has a fleeting taste of one night revelry in the company of a vamp (Nadira). In all such instances of gambling, people think of Sakuni and his exploits in the Mahabharata. The grim sight of Draupadi, chased away from her chamber by Dussasana, who attempts to strip her naked before all, has become the subject of many anxious moments in Bollywood cinema. In *Madhumati*, Madhu is chased by the villain till she jumps off the terrace of the palace to save her chastity. In *Dushman*, the villain tears the edge of the sari of his prey in a godown that symbolizes the menace of the underworld. In *Gangster*, the tribal is raped to destruction by Seth Chandulal. As the show goes on, the faces of the villain change from a zamindar, a hoarder of grains, a smuggler to that of a politician and finally a terrorist.

In the film *Aakhri Raasta* (1985), the villain mocks the girl before raping her, saying that God appeared in the Mahabharata to save Draupadi from her shame at the royal court of Hastinapur. But, in this Bharat, God is not going to appear again. In all such cases, the scene of Draupadi's humiliation shown in the Mahabharata is unfailingly recalled by the audience.

The foregoing discussion shows how the two epics of India supplement one another. If the Ramayana shows the cherished ideals of life and acts of villainy of the *rakshasas*, the Mahabharata throws open the crudities of life—bloodshed, envy among relations, rivalry, vengeance, gambling, horror, and chicanery. The transition from the Ramayana to the Mahabharata symbolically mirrors the transitional phases of the villains in Bollywood cinema. Like the villains garnered their strength down the decades, the ambience of hatred and pogrom was expressed with increasing intensity from the Ramayana to Mabhabharata, responding to the developments through the ages.

Raj Khosla, the director of *Do Raaste*, says in an interview (March 12, 1980), "You cannot escape these two classics—Ramayana and the Mahabharata—in any film. Somewhere a shade will come."[9] Considering film as "the latest form of folk-art," Lothar Ludze, Raj Khosla's interviewer, pays a tribute to the mythological tradition of India, saying "a westerner may feel envious, as he himself belongs to a culture in which such myths have lost their relevance and applicability. India is more fortunate in this respect."[10]

India has indeed been fortunate. We live by our myths and epics, and recognize unfailingly their resonances in literature, film, painting, music—in fact, in everything. This has made empathy and appreciation easier. Our rituals are still a part of our daily lives. When Danny, the villain in the film *Indian* (2001), worships in a temple, he looks frightfully convincing, in spite of his evil intention to grab the entire land surrounding the temple—a desire aired by him to his acolytes immediately after coming out of the temple. When the blind mother in the film *Amar Akbar Anthony* gets back her vision in the mosque, we do not doubt it or even if we do, that doesn't necessarily hinder us from appreciating the circumstances of the film reality. The other reason of this enjoyment possibly lies in the treatment of the narrative by Bollywood filmmakers. This has been superb, nearly always.

With the two epics as our guide, let's now watch the villains in action. Believe it, dear readers, they deserve our attention.

Notes

1. Rajni Kothari. *Democratic Polity and Social Change in India: Crisis and opportunities* (Allied Publishers, 1976), 33.
2. Bipan Chandra. *The Rise and Growth of Economic Nationalism in India* (New Delhi: Peoples' Publishers House, 1969), 467.
3. Ibid., 469.
4. Ibid., 470. For all these references, the author is indebted to Bipan Chandra's book.

5. Jawaharlal Nehru. *An Anthology*, ed. Sarvepalli Gopal (New Delhi: Oxford University Press, 1983), 303.

6. K. Narayan. *The Ramayana: A Shortened Modern Prose Version of the Indian Epic* (suggested by the Tamil version of *Kamban*), (Hermondsworth: Penguin, 1977), ix. Narayan's statement begins with, "It may sound hyperbolic, but I am prepared to state that every individual...." This clearly indicates the celebrated author's conviction and faith.

7. Chidananda Dasgupta. *The Painted Face: Studies in India's Popular Cinema* (New Delhi: Rolli Books, 1991). The vermilion-smeared face of Hanumana and peoples' painted faces have resonance between them as Dasgupta's book would have one believe. Later, Dasgupta has some strong words to say in an article against both Dadasaheb Phalke and Ravi Verma, whom he calls Phalke's mentor: "The form Phalke established in his films was the objective correlative of his fundamentalism. His other mentor, Raja Ravi Verma, used the worst of contemporary standards in art...." "Form and Content," pp. 103–16, in *Frames of Mind: Reflections on Indian Cinema*, Aruna Vasudev (ed.) (New Delhi: UBSPD, 1995). Incidentally, the term "objective correlative," used by the British poet and critic T. S. Eliot while calling Shakespeare's *Hamlet* "a piece of artistic failure" became a much preferred and used tool among the intellectuals in Calcutta dov n the sixties and later.

8. Claude Lévi-Strauss. *Structural Anthropology*, trans. Claire Jacobson and Brooke Grundfest Schoepf (Chicago: University of Chicago Press), 197. The previous quote about the "mythical value of myth" refers to this book. Strauss makes an ingenious study of the Oedipus, calling it essentially structural in mode. He also says that if social life, by virtue of its unconscious structural similarity, validates cosmology, then cosmology is true. Bollywood films, right from the beginning, have responded to peoples' mythical beliefs, representing an unconsciously formed structure based on a solid foundation. This could possibly become the subject of a separate study. However, in the present study that follows, numerous examples from films give one a glimpse of this underlying mythical structure, having their resonance in the film situations.

9. Beatrix Pfleiderer and Lothar Ludge. *The Hindi Film: Agent and Re-agent of Cultural Change* (Delhi: Manohar, 1985), 40. The interview was taken by Ludge, pp. 34–45.

10. Ibid., 40.

Lording over

Shambhu (Balraj Sahni) is helpless in front of Zamindar Thakur Harnam Singh (Murad) in *Do Bigha Zamin*. Murad's fictitious account-keeping later forces the farmer to become a rickshaw-puller in the city, bringing in the *Bicycle Thieves* motif.

Photo courtesy : National Film Archive of India (NFAI), Pune.

"Sone Jab Zanjeer Ban Jata Hain"
The atrocious moneylender Kanhaiyalal crosses all limits
of decorum in *Mother India*. Nargis plays the anguished mother.

Photo courtesy : National Film Archive of India (NFAI), Pune.

The Handsome Baddy

Pran as Ugnarayan in *Madhumati*. For the role of villains vying for the heroines, Pran perhaps suited the role best due to his good looks. Prem Chopra came next.

Photo courtesy : Subhash Chheda/Datakino.

A Thought-reading Villain

Does Pran in *Bluff Master* really want to draw a puff or is he reading the mind of the heroine's uncle whom he blackmails in the film?

Photo courtesy : Subhash Chheda/Datakino.

Nursing a Wound
Nadira in *Dil Apna Aur Preet Parai* looks all set to take her revenge on the heroine who the hero–husband loves.

Photo courtesy : Subhash Chheda/Datakino.

A Chic Villain
K. N. Singh, whom we lost in 2000, was always the stylish villain of Bollywood cinema, leaving a framework for Pran when the latter started on his career.

Photo courtesy : Subhash Chheda/Datakino.

Narad Muni
Actor Jeevan's quaint and macabre mannerisms remind one of Kanhaiyalal.

Photo courtesy : Subhash Chheda/Datakino.

The Seductress
Shashikala is denied her claim by Dharmendra in *Phool Aur Patthar*.

Photo courtesy : Subhash Chheda/Datakino.

Beauty and the Beast
Bindu, playing a vamp in the popular hit *Kati Patang*, instigates Prem Chopra's villainous act in the film.
Photo courtesy : Subhash Chheda/Datakino.

Prem Naam Hai Mera....
Prem Chopra, playing the lascivious villain in *Kati Patang*, teaches the heroine (Asha Parekh) a lesson.
She's ruined by trusting a villain.

Photo courtesy : Subhash Chheda/Datakino.

Hit or Miss

Premnath, playing Ranjit, aka the Rai Saab, in Vijay Anand's highest-grossing film *Johny Mera Naam* is no ordinary villain.

Photo courtesy: Subhash Chheda/Datakino.

Shakaal
Kulbhushan Kharbanda, the tech-savvy villain in *Shaan*, takes on three heroes in the film before he's brought down.

Photo courtesy : Subhash Chheda/Datakino.

Bar No Bar
Menacing Dr Dang (Anupam Kher) is undeterred as Jailer Vishwa Pratap Singh listens to him helplessly in Subhash Ghai's *Karma*.

Photo courtesy : Subhash Chheda/Datakino.

A Bewitching Mother
Can anyone doubt Shashikala's motherly intention in *Samraat* where she plays Ranbir's (Amjad Khan) mother?

Photo courtesy : Subhash Chheda/Datakino.

"Mogambo Khush Hua"
Despite his arguably clownish looks, Amrish Puri's villainous act in *Mr. India* still remains by far one of the most memorable characters of Hindi films.

Photo courtesy : Subhash Chheda/Datakino.

Mad over Mandwa

Vijay Dinanath Chauhan (Amitabh Bachchan) and Kancha Cheena (Danny Denzongpa) engaged in the final battle for Mandwa in Yash Johar's *Agneepath*.

Photo courtesy : Subhash Chheda/Datakino.

Step-motherly Treatment

Aruna Irani (above) tries to kill her step-son (Anil Kapoor) in *Beta* to retain control of her husband's wealth.

Photo courtesy : Subhash Chheda/Datakino.

Part II

THE BADDIES in ACTION

2

The Fifties and Sixties

$\mathcal{T}$he glassy pallor of dawn kept people busy, reveling in the street on the day of the Independence. The odd memory of Partition was still troubling the minds of millions, especially those affected directly by it. The assassination of Mahatma Gandhi in 1948 was ominous to sensitive minds. Farmers, engaged in toiling their land, occasionally debated if everything augured well, and would go on as anticipated. But, there blew a pleasant sensation also, a winged word of optimism as baby cloudlets, not yet having the power to block the ineffably pure prince of the eastern sky, hung out indefinitely. Nehru proposed his plea of a socialist society for strengthening the economic agenda of the country. Between 1951 and 1956, two Five Year Plans were launched. In 1949, Hindi was proclaimed as the official language of India, an event that must have encouraged Bollywood filmmakers to look for a wider market in the distribution of their films. In 1955, India strengthened her ties with the USSR in order to counterbalance the bitter relationship with Pakistan and the USA.

What could the villains do under the new reality of optimism aired by the Nehruvian socioeconomic policies designed to carry the rich, the middle class, and the rural farmers to the promised shore? For a moment, they looked like baby cloudlets that looked both dark and illumined by the new sun. At the beginning, the villains had no choice except hiding and creeping in the dark, disguised in their outward gentility but ready to pounce on the opportune moments. So, a moneylender like Lala Sukhiram in *Mother India* approaches the tormented Radha in apparent appreciation of her struggle, offering his well-meaning amorous assistance. The hawk-eyed greedy son-in-law in the film *Paying Guest* sneaks up on the rich wife to demand money from her. Interestingly, the way the villain shows himself in *Paying Guest* makes him a true successor to Jayant of *Samaj Ko Badal Dalo*, both roles played by Yakub. The plight of India's agrarian economy, along with the crisis of unemployment, received the attention of filmmakers. Toward the end of the fifties, usually described as a decade of dream and aspiration, disillusionment crept in. This was the time when the villains decided to come out of their holes and look more menacing and aggressive. They operated mostly as moneylenders and *sahukar*s, because that was the easiest way to spring into action under the circumstance. Agriculture still remained a major occupation, land being the subject of adulation and worship in India. Concurrently, feudal values continued to rock people's minds. Zamindars retained their hold in villages, and people, having owning lands, needed cash to plough their lands. For them, their laborand crops in the field had to be converted into money. But, to set the process into ignition, they needed hard cash. The village *sahukar* or the moneylender was considered to be a scourge in rural India. Rural indebtedness increased rapidly during the last quarter of the nineteenth century, and it became one of the most acute problems in villages.

This was explored in *Aurat* (1940) in pre-Independence cinema, and again in its remake, *Mother India*. Both films show how the exorbitant rates of interest charged by the rural creditor led to two major evils; first, interest charges absorbed a large part of the peasant's income; and second, this led to his subsequent starvation. The peasant's frequent inability to repay the debt led to a large-scale transfer of the ownership of the land to the noncultivating moneylenders. In *Bandhan* (1969), the hero, pleading mercy of the unashamed moneylender, sums up the plight of the farmers: "*Sood dete dete unke paas kuch nahin rahta*" ("paying interest continually they don't have anything to keep them on"). This shows that the situation, since Independence, hadn't drastically improved for farmers. A report, published by the *Amrita Bazar Patrika* of June 12, 1884, had described the "moneylender, the blood-sucking soukar" as a "creature of the land revenue system of the Government." The zamindars, consequently, managed to grab large areas of land and continued to operate as *thakur*s in rural India for a considerable span of time. In *Do Bigha Zamin*, for example, Murad plays the role of a cruel *thakur*.

An example of a shaky and confused beginning of the villain in the early fifties can be demonstrated by mentioning a Raj Kapoor film *Aag* (1948) that portrays the shattering of the dream of a theater-actor. The *aag* (fire) not only blazes his theater, but in the process it leaves a part of his face charred with injuries. More importantly, the fire that breaks outside symbolically suggests the fire within the minds of the two protagonists, consumed by passion for the heroine of the theater. The role of Deval, the actor-director, is played by Raj Kapoor, while that of Rajan, who finances the theater, is played by Premnath. Given the fact that Premnath plays the villain in a coeval film of the time like *Aan* (1952), and on several occasions again as the decades rolled on—in *Teesri Manzil* (1966), for example—the audience of *Aag* recognizes him as a villain guided by devilish intentions. The girl, first delighted to hear that Deval is alive, screams in agony and repulsion when she sees his contorted face after the fire. At the nursing home, she offers flowers to Deval but announces her marriage to Rajan.

Rajan's ranting in the film when he destroys the canvases reminds one of the raging outbursts of villains in the later decades. Rajan romps away with the heroine of the theater, leaving Deval to pine in the nursing home with injuries, both physical and mental. As a matter of fact, Rajan is not shown in the latter part of the film. He withdraws behind the curtain after throwing tantrums, like the zamindar does in *Do Bigha Zamin*. Raj Kapoor uses a motif where a friend withdraws and sacrifices his love for the sake of his friend, a pattern later repeated in films like *Muqaddar Ka Sikandar* and *Dostana*.

In *Awaara* (1951), a smash hit of the fifties, and a film that was dubbed in Turkish, Persian, Arabic, and Russian, breaking the box-office record in the Middle East and very popular in the erstwhile USSR, Raj Kapoor introduces the menacing villain Jagga, played by K. N. Singh. Jagga, seeking revenge against the judge who had punished him, makes his son an *awaara* (tramp), forcing him to steal and join the group of criminals. When Jagga abducts the judge's wife, he justifies his position by saying, "The rich should feel embarrassed. Your husband killed my son. My father was a dacoit; I wasn't."

With this agenda, the villain makes every effort to ruin the peace of the judge (Pritviraj Kapoor) who repents when he sees his son under trial at the court. *Awaara* takes up a socialist issue, arguing early in the history of Bollywood cinema that those taking to crime, are the products of environment. The judge, however, believes in the claim put forward by feudal standards that say that the son of a gentleman is bound to be good, whereas that of a criminal should in all probablity be a criminal. As a villain, Jagga challenges this prevalent notion, fighting against a society and system that made him an outcast. This theme is later taken up by Manmohan Desai in *Parvarish* where the police officer is guided by a similar notion aired by the judge in *Awaara*. This film sets the trend of villains who, along with the heroes, are often seen fighting against the system. Jagga is a major villain of the time, because he looks like an ideal predecessor of Amitabh Bachchan of the seventies. So, the socialist agenda of *Awaara* is most forcibly stated by the villain of the film, making it a huge success of the time. This point has hardly been noticed, the focus always having been on the hero.

Jagga is a terror of the slum. Even before he appears, people shut their doors in fear. *Awaara*'s social discourse was much appreciated by Nehru for improving the ties between India and Russia. This supports the contention that "cinema in India has evolved as a parallel culture."[1]

In *Aan*, Premnath plays Sham Sher Singh, the villain, who tries to usurp power by killing his father. Dilip Kumar plays Jai Tilak in the film who belongs to the Rajput clan. The film shows a sword fight between the hero and villain, making it very popular at the time. Possibly the ambience of historical romance allows the villain to be reckless in following his path. He feels that in trying to get the throne for himself, he is merely following a cause of his own, like Duryodhana felt in the Mahabharata.

The mood of the villains as zamindars and landlords operating in the fifties was most grimly set by *Do Bigha Zamin*, often mentioned in conjunction with K. A. Abbas's *Dharti Ke Lal*, made under the Indian People's Theatre Association (IPTA) banner in 1946 and considered to be the first Indian movie to have received widespread distribution in the USSR. Remarkably, if the film of the pre-Independence era had shown optimism, *Do Bigha Zamin* ends on a bleak note, leaving no ray of hope for farmer Shambhu. The film finishes with a brilliant filmic suggestion in which all three—the father, the mother, and the child play their roles. Shambhu, blocked by the wire-net guarding his land, takes up a handful of soil. The guard calls him a thief and throttles him, forcing him to let the soil and dust go off his hand. The three trudge up a mound, silhouetted against the sky. They turn back to get a last glimpse of the land that was once their own. The final sequence has the effect of a mise-en-scene in which, as Eisenstein tells us, the "interrelation of people in action"[2] is beautifully suggested by the guard, Shambhu, his wife, and their son.

Ratan Kumar's performance in the role of the rickshawpuller's son, Kanhaiya Maheto, lost in the city from his father's company, not only reminds one of Vittorio De Sica's masterpiece *Bicycle Thieves* (1948), but it also sets the trend of remarkable juvenile petformance, graced by a lot of human sensibilities and boyish imagination even before Satyajit Ray's *Pather Panchali* rocked the screen on August 26, 1955. Ratan Kumar is an ideal predecessor of both Master Manjunath in *Agneepath* 1990 and Arish Bhiwandiwala in *Agneepath* 2012. Balraj Sahni's rickshawpuller still remains a mega performance, an exclusive one of its kind, unparalleled and unbelievable.

Do Bigha Zamin is, in many ways, a remarkable film that remains a milestone for showing the disaster brought about by the ugly roles played by zamindars as villains. The zamindar, Thakur Harnam Singh (another memorable performance by Murad) is shown eating grapes when Sambhu, the farmer, sidles up to his awful presence. Murad is the father of Raja Murad, who has essayed villains in Bollywood cinema, in films like *Tridev* (1989), *Mohra* (1994), *Gupt* (1997), and the role of a terrorist in *Ek Hi Raasta*, a 1993 film.

Shambhu later declines to sign the deed of handing over his land, and becomes a rickshawpuller in the city as he has to pay back a fictitious amount of ₹235, demanded by the atrocious zamindar, in place of ₹65 only. The sight of Shambhu, pulling a rickshaw across the city, provides a scathing commentary on the loss of honor and integrity of farmers in agrarian India after the Independence. The film's strong human portrayal of the agonies of Indian peasanthood was appreciated globally, receiving awards and accolades from China, the UK, the USSR, and such venues as Venice and Melbourne. It was the winner of the Prix Internationale and was nominated for Grand Prize at the prestigious Seventh Cannes Film Festival of 1954. However, the honor (*Palm d'Or*) went to Japan for the film *Gate of Hell* by Teinosuke Kinugasa, a film that tells the story of a samurai who tries to marry a woman he rescues, only to know later much to his anguish and disappointment that she's married to someone else.

While many things can be said legitimately in favor of this film, the anguish of the samurai, being strictly a personal one as he wishes to get his love for a woman satiated, cannot possibly be compared to the height of universal anguish felt by the hapless rickshawpuller, wiping his sweat by the sleeve of his dirty shirt, and separated from his son. This is the position Shambhu has been thrown into by the evil Thakur of the film.

Could it be that such great film personalities like Andre Bazin, Jean Cocteau (the president of the Jury in the 1954 event), and Andre Lang—all from France—were dismayed and distracted by the ugly sight of a man carrying other people on a vehicle pulled along by hands? It is reported that the celebrated filmmaker Francois Truffaut was so disturbed by the sight of Chunibala Devi eating rice with her hand in Ray's *Pather Panchali* that he trotted out of the theater hall, as if struck by a flash of lightning. Truffaut, it should be said here, had words of praises for Ray and Subrata Mitra, the cameraman of *Pather Panchali*.

Ironically, the worries of farmers increased within the feudal and upcoming capitalist infrastructure. People felt like opting for jobs in faraway cities as the crisis deepened. *Naukari* (1954), made by Bimal Roy, who made three significant films in the fifties, shows the hero leaving his village in search of a job. He reaches Calcutta and finds shelter in a mess called "Bekar Block" ("a block for the unemployed"). Later, the hero goes to Bombay and finds a job only to lose it later. Not important from the villain's point of view, this film shows how the time was becoming ripe for villains to become aggressive. Remember *Naukari* was released in 1954, only a year away from the middle of the decade. An important filmmaker, Bimal Roy shows the grim scenario of the country and toward the end of the film pleads for jobs for unemployed youths, withering and rotting in villages.

After *Do Bigha Zamin*, it was left to Bimal Roy to interpret the villain in *Madhumati* within the emerging sociopolitical scenario of the late fifties. Roy was by this time internationally known, and it was probably an honor for Pran to be chosen to play Ugranarayan in this film. *Madhumati*, it's well-known, deals with the subject of rebirth and revolves round the villain as a sinister and lascivious zamindar. The hero arrives at a faraway mountain in search of work, a motif that was established by Roy in *Naukari*. Later, the hero falls in love with the heroine. Pran goes all the way to get the tribal beauty Madhu in absence of the hero, thus showing his predominant motif of thwarting the love interest of the hero, a motif of the villain in the sixties.

Ugranarayan rides into the forest of innocence where Madhu stays. He terrorizes the birds and hides behind a tree, waiting for his trap to work. This is a familiar sight of the villain in the fifties. He never hurries, being impatient. On the other hand he skulks around, waiting to pounce on his prey, unlike the political and terrorist villains of the eighties. Ugranarayan rides twice up the mountain, chasing Madhu. His scaring of the birds acquires a symbolic significance when one sees it in the context of what later happens in the film. Anand, the hero (played by Dilip Kumar), is sent away from the spot by the villain on pretext of work. The father of the girl, too, is out of town. Madhu is summoned to the zamindar's house which looks like a medieval castle, bringing in feudal associations. The villain, knowing Madhu's weakness for the hero, gives out that Anand is back from his work but is injured severely due to an accident. The real accident follows later when Ugranarayan approaches Madhu and chases her, like Dussasana in the Mahabharata. Madhu jumps off the cliff, ending her life.

Later, Anand forces the evil zamindar to confess his crime. The scene is handled with suspense, having all the drama in it and showing the aggressive gesture of the villain till the last moment. The police arrest Ugranarayan, who stubbornly refuses to surrender. It's clear that the villain since the mid-fifties has acquired greater resistance and venom. After all, Pran has arrived on the scene, occupying the center stage. The hero looks pretty ordinary beside him. Dilip Kumar's soft measured articulation which gave him unassailable fame as an actor since the day he had played Selim in *Mughal-e-Azam* (1960) cannot defeat the wily, artful Pran. This is not to take away anything from the ever versatile Dilip Kumar. But, the scenarios down the fifties helped the villains, since the time was now politically and socially favorable for them, at least more than it was before.

Madhumati happens to be the first film where the zamindar's prurience becomes the subject of pivotal interest. Even before the villain appears on the scene, his wayward whims and menace become a subject of discussion by others. The ambience looks grim and threatening, and the happy union of lovers in a far-off mountain looks tragically affected, suggesting the catastrophe. Agrarian economy is already threatened by the march of industrialization and Anand, the hero, arrives at a lonely place, seeking employment.

Naya Daur (1957), a major hit of the fifties, shows the menace of the villain, siding with the crushing consequence of industrialization. The agonies of mill-workers mount when the villain, back from city, introduces machinery into the rural system. Directed by B. R. Chopra, later famous for the *Ramayana* serial, *Naya Daur* is fondly remembered by elders even now. People, riding on bullock-carts from far-off villages and towns, thronged round the movie theater to watch the film. Many reached the hall by sitting uncomfortably in groups on carts. During interval, some, visibly worried about their way back, peeped out to check if the drivers of the carts were feeding the tired animals. The bumpy road used to be lonely at midnight, flooded by the occasional moonlight. People sat silent, drowsing off. When they chose to talk on a rare occasion, they talked about the treachery of the villain in bringing machines into the village. Others hummed tunes like "*Saathi haath badhana,*" or the lusty number, "*Reshmi salwar,*", to keep off the street dogs who barked, annoyed. Bollywood has always taken care of such audiences, and the service has paid off hugely over the years.

What Jawaharlal Nehru had said about agriculture in his speech to the Lok Sabha on September 15, 1952, may be recalled here: "If our agriculture becomes strongly entrenched, as we hope it will, then it will be relatively easy for us to progress more rapidly on the industrial front."[3] As if foreshadowing the agenda taken up by *Naya Daur*, Nehru further said in his speech at the AICC Session at Indore on January 4, 1957: "We do want high standards of living, but not at the cost of man's creative spirit, his creative energy, his spirit of adventure; not at the cost of all those fine things of life which have ennobled man throughout the ages."[4]

What the generous-minded Seth argues about at the end of *Naya Daur*, extolling the creative energies of villagers, echoes the sentiments voiced by Nehru.

So, here is a film that praises traditional technology used in agriculture, claiming it to be as good as the new modernized alternative. *Naya Daur* raises the issue with stunning effect. It's one of the classics of Bollywood cinema, and presents the story having the most ideal pivotal points, articulated through music and acting. *Naya Daur* bagged all three prizes for best story (Akhtar Mirza), best music director (the great O. P. Nayyar), and Dilip Kumar as the best actor.

Kundan is the villain in this film (played by Jeevan) representing new technology. It is he who introduces the electric saw and car into the village. The commitment to bring in the man-machine antithesis in the film is stated when a passage from Mahatma Gandhi is quoted at the beginning of the film. It urges on the use of machinery for easing human labor instead of destroying sensibility. Gandhi, it may be recalled here, was an avid reader of John Ruskin, drawing inspiration from him on the subject of man and machine. As said before, this clearly articulated empathy of the film with the old system becomes pronounced by wedging the villain into the new system. Thus, it's the villain's action that most poignantly brings out the contrast between man and machine. Shankar, the hero, played by Dilip Kumar, is paired off with the villain by making him a carriage driver. Ajit, destined to play the powerful villain in the seventies, taking over from Pran, plays Krishna, who joins hands with the villain, predicting a future possibility. The main debate of the film finally settles on building up a road in the village. A race between the villain's car and the hero's carriage is arranged, suggesting symbolically the man-machine antithesis. It's important to note that the villains in *Naya Daur*, both the treacherous friend (Ajit), and the industrialist (Jivan), play their roles according to the conventions prevalent in the time. They look quite menacing, out to destroy the hero. In the end, they return to their fold.

Mehboob Khan's *Mother India* rocked the screen in the fifties, and brought back the moneylender villain on a phenomenal scale. As said before, this film is a remake of a previous effort by Mehboob Khan, known as *Aurat* (1940), now nearly forgotten. This may be because of the phenomenal success of *Mother India* that revolves round the famous Nargis–Sunil Dutt–Kanhaiyalal combination. This is further complemented by Khan's imaginative handling of the theme of north Indian agrarian feudalism again in the late fifties. Possibly he realized that the social ambience could make the remake relevant in the changed sociopolitical scenario. While the feudal agenda is treated in the context of the country's emerging needs in the post-Independence ambience, the villain as moneylender gets greater prominence in *Mother India*. Even after becoming a saga of the agricultural heritage of India, and released at a significant phase of the country's development, not to mention the phenomenal acting prowess of Nargis and Kanhaiyalal, *Mother India* receives only a passing reference in so-called academic discussions of films, as in M. Madhava Prasad's *Ideology of the Hindi Film*, for example. Prasad considers *Mother India* as being "the source for the thematics of the mother-son relationship,"[5] and one that provides the primary narrative material for the film *Deewar. Ganga Jumna* (1961), he says, is the other.

Prasad considers *Deewar* to be "one of the few film epics produced by the Bombay industry,"[6] but says nothing about *Mother India* that turns out to be a film more about the mother than about the son. The truth is that *Mother India* as a film upholds traditional values, centering on the mother's heroic struggle in which she has to confront an ugly moneylender villain. In *Deewar*, the mother is overshadowed by her towering son who has joined the underworld. It is also to be doubted, as Prasad believes, if Birju belongs entirely to the Robin Hood type. Radha, the mother in *Mother India*, never feels any nostalgia for her dacoit son. As a matter of fact, she shoots Birju in the film. The mother in *Deewar* couldn't possibly dream of it. On the other hand, Haji Mastan and other smugglers, Prasad notes, were arrested after the film *Deewar* was made. Still, the film had nothing to do with it. It became a routine job after Emergency was proclaimed, carried out in the other states also. Whatever little vague ethical status was accorded to Dawar's gang in *Deewar* it was primarily because Amitabh Bachchan was playing the role of Vijay. That necessitated the so-called higher ethical value attached to Dawar and his gang. However, *Deewar* and *Ganga Jumna*, as we'll see later, show some interesting points of similarity between themselves.

After a lapse of four years since *Do Bigha Zamin*, Nargis, playing the role of the mother in *Mother India*, takes a handful of soil up to her forehead. She picks up, symbolically, from where Shambhu had left it in the previous film. If Shambhu ended with a sense of resignation, the mother of Mehboob Khan's film is in no way prepared to cave in, as her epic struggle testifies. She rears up her children all alone, in the absence of her husband and resists the lascivious approaches of the villain Sukhi Lala. The titles appear on the close-up of the mother shown in a ruminative mood, while her face registers the agonies of her past struggle. The busy activity of tractors and cranes are shown in the background. A car without hood passes, carrying the Congress leaders. This betrays a bit of irony, since no one was seen around during Radha's ordeal. The dam is about to be opened. The leaders request the mother to formally open it, garlanding her. She refuses; then agrees, pleaded on with. The mother becomes a tool in the hands of the leaders for putting across their message to the nation. This is, again, unlike the mother of *Deewar*, who merely chooses between her two sons, one belonging to the underworld and the other to the police administration. Thus, her choice is pretty ordinary, like any mother would do in a similar situation. The mother in *Deewar* never questions the system that has turned her son into an underworld don.

This is why the smell of the garland round the old mother's neck in *Mother India* takes her back to the past, the day of her wedding, as if in retaliation against the wishes of the leaders. She thinks of her days of struggle down the memory lane with the help of the same garland which has been offered to her for opening the dam. Khan's handling of the situation deserves attention. So, the curtain goes up to allow us get a closer look at the moneylender villain, Sukhi Lala, an unforgettable face of the fifties in Bollywood cinema.

Significantly, Lala's first appearance in the film is as a debauchee, prying into and commenting on the girls of the village who are out to fetch water. He addresses the other one ("*Arey o Radharani, Zara sambhalke chalna*" ["Hey, Radharani, walk on with caution"]) though his eyes are fixed on the beauty of Radha, newly married to Shamu, the farmer. The conjugal happiness of the couple is shown when Radha brings lunch for her husband to the field, voyeuristically watched by two other farmers hidden behind the bundles of hayrick. Later, the couple is seen toiling hard in the field, producing golden crops.

When the crops are gathered from the field, Lala appears from nowhere. He celebrates his arrival by demanding a large portion of the crop which, like the zamindar's spurious account-keeping in *Do Bigha Zamin*, goes on mounting each year instead of decreasing. The quarrel scene shows the plight and agony of the villagers. Lala, whose crown is spotlessly barren, leaving his wily brain eternally ignited without any encumbrance, growls, "*Police laake saari zameen pe kabza karenge ... satyanash!*" ("I'll call the police, and take over the entire land ... ah crikey, what a violation of truth!") That's Sukhi Lala of *Mother India*. He swears by truth, pleading innocence, and announces his pledge to take care of the farmers' welfare. He claims *only* his due, year after year. His warning shows that the police work for him in connivance, just as they will do far more aggressively in the seventies and eighties. The Lala, who functions within a different sociopolitical scenario, develops into becoming a political and terrorist villain. Sukhi Lalas have many faces.

"*Satyanash*" and "*ram kasam*" are the usual vows of this villain, and he goes on chanting them before plunging into action. The turning point of the film occurs when Lala makes a mockery of Shamu, who loses his hands while trying to remove a boulder. The cow dies, and Shamu loses his hands in this impossible effort. When he is next seen, attending the other cow that is drinking water from a reservoir, Lala appears on horseback, accompanied by his acolytes, holding guns in their hands. Lala mocks Shamu for eating the food of his wife's labor, and takes the cow away. To rile and further humiliate Shamu, Lala puts the harness bells of the cow round his neck. That night, to get rid of his life of shame and humiliation, Shamu leaves the village. He never returns, leaving Radha alone to fight the battle of her survival. The villain has his wish fulfilled. After Shamu's disappearance from the scene, Radha loses her conjugal status. From now on, she's only a mother.

Flood wrecks the village. Radha finds shelter with her children on a fragile platform of bamboo sticks. A snake crawls along the water. It's about to nuzzle Radha's breast. Radha, significantly, is intimidated by the snake and stands still in water. Her younger son Birju, who later becomes a dacoit, sits unruffled, gets hold of the snake, and throws it away. The crawling of the snake and the contrast between the mother and her son, both facing the poisonous reptile, acquires larger significance when Lala enters the frame with a lantern in hand. Lala cannot rest when he knows that others are suffering. Before Lala enters, the youngest child dies. "My children are starving. Give me food, Lala, give me food," Radha says, throwing her *mangalsutra* away. Summoning dignity, Lala assures that he has perfectly understood what she means. The snake, not fended off, slithers in. Remember what Lala Murlidhar says about the moneylender villain: a unique formation of man and beast. Kanhaiyalal plays the villain with insidious cunning and malignity, having truly the "claws of a lion, the brain of a fox, and the heart of a goat." The fifties of Bollywood cinema were certainly not a time of total disillusionment. People, inspired by Nehruvian socialism, were still keenly anticipants, though with apprehensions. Still, this doubt was not one of total distrust. The heroes, by and large, knew that good was to come after initial hurdles. The villains, on the other hand, knew that they didn't need tricks and weapons to get the heroes buckled under pressure. Lala Sukhiram, for example, succeeds in banishing Shamu from the scene by working into his conscience. Only words, coated with venom, are sufficient.

Lala holds the key in every turning point of the film, wrecking Radha's happiness. He's certainly more cunning and circumspective in hatching his plot than the hasty and impatient Ugranarayan in *Madhumati*. He keenly watches every move of his opponent before plodding into action. Sukhi Lala is in no hurry. Discussions of *Mother India* so far haven't looked at the film by placing the villain at the center of the narrative. Significantly, Lala Sukhram, unlike the other villains of the fifties and sixties, is not allowed to go back to his fold. On the other hand, he's killed by the dacoit son in *Mother India*, just as it happens in the pre-Independence film *Samaj Ko Badal Dalo*. Why? Let's try to find an answer.

Since *Mother India* happens to be a major film of the fifties, showing the moneylender as a macabre villain, this issue needs to be taken up. We could possibly get a lead by the fact that Birju, the dacoit son (played by Sunil Dutt) also dies in the film, shot by his mother. Birju says that Sukhi, like him, is also a dacoit. The difference is that he stays in society and acts, wearing a mask. In one sense, it is a triumph of the villain to have had one of the sons of Radha folded up. Lala mobilizes people for banishing Birju from the village in the idealist fifties. The dacoit son does his mother a service when he terminates the life of a man who has caused her so much agony. Still, Radha cannot forgive her son, because he is a social outcast and a killer. The villain's death in *Mother India* facilitates the killing of the dacoit son.

As said before, one typical feature of the villains' operation in the fifties is that they plunge into action when they find their victims alone, separated from relatives. Thus, in *Madhumati*, the villain springs into action when the girl is separated from Anand. Ugranarayan makes plans and succeeds in sending the hero away for a while. When the tragedy occurs, Madhumati's father is also not around. He moves out of the town. In *Naya Daur*, the owner of the mill, the villain's father, playing the role of a benefactor, is also absent for quite some time when the damage to the villagers is done by the villain. In *Mother India*, Kanhaiyalal plots to send Radha's husband away from her. This is because in the fifties the villain, not being an underworld don, has to wait for the opportune moment to start operation.

Paying Guest coincides with the release of both *Mother India* and *Naya Daur*. This film deserves to be noted. The story of the film gathers speed when the villain arrives on the scene. Directed by Subodh Mukherjee, the film first shows the romance between Shanti and Ramesh (played by Nutan and Dev Anand) and the illicit love of the rich wife for the hero. The scene changes when Mr Dayal, played by Yakub, arrives on the spot and starts blackmailing the rich wife. In this film, the villain is a buccaneer, aspiring for money from his father-in-law, who eventually dies with a vague knowledge that his son-in-law is a profligate with little consideration for others, not even for his wife. The film reminds one of a similar role played by Yakub in *Samaj Ko Badal Dalo*, already mentioned in this discussion. *Paying Guest* shows an interesting change in the use of the villain in these two films. In the former film, the villain remained shadowy and played a marginal role in the narrative; in the latter, the villain acquires greater menace, taking control of the situation. The similarity is that in both films the villain is killed. Dayal is killed by the rich wife who targets the revolver at the villain for getting back her *vakalatnama*. Unfortunately, the bullet goes off, leaving her unaware.

The interesting point about the film is that, in this case, the villain finds shelter in the house of his father-in-law in the city. This makes a significant point of contrast with the rural agrarian base of villains found in many films of the fifties. It is in this context that another film *C.I.D.* (1956) should be mentioned. Crime films were nothing new in Bollywood. *Kisan Kanya* was made before the Independence. *C.I.D.* makes a departure in the sense that it's not a rural crime drama like *Kisan Kanya*. Guru Dutt and Dev Anand, together with Raj Khosla, were largely responsible for popularizing the detective genre. *Kala Pani*, released in 1958, was another.

The crime motif gives these films an urban setting and brings the villain to the elite middle class of the city. The feudal base is retained, though it's now pitted against democracy, upholding the cultural values of the capitalist framework. Consequently, the villain in *C.I.D.* plods like an aristocrat, being a stylish and suave middle-aged man, who keeps a vamp with him for facilitating his operation. The role of the villain in this film is played by K. N. Singh, already famous for putting up a smart villain in *Baghban*, made before the Independence. Singh introduced the smart elegant villain, a type in which he excelled.

Mr Dharamdas in *C.I.D.* strides away from us, shoes tapping the floor. His face is not shown even in the next frame. We see him for the first time when he instructs the vamp over telephone to throw the unconscious hero out of the car on the Mumbai–Agra road. Dev Anand plays inspector Shekhar, investigating the murder of Srivastav, the editor of a newspaper.

Dharamdas seems to be a worthy predecessor of Teza of *Zanjeer*. He intimidates by a flick of his eyes, often by a cursory glance, like he does at Rekha's birthday party. His humble claim *"logon ki seva mera dharam hai"* ("to serve people is my religion") suggests his affinity with Teza rather than with Lala Sukhiram. Dharamdas would detest being called a Lala, because operating from a village couldn't be the choice of this smart suave villain.

C.I.D. and the late fifties signal the villain's location shifting from the rural to the urban. The feudal framework couldn't help the villain any more, making his status as a zamindar and moneylender somewhat precarious. The advent of industry brought with it a capitalist set of values, and this made the city an ideal venue for the villain's operation. He had to now put up more sophistication in his manners and appear sprucely dressed in order to win the heart of the heroine, a distinguishing trend of the sixties. This set the scenario for Pran taking over the job from both Kanhaiyalal and Singh.

Meanwhile, another feature was taking place. Remember Dharamdas stamping about in the underground of *C.I.D.* which shows both architectural innovation and emergence of capitalist hegemony, replacing the old feudal system. Tunnels go through walls, and the way goes on, appearing endless. The smart and suave movement of Seth Dharamdas sets an example to the hero to emulate, something that he would excel at doing in the nineties. Sekhar (Dev Anand) observes the Seth from close quarters, and this inspires him to play the new type of hero, looking occasionally like a villain. Thus, the "Dev noir" films came into existence, opening with *Jaal*, and followed by others. Let's look into them for a while.

"*Woh sirf daulat chahta hai*" ("He wants money only")—this is how Lisa, the heroine of the film *Jaal* accuses Tony (Dev Anand). This accusation of the heroine against the hero takes one by surprise at the beginning of the sixties. A spectator, arriving late in the theater, might conclude that the heroine is talking about the villain of the film. *Jaal* makes its intention clear by showing the world of smugglers, joined in by the hero. The "Dev noir" films like *Taxi Driver* (1954), *Kala Bazar* (1960), and the famous *Jewel Thief* (1967) continue the motif up to *Gambler* in 1971. Dev Anand wasn't satisfied with playing the goody heroes. Both *Taxi Driver* and *Kala Bazar* were produced by Navketan, while the story and screenplay of *Jaal* was written by Guru Dutt, who directed the film as well. Guru Dutt must have been inspired to make *Jaal* by watching Anand's performance in the previous films. That's why *Jaal* should be placed in the context of the predecessor films, and those made after. It's well known that the Guru Dutt–Dev Anand combination was responsible for introducing a new concept of the hero, something that was liked by Guru Dutt himself. In *Kala Bazar*, for example, the *kala bazaar* (black-marketing) of tickets at the theater halls suggests the soul-wrecking poverty of the time, following its disillusionment with Nehru's socialist state. It also sends a reminder of how the hero is going to behave. There's a parade of actors and actresses of the film industry. Among others like Nargis, Rajendra Kumar, and Dilip Kumar walking up to the hall, Guru Dutt is also seen. As Guru Dutt walks away to the left of the camera, people shout after him. This parade of heroes might have been intended to show how the hero in *Kala Bazar* was different from others. Guru Dutt, applauded by the crowd, is spotted to be the calling card of the time, not Rajendra Kumar and Dilip Kumar, at least not in the context of this film.

Raghuveer (Dev Anand) turns a black-marketeer when he sees his mother ill, finding himself pitted against the state and society that were supposed to take care of him. Fighting against an alien environment, and probably setting an example to the underworld hero of *Deewar*, Raghu buys a posh, decorated flat and brings his mother and sister to the newly bought accommodation. The poor mother can't believe her eyes, and although she doesn't leave her son, as it later happens in *Deewar* against a bleaker scenario, she suffers from a premonition of her son not following the right path. Raghu is feared by all. He becomes the leader of a gang, confronted later by another don, Madanpuri, once again suggesting the *Deewar* motif. Finally, Raghu decides, as the time is not so fatalistic and agonizing like the seventies, to run a *safed* bazaar, a market where people would sell their wares at a reasonable price. Still, Raghu's previous offense goes against him. He's taken to court and is about to be punished when his case is argued favorably by a lawyer. We are in 1960, dear readers. In another 15 years, this scenario would change drastically.

In *Taxi Driver*, the hero hasn't much time for romance. As a matter of fact, he doesn't do anything that might be called heroic. This new discourse of the hero was quickly exploited by Guru Dutt. In *Jaal*, he shows Dev as a victim of an alien society, someone, who has neither love nor compassion for girls in distress. Tony, on the other hand, cheats girls. But, nowhere else is the critique against the goody hero more ironically suggested than in the scene where Tony mouths the scintillating romantic number "Ye Raat, Ye Chandni," sung by Hemant Kumar. The hero sings the romantic tune and seduces his girl. When asked to choose between gold and the girl, he chooses gold, leaving the girl to her fate. Later he falls at the feet of the girl, seeking her mercy, like any villain of the sixties returning to his fold. The dark photography of *Jaal* illuminates the contrast between good and evil, and finally conveys a Christian message.

Encouraged by the success of *Jaal*, Vijay Anand made *Jewel Thief* down the decade. The suspicion about the identity of the jewel thief is cleverly knotted round the hero, just as Shekhar in *C.I.D.* is misunderstood till at least half of the story. The "Dev noir" films, by their uniqueness, have probably had a lot to do with what happens in the mid-nineties with the arrival of Shah Rukh Khan on the scene. The idea of the hero, usurping the job of the villain, looks significant for the following reasons:

1. First of all, it suggests a change in the idea of the hero, which was by and large unthinkable in the fifties and sixties.
2. Second, these films offer an ironical critique of the social scenario of the time when an individual, unable to find his place in society, was largely misunderstood. This theme was later taken up more virulently in the seventies. The *Deewar* motif of *Kala Bazar* illustrates this.

3. The "Dev noir" films proved for the first time (barring Ashok Kumar's antihero in *Kismet* [1943] in pre-Independence cinema) that the villain's evil design could be better articulated by the hero because he has the camouflage to work his way through. The unexpected turn in the behavior of the hero generates suspense and anxiety in the narrative, taking others unaware. The confirmed villains, yet to become the masters of their guile, couldn't do that. Notice again how Shammi Kapoor finds himself happily wedged in Dev's persona playing the underworld don in *China Town* (1962), two years after *Kala Bazar* and *Jaal*. This too may be cited as a triumph of "Dev noir" films.

The motif of a villain behind the hero also suited Dev Anand's style of acting, looking forward, in a prognostic way, to the films that were to come later. Thus, the "Dev noir" films have their relevance and significance when they are placed not only against the transitional phase of the late fifties and sixties, but also in the context of the future development of Bollywood cinema. Dev Anand, by suggesting a change in the concept of the hero, managed to offer a contrast to both Raj Kapoor and Dilip Kumar, and cut a niche of his own. Shah Rukh takes this up in the nineties to his advantage.

Kala Pani, suggesting black water, attempts to seek justice and solve a crime that took place 15 years ago when the hero's father was wrongly convicted. In spite of betraying the disillusionment that was slowly creeping into the minds of people, *Kala Pani* shows that the villain, too, is aware of the social changes taking place around him. The conversation between the Dewan and lawyer, where they talk about wiping the hero from the scene for digging up the past, shows their concern for the changed sociopolitical scenario. The villain, by this time, was thinking about changing his location from the village to the city. Crime films of the fifties, working on the contrast between feudal hegemony and democratic regulations, did an important job in bringing about the location shift of the villain.

Nehru also felt that everything didn't go as well as he'd anticipated. In a speech to the Lok Sabha, December 11, 1963, a year before his death, Nehru said:

One thing that distresses me very greatly is that, although I am convinced that the great majority of our population have bettered their economic condition a little, with more calories and more clothes, yet, there is a good number of people in India who have not profited by planning, and whose poverty is abysmal and more painful.[7]

In the same speech, Nehru said that setting up factories while ignoring the human consideration was not enough. He couldn't be more specific and candid in diagnosing the malady of the nation as he was facing at the time the opposition in the Lok Sabha. The year 1962 showed that new social formulations had emerged as a result of shifts and mobility in caste-oriented politics. The Swatantra Party of the time, for example—ideologically right-wing, but depending largely on rural awakening—was gaining strength in backward classes, posing threats to the Congress party. There were signs of discontent in villages.

Contradictory ideologies in which the villain has a role to play are shown in *Jis Desh Mein Ganga Behti Hai* (*The Country where the Ganga Flows*). Released at the beginning of the sixties, this movie gives an important lead toward assessing the villain as someone bringing in a cataclysm of events and finally returning to his fold. The role of the hero, an innocuous rustic, is played by Raj Kapoor with his usual upfront spontaneity—known to be his special forte. This puts him in sharper contrast with the monstrosity of the villain played by Pran, who throws obstacles in the union between the hero and the heroine. This sets the trend of the films of the sixties, taking its cue from *Madhumati*, so far as the villain's role is concerned.

Raju the hero, who later becomes a *mehman* (guest) of the bandits in recognition of his service to the Sardar during a raid, is not trusted by the villain Raka, who, along with his acolytes, suspects him to be a spy of police. Significantly, the first introduction of the villain in this film shows him holding an axe instead of a revolver. He bullies others, looking defiant and arrogant. The chieftain's daughter sees Raju with eyes full of wonder, as if he were from another planet. Raka, on the other hand, desires her love. This sets the tension and rivalry in motion. The Sardar is killed by Raka.

When in the end the bandits are asked by the police to lay their arms and surrender, a close-up of Raka shows him miserably resigned to his fate. This makes an instance of the sad predicament when the villain is ruined by the weakness and disloyalty of others, as if ordained by fate—a feature discussed at the beginning of this book. Still, Raka manages to put up a smirk on his lips, looking defiant. The point to notice here is that the villain doesn't change to become a Samaritan, worshipping law. On the other hand, he realizes that making a choice in the situation is like facing a cul de sac. He can't take guns in hand, since others have surrendered theirs. Nor can he give up the struggle easily.

The question of survival in an alien environment, staying marginalized from the mainstream society, forms the theme of *Jis Desh Mein Ganga Behti Hai*. This was going to become a popular theme of the time taken up by other coeval films, like *Ganga Jumna*, for example, that followed the next year. The point to notice is that *Jis Desh Mein Ganga Behti Hai* keeps the issue vibrant till the end, keeping the villain at the center of the narrative and influencing the films of the following decade.

Agriculture didn't do as well as anticipated, forcing the villains to come over to the cities. The new location was well in tune with the disillusionment that was gradually becoming solidified. One should remember also that popular Indian psyche can't function by totally ignoring the existing options or set-ups. If they're to welcome the new, they also show a tendency to accommodate the old within the new system. If industry is good, it doesn't mean that the agrarian set-up should be totally discarded. It's still so now. The much-talked about Indian tolerance about accepting opposing cultures and religions may have played its role in deciding the nature and extent of the changes in the films of the decades. Take, for example, a film like *Ram Aur Shyam*. Released in the late sixties (1967), this film moves round both city and village as its locations, though the villain operates mainly from the house of his in-laws in the city.

Ganga Jumna follows Raj Kapoor's *Jis Desh Mein Ganga Behti Hai*, dealing with the theme of the outcasts as dacoits. The villain in Raj Kapoor's film is a social outcast, pitted against the hero, working on behalf of law. In *Ganga Jumna*, the villain is a zamindar and the hero an outcast. Both features prevail; while feudal family structure, seeking control over wealth accumulated since past years, is retained in films that show the Shammi Kapoor–Pran antithesis in the sixties.

The villain, spruce and elegant, vies for the hand of the heroine. But, the point to notice is that the villain seeks the hand of the heroine not because of love but for property, and becoming its sole heir as the son-in-law.

This becomes the motif of the villain in *Bluff Master* and *Kashmir Ki Kali* in the early sixties, and later in *An Evening in Paris* down the decade. The villain's operation in villages as a zamindar and money-lender was challenged due to the peasant's growing awareness of their rights and privileges, both politically and socially. With the advent of industries in cities as well as in villages, the villain was now in need of liquid cash for leading the comforts of city life. In *Do Bigha Zamin*, the zamindar chooses the option of setting up industry in his village. Remember also the apprehension of the public prosecutor in *Kala Pani* about the gradual disappearance of aristocratic titles. This discourse took place at the end of the fifties. The villain's motif behind claiming the hand of the wealthy heroine appears to be a continuation, therefore, of the developments that had surfaced before.

Let's look at a political feature also. In 1960, the state of Bombay was divided into Maharashtra and Gujarat, forcing the film industry to stay wary about another regional competition within the country. Also, economic challenges were now being felt more acutely by people. Those displaced from their lands, and deprived of social benefits, found it easier to join the band of dacoits for survival, and stay social outcasts. Interestingly, if the sixties opened with *Jis Desh Mein Ganga Behti Hai* (and followed closely by *Ganga Jumna*), asking for a social discourse about bringing the outcasts back to the mainstream society, the seventies opened with *Mera Gaon Mera Desh*, showing a menacing dacoit. All the films, taken together, accelerated force and made way for the gruesome Gabbar Singh of *Sholay*. If in *Mera Gaon Mera Desh*, the villain is called Zabbar Singh, in *Sholay* he becomes Gabbar, making the resonance nearly complete.

Now, watch *Ganga Jumna*, directed by Nitin Bose. The band of dacoits—on horseback, and with faces hooded with black clothes—is chasing a running goods train. The hoofs of horses are seen through the wheels of the moving train. Does anyone need to be told that a rehearsal sequence of what we are going to watch in *Sholay* in the next decade is being enacted here? The difference is that the police officer in *Ganga Jumna* is not helped by any other social outcasts as he's in

55

Sholay. Also, the officer in *Ganga Jumna,* guarding law, shoots at his brother, the leader of the gang. In *Ganga Jumna,* a boy reads aloud, *"Jhooth bolna paap hai."* This boy grows to become the police officer, while the elder, framed by the villainous zamindar (Anwar Hussain) for a crime he hadn't committed, ends up in becoming a dacoit. In *Deewar* (1975), *"Jhooth bolna paap hai"* might sound credulous and self-deceiving. The change of time is shown clearly four years later in 1979 in *Mr. Natwarlal* (1979), for example. The boy, learning the alphabet, can't pronounce violin, since "V" for him stands for Vikram, the dangerous villain of the film. As for the mother–son thematics between *Deewar* and *Ganga Jumna* spoken by Madhava Prasad, and discussed earlier in this argument, let it be remembered that the widowed mother (Leela Chitnis) in *Ganga Jumna* dies early long before the other child Jumna (Nasir Khan) becomes a police inspector, helped by Gangaram (Ganga played memorably by Dilip Kumar)—the dacoit. That's where the similarity with *Deewar* may be said to exist partly. But, it's a *theme* of the *brother–brother relationship,* if at all it is.

Kanhaiyalal plays Kallu, popularly known as Munimji, assisting the zamindar in his evil operations. In the beginning, Kallu hides his face under an umbrella furled wide. The dogs on the street don't like this. They bark at him. Kanhaiyalal plays the comic villain in this film, leaving the venomous mantle for the zamindar. But again, in this film also, the zamindar can't get away with his status. He's chided from time to time by the police officer. This shows the development in the social environment spoken earlier. The villain spends his time in tipsy revelry and dances, wallowing in feudal dreams.

Like the *Deewar* motif, Ganga takes care of his younger brother, and gives him the social benefits so that he may find his place in society. Like Ravi in *Deewar,* the police inspector brother is also torn by conflicts when he's given the charge of terminating his brother. But, unlike *Deewar,* Ganga thinks of surrendering to law, and joining mainstream society. In an emotional encounter, Ganga tells his brother: *"Main ghar se bahar ho gaya, bhai"* ("I've been thrown out of home, my brother"). Remember, in this context, the famous sequence of the meeting of the two brothers at the bridge in *Deewar* and compare the articulations of Ganga and Vijay to appreciate the changes in the sociopolitical ambience. Vijay is in no mood to surrender. The time is out-of-joint for him, and the tragedy, like the fated Prince of

Shakespeare's *Hamlet*, is that he cannot set it right. If we talk about the points of similarity between the two films, we should also notice their differences.

The dacoit's den in *Ganga Jumna* looks similar to the one we see in *Jis Desh Mein Ganga Behti Hai*. There's love, marriage, and birth to complete the cycle. But, it doesn't move to a happy end. The enveloping darkness of the film sends a reminder of the later developments down the sixties. The villain, being a zamindar, and left without much occupation, looks like a thick ring of clouds around the apparent silver lining of the early sixties. Ganga finds it difficult to come out of the sinister trap. He can't go back to society, like the dacoits of *Jis Desh Mein Ganga Behti Hai*. Jumna, wary of her companion, runs up to the police station, and gets a fatal injury in the head. She dies along with the child in her womb, like Anita does in *Deewar*. After Jumna's death, it's all over with Ganga. Dilip Kumar's restrained acting in such moments of emotional crises looks phenomenal again and again; in *Naya Daur*, now, and later in *Shakti* (1982), where he shoots his rebel son. Working within the commercial restraints, these actors of Bollywood cinema have always provided the audience with enviable moments of acting feat that beats the cinematic compulsion of movement, and stays in our memory, like Daumier's drawings, mentioned by Eisenstein in his discussion on cinema.

While the brothers fight—one upholding law, and and the other for preservation of his identity as a bandit and outcast—it's all over with the protagonist. But, this fight is set in a redeeming contrast when we see that Munimji too fights with the zamindar who wants to escape. This makes the villain's position in this film rather complex, if not slightly bizarre. It foreshadows what we'll see in the seventies when the villains fight beween them to take charge of the underworld operation. Munimji shouts that the villainous zamindar is a rotten criminal, and has done all the damage. Ganga, enraged, kills the villain, and by making this fatal choice, loses his chance to go back to law.

Ganga, resting on the shoulder of his brother, murmurs: "*Main ghar aya, Munna.*" This suggestion of having a roof, a house to find shelter in, runs as a motif in *Ganga Jumna*. This is a natural consequence of having the dacoits, the social outcasts, at the center of the narrative.

Still, the villains were looking for new engagements and meeting fresh challenges. One noticeable change was found in his dress. Instead of *dhoti-kurta*, he's now clad in suits and ties, a feature that gives him the kind of niche he was seeking to intimidate the hero. He speaks English and is westernized in manners. This new feature works admirably with the arrival of Pran on the scene. The heroine, not probably liking this get-up of the villain, knots his tie tighter in order to nearly throttle him, as it happens in *Bluff Master*. The decade, seen from this point of view, actually opens with *China Town*, released in 1962. It is a dark film, matched by black and white photography, showing assertively that we have left behind the idealist fifties, at least the first half of it. Incredibly, the release date of this film coincides with the Chinese attack on India, and significantly also, *China Town* appears to be a predecessor film of *Don*, made in the turbulent seventies. Shammi Kapoor plays a double role in *China Town*, those of Mike and Shekhar, the twin brothers, estranged from childhood. Mike is a China Town gangster, while Shekhar a Darjeeling-based hotel singer. There are songs in this film, but not anything like the "Khaike Pan Banaraswalla" number, followed by dance under an addled state due to *bhaang*, in which the hero is later joined by the heroine and a pot-bellied man. Nothing like this happens in *China Town* that shows the underworld operation with uncanny precision and stark cynicism. For a moment, one has the impression that he is witnessing a film of the seventies.

Shammi Kapoor, playing Mike, puts up a cocky face, and dismisses everything unpleasant with a flick of his finger. Like *Don*, Shekhar is asked by the police inspector, investigating into the crime operations of the underworld, to impersonate the dangerous Mike so long as he's in police custody. Before this, there are a few funny incidents in Darjeeling, particularly those in which Shekhar confronts the wayward father of the girl he loves. But once the action shifts to Calcutta and the identity of Mike is revealed to Shekhar by his mother, everything turns gloomy and dark. The way Mike refuses to listen to his crying mother, whom he hasn't seen since boyhood, could hardly be imagined in the fifties and sixties. *China Town* is indeed a surprise package of the early sixties.

This brings Madan Puri, the real dangerous villain, into action. Puri plays Joseph Wong in this film. The way he plays his role makes it obvious that this man is going to create troubles, as he does in *Deewar*. Madan Puri in *China Town* looks like preparing himself for playing the bigger roles. Yet, *China Town* can by no stretch of imagination be called a mini rehearsal of Puri's future shaping as a villain, since he's already one in this film. That is another important point about *China Town* as a film. It is as if this film has all the claims of looking like a blueprint of the Chinese attack to destabilize India.

Wong and the menacing Ching Lee (played by M. B. Shetty) kidnap Mike when he is a boy. They rear him up as a gangster to serve their interest, mainly that of carrying out the risky underworld activities. In keeping with the time, these gangsters are not as fearless and arrogant as they will look in the seventies. They are afraid of police raids, adopt secretive measures to hoodwink the police, and even pretend to be law-abiding people. But, in spite of the dictates of time, *China Town* manages to present characters like Wong and Lee, replicating what possibly was really happening at the time in the China Town of Calcutta. In this sense, *China Town* as a film triumphs over its limitations in a way that many films of the sixties couldn't. Shakti Samanta, the producer and director of the film, was a Bengali, and he knew well the real-life situations of the locality of China Town that was then, and still now, located in the eastern part of the city of Kolkata. This makes the film look very convincing as it was drawn from real-life experience. The underworld operations in *China Town* are carried out on the pretext of running a hotel. And, mind you, this happened quite early in the history of cinema, even before the celebrated director Roman Polanski made his classic under the same title in 1974. *Chinatown* by Polanski is an American neo-noir film, part mystery and part psychological drama, and was nominated for 11 Academy Awards.

Shakti Samanta's Hindi film too has its merits. It created a stir when it was released. The Rafi number "Bar Bar Dekho" went on to become a classic. The hotel entertainments of *China Town* bring the lusty Helen on to the screen, as if she were stepping out to do an item number of the seventies when ritzy hotels would spring up in cities. Helen, playing Suzie in *China Town*, strongly anticipates the arrival of Teza's Mona Darling in *Zanjeer*. We'll take up Suzie in more detail in a relevant chapter. For the moment, let's make a note that Suzie is actually Joseph Wong's woman, though she loves Mike, the gangster, who undertakes the difficult operations under instructions from Wong.

China Town, for all these reasons, appears to be a very important film of the sixties. It catches the mood of disillusionment of the late fifties and is more in tune with the crime motif of "Dev noir" films. Shammi Kapoor looks like emulating Dev Anand, though after this he becomes the rollicking boisterous star of the decade as he's known to be, facing Pran. He is no longer Mike, only Shekhar. Probably, Shammi Kapoor could play Mike when he was facing Madan Puri, but he couldn't do so while facing Pran, since Pran was an older and smarter guy, and more treacherous as a villain than Madan Puri is in *China Town*. The constraint becomes clear when we examine the Shammi Kapoor–Pran films that form the next area of our interest in this discussion.

Pran plays Mr Kumar in *Bluff Master*, directed by Manmohan Desai. *Bluff Master* retains the Desai touch; his favorite ploy to show the hero in slums and his gregarious fraternity with other people, especially the children, and the *tanga-walla*. This brings the Pran–Shammi antithesis into a package of engaging frames of action. Ashok, played by Shammi Kapoor, is a master of deception. A large part of the film centers round the series of masquerades the hero uses to hoodwink others. First, he snatches a camera from a shop in the name of another person and then returns it later to the owner after finding himself in an awkward position. Again, he manages to get the camera back by telling the owner a fictitious story of his distress in conjugal life. Compared to the hero, the villain looks a smarter and decent guy. This makes the villain look like having a better claim for the hand of the heroine in this film.

The villain too starts playing tricks for winning the hand of the heroine Seema, played by Saira Banu. Ashoke stops playing his masquerades when the villain springs into action. Seema's uncle joins hands with Ram Kumar, the villain, telling her, "*Pitaji ne kumarbabu ko chuna tha*" ("your departed father chose Kumar as your husband"). Back from London, Kumar has an obvious advantage over the hero who lives in a slum.

The villain employs people to bump Ashoke off from the scene. Later, Kumar steals a huge sum from the iron chest of Seema's uncle. He isn't fooled like others by Ashoke's deception of playing the role of a rich merchant as his father. Seema's uncle and the owner of the camera shop are duped by the hero's masquerade, but not the villain. Ram Kumar exposes the hero before others by bringing his mother on the scene. Ashoke's hopeless status as a slum-dweller is revealed to all, justifying the villain's claim for the heroine. But, alas, what a pity! Ram Kumar is denied his claim, though he possesses the qualities. Dear reader, you might well pause to commemorate Mr Ram Kumar of *Bluff Master* and the injustice done to him by the scriptwriter of the film. During the breathless encounter between the villain and the hero, Tun Tun, the woman of the slum, plays a waggish role by slapping the henchmen of the villain down the valley, and in the process, her husband on the bottom, an offense that might be excused in view of the urgency of the situation. This provides another instance of rollicking fun provided by Bollywood filmmakers again and again—something we have spoken of in this discussion. Tun Tun can be irresistibly hilarious on such occasions, providing pure entertainment. Accordingly, she was well taken care of by the directors of Bollywood cinema. In *China Town* also, Tun Tun plays the role of a Bengali wife, pestering Shekhar's girl again and again for using *sindoor* on the parting of her hair. There are many such actors in Bollywood, and they all deserve mention. The villain is later handed over to the police in *Bluff Master*. The social ambience of the time didn't ask for wiping out the villain. Therefore, Ram Kumar returns to his fold.

Kashmir Ki Kali was released in 1964, establishing the trend (except *Junglee* which was released in 1961) of casting Pran as villain against the boisterous Shammi Kapoor, the flamboyant hero of the decade of the sixties, offering a contrast to the despondent and romantic Rajesh Khanna. As a villain, Pran reigned supreme in this period till *Upkar* (1967), often cited to be a turning point in his career.

Kashmir Ki Kali revolves round the same theme more or less, though the scene of action this time shifts to the scintillating valley of Kahmir, quiet at the time, but was soon going to be troubled as a result of the second Indo-Pakistan war of 1962. Meanwhile, the Indo-China war of 1962 created apprehension in the minds of people, though one great advantage of it was that people felt united and resolved for upholding the stability of the nation. Prices bumped up, yet people didn't mind, at least for the time being. In *Kashmir Ki Kali*, the hero, trying to win the heart of the heroine selling flowers, gives her ₹20 as a cost of the bunch he buys from her. Later, under instruction from her surrogate father, she returns ₹15 to the wealthy hero, keeping ₹5 to herself as the actual cost.

Significantly, the film opens with Raju, the hero, son of Seth San-jiblal, about to take over the mill as the natural owner. He addresses the workers, telling them, *"Yeh mazdoor ka zamana hai"* ("It's the time of workers now"). This shows the trend of the time when workers were getting united to claim better wages and privileges. The hero's speech doesn't please his mother and Shyamlal the accountant, both representing feudal heritage. Raju declares that ₹500,000, which is the dividend of his company, should be distributed among the workers. We are still away from the turbulent seventies when the cities will witness labor unrest and economic repression; when the villains will show their ugly faces.

Raju goes to Kashmir to avoid his mother because she insists on his marriage. In Kashmir he finds his girl, Champa, the flower-woman. This brings the villain Mohan Seth to the scene. The film takes a turning point when it's discovered that Champa is actually the daughter of the Rani-ma, the rich woman of the city. Mohan's subsequent actions keep the film alive till the end. Pran takes away much of the film space from the usually unconquerable Shammi Kapoor. Mohan threatens Champa's surrogate father to marry him off to Champa and starts blackmailing him. The surrogate father, now blind, is unwilling to release the girl from his custody. The flashback begins on the windscreen wiper of a car, handled imaginatively by the director. Mohan seeks out Dheeru's sister Karuna and learns about Champa's real parentage. The money interest comes to play its role. Mohan abducts Champa and hurriedly calls a priest for holding the marriage ceremony. He snaps, *"Shaadi paanch minute me honi chahiye"* ("The marriage has to be finished within five minutes").

Before this, Mohan is fooled by Raju and Champa at the fair, being unable to spot the heroine, who disappears with the hero, reminding one of a similar situation in *Nagin*. It turns out later that Raju is an ordinary guy, the son of Champa's poor surrogate father. Mohan Seth, in the circumstance, looks all set to win Champa; but again the villain's claim goes frustrated. This happens again and again in the sixties. It is, after all, Mohan Seth, who plays a pivotal role in unraveling the real identity of the hero and the heroine. The film, needless to say, hinges on this discovery. Still, the villain's effort goes unrewarded. Undaunted, he puts up a fight to the finish before being handed over to the police.

In *Ram Aur Shyam*, Pran plays Gajendra, the awesome brother-in-law of the good Ram. Dilip Kumar plays a double role. Having Ram in the house, Gajendra finds it easy to stomp in the rich in-laws' house where he stays with his mother and tortures his wife and daughter. Property issues surface again when Gajendra wants Ram to sign the property over to his name. Ram escapes, and enters a hotel after Shyam, his twin brother, not yet discovered, moves out without paying for the sumptuous meal he has eaten. The identity confusion keeps the narrative vibrant from now on. Again, it is the villain who exposes the brothers' real identity. It's difficult to keep Gajendra longer in the dark.

Ram, in course of his wanderings, finds shelter in Shyam's house in the village, while Shyam is mistaken for Ram in the rich house of the city. Shyam, a smarter guy, beats Gajendra mercilessly, something that takes everyone by surprise. Finally, Gajendra unravels the mystery of the twin brothers, keeps Ram in his custody in a godown, and beats him severely for having the property written in his name. Gajendra tells the police that Shyam has murdered Ram, and is staying in the house by using the look-alike image of his brother. Shyam escapes from prison and comes to know that Ram is his brother. The lost parentage of Shyam is narrated by his surrogate mother.

The role of Gajendra is played with great menace by Pran. There are moments in the film when he looks thretening, like when he throws the birthday cake of his daughter away, and whips the innocent Ram, causing a dent in his psyche. One important feature of this film is that here the villain not only returns to his fold, but he's also shown apologizing for his misdeeds. This is because the structure of family as a homogenous entity is preserved in this film. The villain too endorses feudal values and stays loyal to them. However, things start looking favorable for the villain two years later.

Raj Khosla, the director of *Kala Pani*, later made *Do Raaste*, a family drama that drew heavily on the values demonstrated in the Ramayana. Released in 1969, this film was followed by the victory of the Congress party under Mrs Indira Gandhi's leadership in 1967. The country was basking in the dream of witnessing positive economic reforms after the disillusionment of Nehruvian socialism. The villain's function in *Do Raaste* is taken over by the housewife (Bindu in a major role), who instigates her husband Birjuprasad (Prem Chopra) against the family.

She is contrasted with her good sister Rina, played by Mumtaz. The family accepts the legal marriage of Birju, though on the whole they want to retain traditional values. This sets the theme of the film in motion. As it happens in *Junglee*, the photo of the dead father becomes a subject of debate and adulation. In *Do Raaste*, it takes on an ugly turn. The evil housewife, spurred on by vengeance, removes the photo from the wall of the room allotted to her. Birjuprasad questions the values stuck to by his idealist elder brother Navendu (Balraj Sahni in a memorable role again), and later leaves the family. Toward the end, Birju realizes his mistake and the villainous role played by his wife in disrupting the peace and stability of the family.

The film became a blockbuster at the box office and got a Filmfare Award for the best story. Bindu was nominated as the best supporting actress. She delivered several powerhouse performances mainly as a vamp (discussed later in this book) and had a sizzling score "Mera Naam Shabnam" to her credit the very next year in Shakti Samanta's *Kati Patang* (1970). *Do Raaste* not only shows a villain-woman, but it also dramatizes the contemporary clash between the old and new emerging set of values during the late sixties, mentioned earlier in this discussion.

Meanwhile, the Shammi Kapoor–Pran antithesis went on in great guns, in *An Evening in Paris*, for example, with greater virulence against an international scene, forecasting the trend of the later decades.

Pran begins from where he left in *Bluff Master*, exposing the hero's masquerade before all, and leaving him to a life of shame and humiliation. And, this time in *An Evening in Paris*, he retaliates by romping away with the heroine, offering her drinks and dancing with her, watched hopelessly by Sam, the hero. Shekhar (Pran) looks as suave and smart as any romantic hero does in a film, once again justifying his claim over the heroine. The story remains incomplete if we don't consider Shekhar's fight with the other fierce villain of the film, Jack (played brilliantly by K. N. Singh) and the no less menacing Jaggu. Jack kidnaps the heroine Deepa, and demands a huge sum from the Seth, Deepa's father. This leads to the exposure of the missing twin Rupa, now known as Suji, a cabaret dancer, adored by Jack.

Shekhar, fighting for the hand of the heroine, cables the Seth, and it's the Seth's arrival on the scene that encourages Jack to ask for money. Thus, the film space is largely occupied by Pran, leaving

Shammi Kapoor again an observer most of the time, though he's aided by the mellifluous Rafi number "Akele, Akele." This is an important feature of this film. *An Evening in Paris* is a significant film of the decade as it shows the villain's cool calculating menace in which he's substantially aided by the vamp—a feature that looks much ahead of the time. Importantly, a foreign land becomes the center of action in this film. This point should be noted also.

Finding Jack in action, Shekhar approaches Suji to take over the place of Deepa, now missing. They agree to share the money between them when Shekhar succeeds in claiming the hand of Deepa. Shekhar is encouraged by the Seth, who considers him to be a worthy son-in-law, in spite of protests from Shekhar's well-meaning father who looks after the Seth's property in Paris. The Seth recognizes the merits of the villain and thinks that he has a greater claim for the beautiful and wealthy heroine. But, in no time, he too is pulled away from behind by the wily scriptwriter, discrediting the claim of the smart good-looking villain—a prominent feature of films showing Shammi Kapoor–Pran antithesis.

The underground, where Shekhar meets Jack with money, looks like those found in the films of the seventies and eighties, in *Mr. India*, for example. It gives the creepy sensation associated with all such places, where doors through walls are endless, one leading to the other. In *An Evening in Paris*, a clock indicates the time of entries and exits through the doors. Finally, the mighty occupant is seen relaxing in his chair. Jack appreciates Shekhar for being smart and takes the money with a little bit of suspicion. Shekhar wastes no time and shoots his rival from inside the briefcase containing money. The plan works admirably, and is later emulated by Prem Chopra in *Dostana*, making an innovation in the previous trick, for Chopra shoots in the later film from inside the hole of his pocket, leaving others staggered with disbelief.

During a final encounter between Sam and Sekhar in *An Evening in Paris*, the villain is swept away by the mighty current of the lake, suggesting the villain's resurrection on a foreign soil as a terrorist in future. This shot deserves special mention, since the trend of the villain's return to his fold in the sixties is handled imaginatively here, leaving behind a whole range of possibilities. The second half of *An Evening in Paris*, as said earlier, shows Pran in action. In the Shammi Kapoor–Pran starred films, the villain always fights the hero on equal terms.

Brahmachari (1968) is an important film of the sixties for many reasons. First, it shows the vamp, played by the enchanting Helen, a cabaret dancer, seen in a new dimension. We will take up the subject in a relevant section of this book. Second, the Pran–Shammi Kapoor antithesis is shown in *Brahmachari* most eloquently and with greater resonance. Pran in this film is a sleek yuppie in his city suit, claiming and plotting to get the hand of the heroine, a motif that was right in tune with the villains of the sixties. Apart from this, *Brahmachari* shows how it might have influenced Shekhar Kapoor's thinking in using the children as orphans in a later film like *Mr. India*, starred by Anil Kapoor and Amrish Puri. As said before, *China Town* too looks like being a forerunner of *Don*, both showing the menace of underworld smugglers. These possibilities have so far escaped our notice because we haven't looked at the villains from the right perspective. Let's look at *Brahmachari* in detail.

Glossed by the presence of the ever boisterous and rollicking Shammi Kapoor, who certainly deserved greater attention in his lifetime, *Brahmachari* is further enriched by the smart and suave Pran, who looks disturbingly elegant, seeking to capture the attention of the heroine of the film. As a matter of fact, the parents of both had decided for the match when they're children. It is also interesting to note that the heroine is madly in love with Ravi Khanna (played by Pran). The hero spends a lot of time in training the heroine, a country wench, so that she could attract Ravi's attention. On her arrival in the city, the heroine had met Ravi, now enormously rich, only to be rejected by him in the vilest terms. And, mind you, Ravi hasn't amassed his wealth by any unscrupulous means. At least this film doesn't show this. This is important. This film hasn't been discussed from the villain's point of view either.

So, Ravi denies a previous pledge (not made by him) when he's confronted by the heroine at his posh residence. The heroine looks pretty ordinary, compared to the smart and good-looking villain. He says that there are many maids working in his house, and clearly he can't marry them all. His words are arrogant and proud, both attitudes going well with his position. Ravi is a man of the city. Not many films possibly show how the villain's location shifting from the rural to the urban boosts his stature. Remember also that the heroine in this film hasn't been made pregnant by Ravi Khanna, which is the usual way of forcing a marriage, decrying the villain's reputation. Nothing of this sort happens in *Brahmachari*. So, Ravi Khanna is not amoral, at least not at the beginning of the film. We mention Pran by the character he plays in this film, because it sounds somewhat spurious to call him a villain till we have reached the end of the film.

Pran, as many know, was booed whenever he walked down the street. Fretfully enough, the man was gulped by his on-screen persona. A hero, on the other hand, receives welcome and thunderous applause whenever on some rare occasion he too glides across the street. He's aided by camera and screenplay, but the villain who contributes to the hero's feat is looked on with distrust and fear. This feature in a profound sense is the consequence of our illusion and deep involvement with on-screen film-reality that continues even after a film has ended. That this happens speaks volumes of the scintillating Bollywood show. This is not usually seen anywhere else in the world. Hero worship and villain revulsion has kept our peoples ever vibrant and alive. That also contains much of the fun.

Denied by Ravi Khanna in abusive yet valid terms, the heroine, Sital Chaudhury (played by Rajshree), who is handled wretchedly by her mother and maternal uncle in their rural home, decides to commit suicide. It is then that the hero, looking for the best of snaps as a professional photographer, meets the girl and saves her from imminent death. Shammi, as usual, is his own self. He asks the girl, standing on a cliff before the sea, to bring her hair in position, and take the edge of her sari off her chest. Shammi's approach brings a lighter mood in the film, rescuing the girl from her suicidal trance. She starts taking an interest in the stranger, and reaches the Brahmachari Ashram, an asylum for orphans. The hero is a *brahmachari*, whose life is dedicated to taking in waifs and strays in the asylum where he stays too. He's himself one, as the film shows later.

While discussing Shammi-starred films, let's take an opportunity to pay our tribute to this excellent actor, who passed away recently. Shammi Kapoor gulped the film space in a way that no other actor did before him, not even the great Dilip Kumar, noted for playing the sad, heart-broken hero, something that Rajesh Khanna later took over. Amitabh Bachchan is mentioned by Amitabh fans for dominating the film space. On deeper scrutiny, however, it appears that Shammi Kapoor was more naturally gifted in taking the space all alone, providing hilarious comedy, fun, and enjoyment, not to speak of the frolicking "Yahoo" tune in *Junglee*, followed by his unique somersault that instantly captured the heart of Saira Banu in the film, and probably many others outside the screen. Those days' the media wasn't as alert and active as it is today. Therefore, the glamor story might have been written differently had the situation been otherwise.

In many films like *Muqaddar Ka Sikandar* or the mighty *Sholay*, for that matter, Amitabh, like Dilip Kumar, plays the sad, pensive lover. It has been given out that Amitabh too, along with Rajesh Khanna, was a contender for death in a film, because that elicits audience empathy easily. But, Shammi rarely dies in a film. In *China Town*, Shammi is about to succumb to his injuries but finally survives, as that would have been most unlike of Shammi Kapoor, who was a staunch believer in the vital force of life and the pleasures it offers. So, in the film, Shammi goes to prison, leaving his brother (a look-alike; Shammi in a double role) behind him for the comfort of the audience.

A number of Amitabh roles show the hero contemplative; someone cocooned from the outside world and mired in thoughts. He nurtures his wrath and finally takes upon himself a Hamlet-like responsibility to set the world right. This glorifies his image in the turbulent scenario of the seventies when the hero had to behave differently for the sake of encountering his strong adversaries. In reality, the villains made it necessary for the emergence of the new hero and not the hero for the villains to become stronger. Anyway, both Dilip Kumar and Rajesh Khanna had to quit, the former switching over to character roles.

Thus, Amitabh begins from a vantage point, giving him an elevated status, making it easy for him to lick other actors and dominate the film space. Shammi Kapoor, compared to this, had a quiet beginning. This was natural, because the time wasn't ripe yet for the hero to behave like a superman. So, Shammi had to diligently create his own persona, both boisterous and thoughtful, according to the demands of the narrative. Shammi too can be thoughtful and contemplative along with the developments of the narrative, like he's in the latter half of *Kashmir Ki Kali* and *Bluff Master*, even in *Junglee*. This speaks highly of this actor, known usually for his boisterous acrobatics. The Rafi numbers helped him. But, it was never easy to lip the songs, especially when the everlasting and incomparable Rafi Saab could sing a particular song in different voices, like the one in *Brahmachari*. Toward the end of seventies, Amitabh too plays his role with comic flair, in *Amar Akbar Anthony*, and later in *Toofan* (1989), for examples. A fine gentleman that he was, Shammi Kapoor will always be remembered by posterity.

To go back to *Brahmachari*, Shammi teaches Sital the tricks to impress Ravi and transforms her from a village girl into a coy woman of the society. Ravi is known to have weakness for such girls. So, he is hooked easily when he sees the new Sital Chaudhury. *Brahmachari* is possibly a rare film of the sixties in the sense that here the villain moves like a hero. It's later that the villain is known to be a lady-killer, much like the turns in an Arthur Conan Doyle story, "The Adventure of an Illustrious Client." The real hero behaves like a booby and is in no way near to the villain in terms of money and smartness. Many Bollywood heroes are shown to be without money (on the screen, hopefully)—mendicants—but each one is sufficiently adventurous and enterprising so as to impress the heroine, rescuing her, single-handed, from the clutch of criminals. That usually settles the game in the hero's favor. The screenplays rigorously work it out. But, Shammi Kapoor in *Brahmachari* is noted for his simplicity, much like Anil Kapoor in *Mr. India*. Shammi admirably fits himself into the persona with a special style of walking, occasionally treading on the ground with short heavy steps. This was a clever move of the actor.

When it comes to casually sipping the soup in a posh restaurant, Shammi does it like any rich man. This is because Shammi is now playing the role of a trainer, instructing the girl how to behave elegantly among rich people. As anticipated, Ravi is soon trapped into developing a mad liking for the girl he rejected once.

Dressed in her new attire, Sital undergoes a complete change. Ravi has a faint memory of having seen her before but fails to trace her down the memory lane. Soon, Sital discovers Ravi in the company of other girls, saying the same words of tribute to their beauties and promising each to marry. Mumtaz happens to be one such victim, now made pregnant by Ravi, and discarded by him. Mumtaz is in possession of Ravi's letter to her. This letter of confession leads to his downfall.

Now is the time to call Ravi a villain. He looks menacing and handles every situation to his benefit. "*Main bahut bura aadmi hoon*," the villain hisses. He asks Mumtaz not to meet him again in future. From now on, *Brahmachari* is the villain's film. The man who looked like a hero is now discovered in his true image, while the unassuming hero is worshipped by Sital. This reversal of identity has been brilliantly handled by Sachin Bhowmik, who writes the story and screenplay of this film. What the Selim–Javed duo did in the seventies was done by Sachin Bhowmik in the previous decades. Ravi has now nothing to hide about himself, and he's rejected in exactly the same terms by Sital on the same spot in his house where she was once rejected by Ravi. She has her revenge now, watched and heard by the other girls, all Ravi's victims. They pounce on Ravi with their flip-flops. Ravi frees himself from their insulting attack and clears the dirt off his dress in order to get back his dignity. One remembers a nearly similar scene from *Ghayal* (1990), where Amrish Puri, after being throttled by Ajay (Sunny Deol) in an alfresco party gathering, soon gets into position, summoning dignity. As his assistant, to please his boss, starts straightening his crumpled shirt, he shoos him off, asking the party to continue as before. Great fun, once again!

When Ravi's identity as a villain becomes clear to the audience, he goes on spreading his net and getting Sital back to his fold. He knows now the identity of the girl. The lascivious nature of the villain is best understood in the scene where he watches Sital dance lustily. Deeply engaged in his diversion, Ravi forgets to light his cigarette. Pran uses some of his magic properties as an actor he'd amassed in *Madhumati*. The story takes an ugly turn. Ravi meets Sital's mother in their rural house and reminds her how his marriage with Sital was previously settled by their fathers. Sital is forcibly brought back to her rural home. She is locked in a room. Ravi bribes the greedy uncle and forces him to do what he wants.

In 1968, a program of "New India Cinema," urging state funding for promoting what at the time was called "auteur" cinema, was announced. This, along with some other developments, created a breathing space for a while, assuring a democratic distribution of wealth by terminating the huge amount of private property held by the landed gentry. The move to make economic reforms was already on. Navrangilal in *Khandaan* (1965) mentions to his aunt a government threat for taking over the excess lands owned by the privileged class. He insists on her selling out some of the lands and giving him the money he wants. We'll come back to this film for looking at a different and unforgettable Pran. In 1969, the Congress party was divided by Mrs Gandhi to gain control over the party, and give it a new look. This created hope as well as apprehension in the minds of people. While many were relieved to see the disappearance of some known and old faces in the party, there were others who were confused about the outcome of the political move. The division, significantly, was made two years after Mrs Gandhi's victory.

The villain, too, felt dubious and confused about his intention. Both Jeevan and Kanhaiyalal play villains in the film *Bandhan* (1969), released toward the end of the decade, showing the villain's operation a little bizarre and complex, unlike the Shammi–Pran films. The moneylender Malikram (played brilliantly by Kanhaiyalal) can't become as ruthless as he was twelve years back in *Mother India*. This is because of the change in time. In some sweeping summaries of *Bandhan*, Malikram is described as a wicked moneylender. This gives a misleading idea about the complex character Kanhaiyalal plays in this film. As a matter of fact, his phenomenal feat in presenting this character could be placed at par with the performance he gave portraying Lala Sukhiram in the previous film. Malikram is not the villain in *Bandhan* in the usual sense. The real villain is Jeevanlal, played by Jeevan.

The strained relationship between Jeevanlal and his son Dharma (played by Rajesh Khanna) begins when the son discloses to the police that his father has stolen someone else's money. So, Jeevanlal is not a moneylender, but a pickpocket and ruffian villain, looking forward to the seventies. Jeevanlal goes to jail. When Dharma's mother approaches Malikram for money, he wants her land instead of the house. But, Malikram hesitates. He never betrays his lascivious intention in this film like Lala Sukhiram in *Mother India*. Even when Malikram locks his daughter up in a room to prevent her from meeting Dharma, Malik shows his anguish as a father.

This makes Kanhaiyalal work out a complex range of emotions in this film. Jeevanlal, on the other hand, looks unashamedly fierce and arrogant after he comes back from jail. The marriage of Dharma's sister is abruptly stopped by the groom's father for lack of receiving sufficient ornaments as dowry, especially a necklace, bought by Dharma for the purpose. Actually, it is stolen by Jeevanlal for pursuing his libidinous pursuits at a courtesan's house. Pleaded on by his wife, Malikram approaches the groom's father, arguing on behalf of the distressed family and the honor of the village Balrampur.

So, it's Jeevanlal, who's in conflict with Malikram in this film. Jeevan's atrocious villainy, much like the decade of the seventies, is shown when he tries to rape Malik's daughter, engaged to his son. This is something to be carefully noted, since *Bandhan* was released a year before we enter the seventies, known to be a major decade of villains. Dharma saves her, but in the process Jeevanlal dies, receiving an accidental injury. Dharma is accused of murder by the court. He's later released after the appearance of a smart lawyer (played by Sanjeev Kumar) from the city on the scene, the brother of the lady doctor of the village, whose love for Dharma remains unspoken in this film.

As long as he is alive, Jeevanlal does everything to wreck the happiness of his family, even selling the family cow for his interest. He shows no concern either for his children or his wife. His villainous activities threaten the peace and harmony of the village, making the story move to its end. In presence of the police inspector, he thrashes the old Malikram. The *munim* poisons Malikram from time to time, and prompts him to take over the land of Dharma. But, in this case, it was done more for the apprehension that the land of the family was going to be given to the vicious Jeevanlal, the hero's father. The *munim* warns Malikram about the possibility, and the latter, hearing this, springs into action to thwart the interest of Jeevanlal. Had he known that the land was going to be in the name of either the mother, or the son, which indeed later happened, he wouldn't have chosen the action. Malik is told by the *munim* that, by taking over the land of Dharma, he could separate Dharma from his daughter. The plan works for a while, since Dharma goes to the city after this in search of work.

Thus, the activities of Malikram as a moneylender in this film are curbed, both socially and narrative-wise. That's why the more confirmed villain's role is taken over by Jeevanlal. Released at the end of the sixties, *Bandhan* shows a villain who cares only about himself, and prepares the viewer to meet the powerful villains of the seventies. The decision to rape the girl in love with his son symbolizes how things started looking gloomy during this time. Naxalite agitations in different parts of the country began and there was a general mood of discontent among people.

We will go back to *Khandaan* before closing this dialog. Coming exactly in the middle of sixties, this film shows Pran, the villain of the previous decades, playing now a different kind of villain in the character of Navrangji Lal. In *Khandaan*, the narrative space is occupied entirely by the villain once he comes back from Singapore. The role of the senior brother Chaudhuri's wife is played by Lalita Pawar, and she supports unknowingly her nephew's misdeeds. But, as in *Junglee*, she realizes her mistake later and breaks the wall that had separated the family. This wall was set up at the behest of the nephew. The villain is accompanied by his sister, played by Mumtaz. Significantly, this film is not primarily concerned with showing either the feats of the hero, played by Sunil Dutt, or his romance with the heroine Radha, played by Nutan, a poor orphaned girl, who's brought to the house by the younger brother's wife. Nutan works as a maidservant in Chaudhuri's house. When the audience feels bored with the peace and harmony of the family, Navrangi Lal arrives on the scene.

Pran keeps a short mustache, and a flattened hairstyle, looking somewhat funny, which is in sharp contrast with the roles he plays in the Shammi Kapoor-starred films. His acts of villainy in ruining the family acquire a grotesque and macabre dimension. Pran creates a new persona of himself in this film. First, he wins Shyam to his side, the brother of Govind (Sunil Dutt), and then gets him married to his sister. Later, he manages to get ₹50,000 from his obliging aunt and burns the bulging crops of the family. Finally, he takes away Radha's (married to Govind) child in his arms for using him in the elephant show of his circus. The police arrive and arrest Navrangi Lal, who protests by saying that they don't know how to behave with a learned man like him. The villain shows his preference to be called educated. This is a new development so far as the villain's putting up a camouflage is concerned. Navrangi Lal shows the way to others who follow him in the next decade. By the sixties, the villain becomes not only a man of the city, but also someone who belongs to the world. Like *An Evening in Paris*, the villain in *Khandaan* boasts of his international upbringing. The whole world is advancing fast, whereas "*hamara desh peeche ke peeche rehta hai*" ("our country falters, and lags behind more and more"), laments Navrangi Lal. Even before *Do Raaste*, stability of family values is seriously threatened by the villain in *Khandaan*. A. Bhim Singh writes the screenplay and directs the film. One remembers the stylish villain of *C.I.D.* while talking about Navrangi Lal.

Thus, the sixties took over from the fifties, and now the seventies were getting ready to follow. By this time, family values were seriously

73

questioned. Prem Chopra was waiting to spring into action, whetting his calm and sedate gestures. Later, both Ajit and Chopra took over the mantle from Pran. Dev Anand's production *Des Pardes* shows how the duo occupies the center stage as villains. Ajit too was waiting to calmly replenish his glass of whisky when the hero will be breaking into his den in *Zanjeer*, the gateway to the decade of violence. The vamp too was hovering in the background, as Suzi (played by Helen) made it clear in *China Town*, and later Bindu in *Do Raaste*. They're all going to be engaged in a bond of camaraderie as Gabbar Singh will be heard roaring and spitting in his den down the valley.

The green pastures of villages become charred due to poverty. Farmers stream into cities, looking for new avenues of earning. Unfortunately, factories witness lockouts as a consequence of economic uncertainty and labor unrest. Integrity and harmony of families, seen before, loses its previous promise and shine in the seventies. The upshot of all this is that the hero from now on will find little time to sing and dance with the heroine. A superstar's arrival on the scene is needed to take on the mighty villains who are going to roar and stomp the screen. And, what villains they all are! Where would have been our heroes if the villains weren't there, composing half the music of humanity?

Notes

1. Lalit Mohan Joshi. "Bollywood: 100 years," in *Bollywood Popular Indian Cinema*, ed. L. M. Joshi (Piccadilly, London: Dakini Books Ltd, 2001), 8–56, 211–12.
2. Sergei Eisenstein, *Film Form*, Jay Leida (ed. and trans.) (London: Harcourt Brace and Company, 1949), 16.
3. Jawaharlal Nehru. *An Anthology*, ed. Sarvepalli Gopal (New Delhi: Oxford University Press, 1983), 310.
4. Ibid., 316.
5. M. Madhava Prasad. *Ideology of the Hindi Film: A Historical Construction*, (New Delhi: Oxford University Press, 1998), 152.
6. Ibid.
7. Nehru. *An Anthology*, 317.

3

Sholay and the Seventies

*W*ith the seventies, the age of innocence was over. People, anguished by the failure of Nehruvian idealism, started questioning the system that failed to guarantee jobs, legal protection, and adequate supply of foodgrains. The image of the state as provider and benefactor was eroded. Power in politics and society became centralized in a few hands. There was disappointing inequality in the distribution of wealth. Farmers felt deprived, and the Naxalite movement was gaining momentum, leading to guerilla warfare. Students joined politics to lead the agitating farmers. In Bombay, the road to Mantralaya outside Churchgate station became a favorite venue of protesters for various causes like trade union disputes, closure of factories, and other burning industrial issues, just as College Street in Central Calcutta regularly witnessed students' agitation.

The consequence of all these is that an intrepid and honest trade union leader in *Deewar* cannot survive. In *Zanjeer*, a girl sharpens tools made of iron out in the street on her whetting machine. She complains that change of coins is hard to get. Her profession and utterance gain importance when she sees hooligans romp in the street, running over a group of innocent children. Down the decade, in 1977, heroines become pick-pockets (*Parvarish*). This speaks eloquently about the changed scenario. In *Zanjeer*, smugglers and bootleggers walk free. Emergency hits the nation. The resentful upsurge of people, resulting in the formation of the Janata government, and its disastrous failure later to provide an alternative, leads to Mrs Gandhi's historical comeback in 1980. All these, garnering greater strength, pass on to the decade of the eighties, making the scenario look further grim and violent.

Zanjeer is the gateway to hell. With this film begins the decade of villains in the seventies. Ajit, playing Teza, looks suave and awfully relaxed, giving one the creeps. He has a moll to entertain him at the swimming pool. One new feature of this villain is that he tries to win over Vijay, the police inspector. Amitabh Bachchan starts with this name that will be repeated in many films later, symbolizing the grand continuity between the seventies and the beginning of nineties, till the assassination of Rajiv Gandhi. Pran in this film appears as the owner of a gambling den but changes later, and helps the hero in his mission. This shows that the villain of the previous decades is now ready to leave the mantle to someone else.

Amitabh's encounter with the villain in which he's aided by Pran looks less heroic for the superstar and speaks more eloquently about the villain. There is little doubt that the villains in the seventies, receiving the thrashing every time, added charisma to the hero. In *Zanjeer*, Vijay, beaten severely on a lonesome road by Teza's men, is taken care of by Pran. Toward the end of the film, they join hands to raid Teza's house. This leads to a grim battle in which Vijay is again helped by Pran. Later, when both are overpowered by Teza, it is Mala's (the heroine) presence of mind that saves both. One might say that it is the villain who starts the decade with a bang, not the hero.

Interestingly, this was also the time when Prem Chopra was emerging as a villain. *Daag* (1973), also called "A Poem of Love," and considered to be an adaptation of Thomas Hardy's famous novel, *The Mayor of Casterbridge*, centers around Dheeraj Kapoor's (Prem Chopra) attempts to rape Sonia (Sharmila Tagore). Sunil (Rajesh Khanna) arrives in time and kills Dheeraj, his boss' son, but in the process he is charged of murder and is sentenced to death by the court. Although Prem Chopra plays a smaller role in this film, the main plot hinges on his action. Prem Chopra begins the decade as a lascivious villain, which later becomes his forte, though this versatile actor achieves many other dimensions as a villain during his long career. *Daag* is also important because it is produced and directed by Yash Chopra, who begins his debut as a producer, laying the foundation of Yash Raj Films that gives villainy a new definition in the nineties.

In 1975, more popularly or awesomely remembered as the year of Gabbar Singh, Prem Chopra plays the bad man Poppy Singh in *Kala Sona*. He runs an underground business empire of cocaine. The hero Rakesh, played by Feroz Khan, for a long time believed that his father's assailant had been killed. But, after many years, he comes to know that his father's killer is alive. Importantly, the hero finds little time to romance in this film with the girl (Parveen Babi as Durga) he loves. In the bleak environment of the seventies, this is the penalty the hero has to pay, a distinguishing feature of films where Amitabh Bachchan takes on a good number of villains in the decade. In *Sholay*, for example, Jai has no time to express his love as he, along with his friend Veeru, becomes actively engaged in catching Gabbar on behalf of Thakur Baldev Singh (Sanjeev Kumar). *Kala Sona* shows this motif also, since Feroz has to track down the killer of his father. Another major feature of this film is that here the hero joins hands with Poppy Singh, becomes a part of the underworld he fights with, and kills a police officer to earn the trust of the villain. Prem Chopra plays his role with great menace. The selling of cocaine suggests the overall gloom and smuggling bully of the seventies. The film is directed by Ravikant Nagaich.

Sholay makes a frontal attack on sensibilities by showing gruesome violence on screen. For the first time, the villain is located at the center of the narrative. The writer-duo Salim Khan–Javed Akhtar, after the huge success of *Zanjeer*, doesn't try a similar story but a different one, in which the villain is a rural dacoit, straddling the screen like a colossus. The larger screen suits Gabbar Singh, as he needs more space to roar and move like a predatory animal. There's no jail to keep Gabbar longer than he wishes, he warns Thakur Baldev through clenched teeth. Finally, Gabbar does break the jail and kills Thakur's relatives in retaliation against Baldev's previous temerity to arrest him. Back in his den, Gabbar chops Thakur's hands, those hands that wanted to send him to the gallows.

When *Sholay* hit the screen, people were stunned to watch a villain occupy the center stage. The *Sholay* universe, ruled by the villain, doesn't allow an individual like Jai (Amitabh Bachchan) to become introspective and survive. In *Zanjeer*, as said before, the hero was helped by someone running a gambling den. In *Sholay*, again, Thakur hires two henchmen, actually social outcasts, to catch Gabbar alive. But Gabbar is a mighty villain. He's ruthless, cruel, and desperate. He knows of Veeru's (Dharmendra) love for Basanti (Hema Malini), the *tanga-wali*, but nothing about the unspoken love of Jai and Radha

77

(a name having mythological resonance and reminding one of the anguished longing for union). Finally, Gabbar succeeds in wiping off Jai from the scene. The world occupied by Gabbar shows no concern for finer sensibilities.

Everything in *Sholay* is controlled and manipulated by what Gabbar thinks and does. Every move taken by others depends on how he reacts. The implicit threat of Emergency is mirrored by the dumb reaction of the villagers of Ramgad that becomes a microscopic projection of what others at the time were thinking. Gabbar Singh, a diabolical villain, wants all power and authority to himself. He coerces the villagers into giving him the produce of their labor in the fields. In *Mera Gaon Mera Desh* (1971), the dacoit villain growls when he sees the panic he'd created among the villagers is questioned by a stranger, the hero. In *Sholay*, Gabbar shoots his assistants one by one when they fail to bring him the food stuff from Ramgad. The price of his head declared by the government pleases him, adding to his megalomania.

Gabbar may feel insulted if anyone, getting the wrong end of the stick, calls him a *bhaddarlok*. Let's watch the scene of pogrom in *Sholay* after Gabbar, keeping his word, escapes from prison. He rides to the Thakur's sprawling bungalow in the valley, kills every one of his relatives, barring the daughter-in-law, who luckily isn't present on the spot. Finally, he slays Baldev's grandson, as he stands watching Gabbar in awe and disbelief. There's a custom of having swings in front of the houses of noblemen in villages of India. Thakur has one also. The camera tilts down (from Gabbar's perspective), and shows the swing, screeching in midst of drop-a-pin quietness after the brutal killings. The same effect has been achieved to a different purpose in a recent film (*Omkara* [2006]) in the final shot of the film where the swing in the room is used with visual imaginativeness.

Before Gabbar's arrival, they were all chatting; some chopping vegetables. It appeared as a happy family unit, everyone attached deeply to one another. Now, everything is silent. Gabbar shoots first the Thakur's younger son, Radha's husband, up on the cliff, and then the family. The cinematic language conveys acutely the heinous bloodshed, carried out with skill and perception. The whip-pans establish the locale with reasonable clarity, while the top-angle shot, using the dacoit's perspective, portrays the helplessness of the tiny men residing in the valley. And, think of actors like Sanjeev Kumar, Dharmendra, Jaya

Bhaduri, and Amitabh Bachchan's presence in this film. Amjad Khan, playing Gabbar, makes his debut appearance among a bevy of stars. Yet, he holds the center stage and takes away much of the kudos. This is enough to suggest the menacing stature of Gabbar Singh in this film. Gabbar spits, roars, and howls, much to the fear of others.

The world of violence displayed in *Sholay* is one of democratic violence that seeks to restore a meaningful code with society. *Sholay* shows why making a distinction between nihilistic violence that seeks nothing but disruption, and democratic violence, laced with a crea.. purpose, is essential for appreciating this film's effort to reinstate two lost men like Jai and Veeru into the mainstream society. When they're contrasted with Gabbar's diabolical villainy, the message becomes clear. The villain contributes to the unfolding of this message. This is another strong point of the script written by Salim–Javed.

The moment Gabbar is introduced he steals the show, justifying his superiority over the galaxy of stars in this film. Gabbar's men stand on the cliff, guarding his den. A macabre drama is enacted below. Three men, Kaliya being one, stand petrified. Gabbar, enraged at being dishonored by Baldev, screams and hisses, altering his voice according to the mood and words he utters. He snatches a revolver from one (he doesn't keep a revolver to guard himself) who watches the show with fear and tension. "How many bullets are there?" Gabbar asks. Someone says, "Six." Six for three. So, the bullets are in excess. Gabbar fires in the air: one, two, and three, getting the extra bullets spent. Now, the arithmetic becomes equal. Gabbar never misfires. The three offenders stand looking in the other direction. Gabbar brings his revolver close to each one's neck. The trigger doesn't apparently work. They survive. Gabbar spits, leaves the cowards, and paces round, hooting in laughter.

Soon he's joined by others, including the men guarding the cliffs. The chorus of laughter reverberates through the valley, everyone joining in the fun. It rents the air. Gabbar, laughing down on his knees, manages somehow to keep his balance. The offenders, terrorized, are at a loss about showing their exact emotion. Should they laugh also to please Gabbar? The contours of their faces slowly change. Finally, they join in the peals of laughter, looking a bit foolish. Gabbar turns round and shoots all three. Amidst drop-a-pin quietness, Gabbar asks, "When's *holi* due?" This is a new tone of violence, macabre, and hideousness.

There's also fun in this film. Jai is entrusted by Veeru with the job of approaching Basanti's old aunt with the marriage proposal. Jay does the job to the best of his knowledge. Is the bridegroom employed? The woman asks, hunching eagerly. Yes, he does earn; but not always. She looks on, gobsmacked. Well, the groom gambles, and obviously he cannot win every day: *"Kabhi kabhi haar bhi jata hai, bechara."* "Feeling anguished, my friend," Jai says, spilling the beans, "drinks, and goes to a tart's house." It's time to leave. "The marriage, then, is *pukka*; isn't it Mousi?" Jai asks. Mousi's reaction is for all to see! This is rollicking fun. No other film industry of the world can give so much in exchange of money.

It's little surprise that *Sholay* should make an impact on the films that followed. There was a weak imitation of it in a film called *Ramgad Ki Sholay* as late as in 1991. Amjad too was tried in many other similar roles, for example in *Mr. Natwarlal* and *Suhaag* (1979). But, the Amjad of *Sholay* never returned. It came once, only once, in the history of Bollywood cinema, and it is probably still without its peer in the history of world cinema also.

Deewar, released in the year of *Sholay*, shows villainy inherent in the system, and to suggest that symbolically, the film shows two warring underworld dons—Dawar and Sawant, both engaged in smuggling. Vijay's role, played by Amitabh, is believed to have been modeled on Haji Mastan, the real life smuggler and slumlord of Bombay. Set in the political tune of the time that was disillusioned with Nehru's utopia, *Deewar* shows a world where all values turn void and meaningless. It's bleak and dark, killing the hero in the process. The heroes in this film are brothers: one a police officer, guarding law, and another, an underworld don. As said before, the seventies were a time of smugglers and criminals, making it a decade of villains.

The two-hero formula was introduced in *Sholay*; but the two-villain formula, one fighting the other (an important point of contrast with the heroes who work together), is used in *Deewar*. Dawar is played by Iftekar; Sawant by Madan Puri. There is very little romance in this film. There cannot be any, since the villains don't allow it. As the two dons fight one another for getting control of their smuggling business, the hero is gulped and has to exit from the scene. Anita, Vijay's girl, cannot deliver her child, and is killed by Sawant's men. The pessimism is complete, reminding one of the dead child in Hemingway's famous

A Farewell to Arms and the children in Hardy's *Jude the Obscure*. The latter novel so irritated a bishop that he threw it into fire! *Deewar* begins on an unpleasant note. Vijay's father, escaping from a life of shame, deserts the family. Vijay goes to work in the dockyard, after having had a brief stint as a shoeshine boy (like the boy in *Do Bigha Zamin*). His struggle and experience urge him to take on the extortionists all alone when a worker refuses to part with his earning. The death of the fellow worker in the hands of the goons forces Vijay to take action against the criminals (later known to be Sawant's men). The death of a minor character in the film thus provides a turning point in Vijay's career. Dawar seeks Vijay out and employs him to look after his underworld operation. Thus, the villain engulfs the hero. On the other hand, Ravi (Shashi Kapoor) is helped by his would-be father-in-law to join the police force. The *deewar* (wall) between the brothers is built up. Villainy in *Deewar* is so ubiquitous that it succeeds in ruining the brothers' love.

In *Adalat* (1976), Dharma, the hero, ploughs his field at the beginning. But soon, he too is engulfed by the villains and is consumed in the end. The villains are all smugglers in this film.

In *Kalicharan*, Subhash Ghai, the maker of the prolific *Karma* down the eighties, pursues the theme of terror and violence shown in *Sholay*. *Kalicharan* shows a villain (Ajit) who's lionized in the film: *"Sara sheher mujhe lion ke naam se janta hai"* ("The entire town knows me in the name of a lion"), Seth Dindayal, the villain, roars. This dialog, like Teza's "Mona darling," became famous in a decade that showed the mighty Gabbar on the screen. This is a great achievement. Ajit plays his role with the same guile and menace of Teza. Prabhakar, the police inspector and hero, is killed in the film by the villain. To appreciate the villains' status in the decade (no less than the superstar's), we should remember that in all these films—*Sholay*, *Deewar*, and *Kalicharan*—one of the heroes dies. The villains are so strong that both heroes cannot survive. One must quit.

A second Prabhakar, actually a criminal, but a look-alike (Shatrughan Sinha in a double role), is picked by the IG Mr Khanna (Premnath) to carry on the task of the departed hero. This looks unjustified from the villain's point of view, but this becomes the trend in the seventies. In the *Sholay* decade, they hire criminals and have two heroes for harassing and trapping a single individual. Dindayal, a confirmed villain, cannot believe that a criminal is ever capable of becoming a gentleman: *"Iss duniya mein ek aam aadmi achcha naagrik nahin ban sakta"* ("An ordinary folk in this world cannot become a good responsible citizen").

The IG tries best to reform Kalicharan. If Kalicharan's defiant cynicism echoes the disillusionment of the seventies, then the IG's dogged persistence in making him a good citizen and reinstating him in the mainstream society justifies what we meant by democratic violence in *Sholay*. Finally, Kalicharan starts behaving like a gentleman and becomes a police inspector, like the dead son-in-law of the IG. This is, however, not enough to vanquish the villain. By a turn of events, the villain comes to know about the identity of his adversary and challenges him to a gruesome battle. One significant point about this film is that Kalicharan is aided by the senior IG in vanquishing the villain. The reincarnated hero can't do it alone. He needs the help of someone else to finally defeat the lion in his den.

Another point needs attention. The hero fights on behalf of the IG, reminding one of the *Sholay* motif where the heroes were fighting someone else's battle. This is, again, from the villain's perspective, ethically wrong, since he hasn't wronged the hero, who merely takes up another man's agenda and becomes a henchman to someone else, a sidekick. This makes the hero's position vulnerable both in the seventies and eighties when the villain grew truly menacing. Even if one remembers Kalicharan's personal agenda of revenge against the man who had once raped his sister Geeta (maybe a self-defeating alibi), it's also true that the offender was a henchman of the villain, not the villain himself. Danny plays Saka in this film, a lame bootlegger, who, like the *Zanjeer* motif, is won over by the hero to his side.

In *Trishul* (1978), Prem Chopra plays Balwant Roy, the villain. It is his deeds that keep the narrative going, apart from those of the hero, where he is out to ruin the happiness of R. K. Gupta (Sanjeev Kumar) and seek revenge on the injustice done to his mother Shanti years back. Thus, the hero's agenda of revenge brings him to the villain's platform, and for a while, the hero behaves like a villain. Later, they fall out, and Balwant alone turns the story to its nail-biting finish.

Desai uses his favorite lost and found theme in *Parvarish* and *Suhaag*. The debate of class and family legacy is examined two decades after *Awaara* against a bleaker social scenario. Two children, brought up together in a good environment, grow up to become different. The dacoit's son becomes an honest police officer in *Parvarish*, while the IG's a smuggler. The lost and found theme of *Parvarish* wishes to examine society from scratch, extolling the efforts of responsible men, who volunteer their duties as citizens without asking for any intervention from social institutions.

Amjad plays dacoit Mongal Singh, who's hotly pursued by the police inspector (Shammi Kapoor). Unfortunately, Mongal cannot stay with his wife, who's about to deliver his child. Later, the wife hands over a locket and the baby to the inspector. When Mongal comes back from jail he is not allowed to get back his son. The inspector fears that the innocent boy would become a criminal if he is left to the care of Mongal. One may question this stand taken by a person who keeps a boy to himself, though he isn't the boy's father and, in the process, denies the claim and affection of a real father. This feudal constraint denies the democratic right of Mongal Singh, the dacoit. The irony is that the dacoit's boy, being in the custody of a police inspector, grows up to join the police force. The other one, in reality the son of the inspector, and often reproved by his parents, assumes Mongal to be his father. Later, he joins the convict secretly to turn into a criminal. This reversal of fortune provides a sharp commentary on feudal beliefs.

The roles of heroes are played by Amitabh Bachchan and Vinod Khanna, while those of pickpockets by the heroines Neetu Singh and Shabana Azmi. This is also the film where the sisters, during their childhood, watch the villain shoot their parents. Amjad occasionally reminds one of Gabbar in *Sholay*. His menacing image does on occasions offset the decade's biggest superstar, Amitabh Bachchan. In accordance with the thematic need, Mongal is aided by Kishan (Vinod Khanna). Their presence unleashes fresh menace in the film, challenging the superstar in his role of the police inspector. Mongal, as villain, is unusually crafty, and believes that Amit, his real adversary, is feigning blindness. When Amit is brought to Mongal's den and is tested against a death-trap below, while up at the center he's about to be crushed by sharp iron hooks, Kishan runs to his aid. In keeping with the villain's larger image shown in this sequence at Mongal's den, Amit's position as an investigating officer looks insecure for a while.

The final sequence of the film is full of drama. Mongal's real boss, an international guy (Kader Khan), arrives on the scene, forecasting the villain's status as an international terror in the eighties. The submarine sequence of *Parvarish* reminds the audience of the smuggling menace of the underworld in the *Sholay* decade. Filmed with precision and expertise, the submarine sequence offers a revealing commentary on the feelings of both the father and the lost son. Mongal hopes that his own child would allow him to escape. He doesn't. In fact, Amit and Kishan join hands in the final battle, apart from the IG himself, making the fight look yet again uneven and fated for the villain.

Don continues the smuggling menace of the *Sholay* decade, giving it a new twist. The villain, an international smuggler, introduces himself in this film as an Interpol officer. He starts functioning from within the police administration by having the real officer R. K. Malik imprisoned in his custody. Om Shivpuri plays the role of Vardan with style and elegance, ably supported by Kamal Kapoor as Narang, and M. B. Shetty as the dangerous guy Shakaal. As a matter of fact, M. B. Shetty has always made an impact in short appearances, like Mukesh Rishi and Sharat Saxena, the latter two playing, of course, bigger roles, and making the canvas of villains look ugly and frightening in Bollywood cinema. Probably, time has come to recognize these excellent actors of Bollywood cinema, a job we have essayed later in this book.

The world of *Don*, occupied by smugglers, is different from the previous films in the sense that here children, victims of the gloomy scenario, play important roles till the end. They're the children of JJ (Pran), a performer in a circus company, and leading a happy life of his own, till one day he's trapped by Narang, a criminal of the underworld, into doing their work of breaking lockers of cash in a bank. In trying to escape, JJ is shot in the leg. *Don*, in many ways, could have been JJ's film, had not the villain been unusually crafty, occupying a major part of action.

The hero, of course, is aided by songs and romance, as usual. But, he has to feign an identity and stay in a far worse position than the villain. The real don dies in this film, and Vijay (Amitabh), a lookalike, is employed by Iftekhar to track the smugglers in their den. Ironically, both the villain and hero play masquerades in *Don*, having equal status—something we have been suggesting in this narrative. This makes *Don* an important film of the decade. The *Bluff Master* motif, involving the hero and villain of the sixties, assumes a bleaker turn down the seventies. This raises the stature of villains without making them look vainglorious against the heroes. This implication has so long escaped our notice because we had never bothered to look at the number "6" from its opposite angle.

The villain, acting as the police administrator in *Don*, makes ingenious plans to protect the criminals. Vijay, like his predecessor Kalicharan, plays the role of someone he'd never seen. He takes up the agenda of someone else (Iftekhar's, in this case) and gets involved in actions he wasn't remotely connected with. This makes the hero's position both ambiguous and uncertain in *Don*. Having no clear agenda under his belt, he says funny dialog, sings, and dances. The "Khaike Paan Banaraswala" number, sung by the hero, is probably the consequence of having no positive engagement. Vardan, on the other hand, has no time to waste.

The wily operation of Vardan, the linchpin of the smuggling organization, gets stronger focus against the uncertain image of the hero. He tackles each crisis with confidence and shows how the villains of the seventies became smart guys, assuming any role with ease. In *Don* it turns even bleaker, because the villain operates from within the administration. Vardan, Bikram, Shakaal all make up the canvas of the menacing world of smugglers in the seventies.

Take, for instance, the scene where the crafty Vardaan is confronted by the DSP, about to arrest him and his gang. The villain shoots the DSP (Iftekhar) and asks inspector Verma, who arrives after the killing, to take away the body, implicating Iftekhar in the smuggling racket, having links with the underworld. Later, Verma meets the villain to tell him that he's received a letter informing him that the man, occupying chair, is in reality a smuggler. Vardan, unperturbed, represents a complete volte-face in his thinking and says casually that he too has received a similar letter about Verma's alleged connection with the underworld. When Vardan and his gang go to meet the real Malik, imprisoned in their custody, Malik warns the villain for his offense against law. Vardan chuckles and says that if Malik had known the range of offenses committed so far by him, he would have dismissed this one as a minor peccadillo.

This dangerous move of operating from within the police administration makes *Don* different from the other films of the decade. Compared to the villain, Vijay is a simpleton, falling easily into the trap set by Vardan. When Vijay goes all the way to meet Vardan, hoping to be helped out of trouble by him, Vijay sees himself surrounded by goons, all Vardan's men. Confounded, Vijay says: "We're surrounded by enemies, sir!" "Not we; only you," retorts Vardan. This is great piece of cunning, even a bit outrageous. Salim Khan–Javed Akhtar wrote the screenplay and dialog of this film.

When the hero springs into action to save himself from the indignity of being pursued by police, he's aided by JJ. The heroine too lends support. And, mind you, the diary that contains the names and addresses of smugglers and becomes the target of a hilarious catch-game at the graveyard is actually retrieved by JJ, not by the hero. If one looks at the seventies from the villains perspective, one understands how much the villains (even others also, occasionally) contributed to the image of the superstar. *Don,* as a film betrays the impression that it was initially intended to exploit Amitabh's image as a playful frolicking hero, explored a year before by Manmohan Desai in *Amar Akbar Anthony.* Curiously, Chandra Barot, the director of the film and previously assistant director to Manoj Kumar, is not heard of again after the encouraging success of *Don.* He preferred to be remembered by *Don* only; that must have been a good option to choose, since *Hong Kong Wali Script,* Barot's intended subsequent venture, didn't see the light of day.

The world of violence in the *Sholay* decade is suggested by Natwar, a child, learning alphabets in the film *Mr. Natwarlal.* The boy has no difficulty in identifying "S" for sheep, "T" for tiger, or "U" for umbrella. But, coming to "V," he can't pronounce the word "violin." For him, "V" stands for Vikram, the diabolical villain. The soft and pensive tune of violin has no place in the seventies. The smuggling menace of the seventies influenced everyone's psyche, children and adult alike. Amjad Khan plays Vikram in this film. Natwar, grown up, goes to Chandanpur to fight Vikram.

Inspector Girdharilal, Natwar's elder brother, is after the villain, but *"saboot ke taur pe usko kuch nahin mila"* ("running after evidence, he couldn't get anything")—the voice-over informs the audience. The film opens with violence, showing a poisonous snake in the bed of the inspector, a gift sent by Vikram. His den in the hilly areas of Chandanpur is reminiscent of Gabbar's recluse in the valley of Ramgad. The wooden bridge, the steep rough hills, and the dacoits riding fast to raise thick layers of dust suggest that there's a conscious effort to bring back the image of Gabbar Singh. Added to this is Bharati, the tigress, mentioned in the title of the film, and used by Vikram for intimidating the villagers. Gabbar, however, needed no tiger; he was one himself. Bollywood has tamed wild animals through the mighty villains over and over again.

The *Sholay* motif is also seen in *Mr. Natwarlal* when the heroine (Rekha), like Basanti, is abducted into the villain's cave. She's asked to dance before the villain and his men. This time, they throw round her feet a snake instead of shards of glass. There has been no lack of innovation in Bollywood.

The seventies are often described as the decade that showed a trend of making films on natural disasters, probably taking the cue from Hollywood. The film *Towering Inferno* is cited as providing the inspiration behind the making of *Kala Patthar* (1979). A multistarred venture, with Shatrughna Sinha in the role of Mongal, a convict, apart from casting Amitabh Bachchan and Shashi Kapoor, *Kala Patthar* was shot in Dhanbad of erstwhile Bihar, a region known for coal mines. It is said that the technicians used in *Towering Inferno* were brought in from Hollywood. Prem Chopra plays the villain in *Kala Patthar* that captures the agonizing moments of workers deep down the mine. The villain's cruel treatment of hapless workers forms the main subject of this film. Once again, the villain tackles as many as three men in *Kala Patthar*.

Riding on the social discontent and Naxalite agitation of the country, "parallel cinema" or "realist cinema," as it has often been called, thrived in the seventies. This was a new film genre that offered a contrast to the larger-than-life image of Gabbar Singh and brought back the menacing landlords of the past to a recognizable social scenario. The realist cinema got its momentum with the arrival of Shyam Benegal on the scene. The formation of Film Finance Corporation (FFC) gave a new direction to the availability of state funding. In 1971, after the expiry of the five-year contract for importing Hollywood films, a renewal of the contract was refused on the ground of showing Indian films in foreign film theaters. The demand was in the air for quite some time. Finally, the FFC caved in. With the success of Mrinal Sen's *Bhuvan Shome* (1969), the mood and viability of realist cinema' garnered strength. *Ankur* (1974), *Nishant* (1975), and *Manthan* (1976) followed on close heels.

Ankur's agenda is feudalism of the past, while *Nishant* is set in 1945. *Ankur* shows that feudal oppression forms a part of its illusory promise and pretension. Surya, a young landlord (Anant Nag), is sent to look after their land in a remote village by his overbearing father, a zamindar. Surya, already married, manages to trap Lakshmi (Shabana Azmi), the maidservant of the house, to his fold, and promises to look after her for the rest of his life—an illusory promise, but alluring enough for a village girl.

After marriage, the wife of the zamindar's son goes to stay in her father's house, as the custom then was. Lakshmi, the maidservant of the village, is married to a mute man, Kishtayya (Sadhu Meher), who works in the same house with his wife. Soon, Lakshmi's mute husband is dismissed from service by Surya for a minor offense. This clever move brings the wife under the care of the feudal umbrella. This is like what happened in the fifties, the *Madhumati–Mother India* pattern, discussed before. In this sense also, *Ankur* revives a feudal agenda by looking back to the past. And, the girl seems to be well taken care of, apparently. She's cajoled into accepting the young landlord as her benefactor. Gradually, but steadily, Surya's act of villainy dawns on the viewers. In absence of the husband, Surya seduces the girl, having her in his bed. Lakshmi becomes pregnant, though she'd failed to conceive for her husband.

Benegal carefully and minutely builds up the details of the narrative in which the seeds of amoral cohabitation gradually exfoliate. Following the act of voyeurism of the landlord, the audience gets a glimpse of what the servant girl does throughout the day. The film language is used with precision to show how the villain, within a realist framework, sneaks up on his prey to destroy her happiness. This move, backed up by feudal aggression, turns out to be more cunning than the usual rant of villains in the *Sholay* decade. The camera, handled brilliantly by Govind Nihalani, shows from above how the girl washes her feet, fills her pitcher, and trudges her way back to the house. They look like a series of stills, generated imperceptibly with movement from within. Every frame is shot and slid with inner tension.

Surya has no work except watching Lakshmi. He quarrels with his neighbor for a petty offense like when a cow plods into his garden. He stops water supply to the land of his father's mistress. Taken together, they provide nice details to understand how feudal hegemony envelops one's psyche. Later, Surya brings a gramophone to the house and starts listening to popular Hindi songs. Like any villain, he goes on spinning his web. The film takes a turning point when Surya's wife arrives on the scene.

As expected, the wife takes over the charge of the house, not allowing Lakshmi to prepare tea or food for her husband. She drives her out of the kitchen, forcing her to do the chores. She has an imposing politeness about her; never arrogant, but effective. Suspecting Lakshmi to be pregnant, Surya's wife asks her to go on leave for a few days. The feudal camouflage, however, doesn't work longer. One day, the wife finds Lakshmi stealing rice from the kitchen. As she throws a tantrum, Surya appears on the scene and admonishes Lakshmi, reminding her that such offense invites both beating and police custody. Lakshmi stares arrogantly at her one-time benefactor and bedfellow. Feudal balloon pops.

One morning, Lakshmi discovers her husband lying in the shack by her side. He shows her the money he's earned during his absence from her. Pathos deepens. The wife's conscience is roused. She breaks into tears, body shivering. The viewers' active participation in this tale of woe mounts when Kishtayya becomes excited to know that Lakshmi has finally conceived. He cannot talk (a filmic advantage); so he grabs his wife by her hand and takes her to a temple for expressing his gratitude to God. A job is necessary, the husband gesticulates, for looking after the baby due to arrive soon. He goes to meet the landlord, seeking his apology for the previous mistake. The stage is set for the final drama. As we watch Kishtayya, striding along through the edges of the paddy field, stick now in hand, then on shoulders, arms resting on the stick, we realize that this scene is different from the one we'd seen in *Sholay*, where Veeru, after the death of Jai, challenged Gabbar in his den. He rode off, hollering "*Ek ek ko chun chun ke maroonga. Gabbar Singh, aa raha hoon main.*" In *Ankur*, a mute protagonist walks on within a realist framework.

Kishtayya's approach to the house gives Surya the creeps. He's engaged in kite-flying with a local boy. Good pastime for a young landlord. Like Gabbar in a different scenario, Surya asks the guard to hold Kishtayya and withdraws into his room. He emerges after a while with a thick coil of rope and starts beating Kishtayya mercilessly till the fellow, like a mute animal, bleeds profusely. After his enraged outburst, Surya locks himself inside a room. His wife slides in, like an apparition.

Lakshmi, meanwhile, trudges her way on to the scene a trifle late, unable to understand from her shack what exactly is going on at the other end. She curses the landlord from the patio, saying that her husband had come to seek his apology and get a job: *"Tu kabhi nahin bachega, kabhi nahin bachega"* ("You aren't going to survive; never")! The landlord's wife, shut in the room with her husband, glares silently at Surya, searching for the missing clue. Her looks show she's got it.

Everyone watches the scene in the patio. Then the crowds disperse, slowly but reluctantly. Outside the gate of the house, the young lad who'd played kite with Surya and was a witness to the moving spectacle, retreats; eyes on the house. He stops, picks up a stone, and throws it at a window, breaking the glasses. This is not much different from what the aggrieved boy does much later in *Agneepath*, throwing fire at the petrol station. In *Ankur*, sounds of birds fluttering their wings and flying off are heard on the soundtrack. Things fall apart with greater density and vibration.

The atrocity of the young landlord, like any villains of the seventies, has been unmistakably shown in *Ankur*. Satyajit Ray, however, cannot see any "monstrosity" in the landlord's psyche and finds the end of *Ankur* not convincing. This is probably because he sees Surya as a hero, not someone behaving like a villain. His humanist concern allows a ray of sympathy for the young landlord, as it happens with the wretched zamindar in his own film *Jalsaghar* (*The Music Room*), released in 1958. In Benegal's film, the real protagonist is the couple, the mute husband and his wife.

Nishant is placed in the feudal ambience of 1945. Shyam Benegal is reported to have once said that the "new cinema" thrives when there're demands for it. It's relevant to remember that all three films of Benegal were not financed by the FFC. *Ankur* and *Nishant* were financed by Blaze advertising, while the third, *Manthan*, was financed by the members of a milk cooperative in Gujrat, showing in all three instances that private finance could be available even for "auteur" ventures. This in itself is a great achievement.

In *Nishant*, we have no difficulty in identifying the villains. In *Ankur*, the villain was shrouded in the feudal aura of mystery and false promise. He had to be identified after a tenacious cat-and-mouse game. In *Nishant*, which looks back to a vast stretch of time, the villains are easily identified right from the word go. All four brothers stomp noisily about the town, terrorizing innocent people. The eldest (Amrish Puri) chides (again, a feudal pretension) his younger brothers for crossing the limits of liqor which he himself consumes every night in his room, alone. This betrays his ostentatious and fragile conscience. Unlike many films of the seventies, we have in *Nishant* as many as four villains, all united to destroy the middle-class stability and values.

Looking stern and feigning the role of a disciplinarian, Puri says nothing when a schoolmaster's wife is abducted into the manor. The first two brothers, Anjaiah and Prasad (Anant Nag and Mohan Agashe), are noted from the beginning for their love for drinking and lasciviousness. After forcefully abducting Susheela (Shabana Azmi), the lascivious brothers rape her. The two brothers again enter her cell in the manor and helps one another for satisfying their carnal desire. The ghastly nature of this crime makes a forceful commentary on the violence of the seventies, even the eighties also.

One should get a look at the saunter of the brothers in the local market. They lift two live chickens from the basket of a woman without paying her. When she asks for payment, they laugh at her and ask Shamsuddin, the policeman, to explain the act on their behalf. The audience of the seventies of Bollywood cinema easily empathizes with this act of larceny in a marketplace. The schoolteacher (Girish Karnad) looks on with surprise, like someone, watching a naughty schoolboy's game. When the two brothers enter the manor with their plunder, Puri looks on. He watches the live bird but inquires about the price of rice. This is how feudal pretense is presented, featuring its inherent contradictions. Vijay Tendulkar's screenplay exposes the inconsistencies with razor-sharp precision. The final sequence, showing the peasants' rebellion, ends in violence it wanted to set right, probably offering a critique of the Naxalite movement that was often believed to have lost direction. *Nishant*'s theme has epic dimension, symbolized by the enactment of events from the Ramayana before the villagers mobilize their strength for the uprising. The buffalo fight and the Ramayana event serve the purpose of having a play-within-play motif in which the monstrosity of the villains is highlighted, encouraging action against economic and sexual oppression.

The abduction scene in *Nishant*, a major turning point of the film, is smartly handled by Shyam Benegal. It shows the surrounding gloom and helplessness of the community, languishing in panic. Violence here is not so much an occurrence as something people anticipate. They're left numb and moronic when something actually happens. Watch any scene of violence in the seventies and eighties. The scene ends, apparently. Actually it stays, affecting the psyche. Benegal's succinct handling of the situation leaves the spectator irritated and restless, ensuring involvement. The situation grows suffocating from one sequence to another, like any film of the *Sholay* decade. Remember the scene where the schoolteacher leaves his umbrella on the ground and decides to throw stones in air, having no one in particular to target at. Losing direction is fatal. *Nishant*, one feels, should be telecast for the present generation of viewers.

Manthan makes a refreshing contrast to Benegal's previous attempts. The film is based on the Emergency. Amrish Puri plays Ganganath Mishra, who buys milk from the villagers at a cheap rate and makes huge profits. Mishra upsets the socialist agenda for which a bureaucrat is sent to the village. Mishra and the *sarpanch* (a village leader by tradition) act together and disrupt the image of the state as provider.

Acting on hindsight, one has to confess that Benegal's one major contribution (in view of the present context), among others, is his presentation of Amrish Puri as a powerful villain. Puri works on this image and plays it to monstrous perfection in the decades to follow after Amjad's exit from the scene. "Parallel cinema" shows the other face of villains—cool and cautious, spreading the net slowly but steadily. The realist framework makes the whole plan look subdued and effective. The landlords of *Ankur* and *Nishant*, coming back in the seventies, make one familiar with the feudal legacy of the country at a very important sociopolitical phase of India.

Mainstream cinema continued as before, unperturbed by whatever waves, new or old, lashed the mighty shore of Bollywood cinema. The other reason might be that mainstream cinema got a tacit approval from "parallel cinema" for what it was doing within its commercial constraints—a point we will come back to very soon. The villains, in particular, continued to challenge the heroes, as it happens in *The Great Gambler* (1979), a film of the late seventies, spelling out what the *Sholay* decade was meant for. This time Prem Chopra occupies the screen, aided by Sujit and Utpal Dutt, the versatile actor from Bengal, playing comic and evil roles with equal flair. Anupam Kher of Bollywood seems to be closer to what Utpal Dutt was doing in Tollywood and Bollywood.

It is actually Chopra who does most of the damage to the hero in *The Great Gambler* where Amitabh plays a double role—those of Jai, the gambler, and inspector Vijay, his twin brother. Shakti Samanta, the director of the film, once again tries to exploit Amitabh's image for playing a smart don of the underworld, like he did before with Shammi Kapoor in *China Town*. The result is that the hero, playing two persons, is better equipped in tackling the villains of this film, though Saxena (Utpal Dutt), being the boss of the underworld, is most often out of action. He's seen toward the end when he's confronted in his den in Goa by the hero, accompanied with armed police.

Chopra, already noted for his performance in *Kala Patthar*, plays Ramesh with greater assurance. He is not ready to succumb to the tricks of Jai and Vijay on the train when the brothers unite together. Iftekhar, playing Deepchand in this film, helps the brothers know their true identity since he's a friend to the father of the brothers. Once again Amitabh is Vijay, completing the cycle of *Zanjeer*, though for this decade only, since he'll be assuming the same name in the next decade also. Maybe, the hero grew a bit superstitious about taking on the mighty villains, and thought it safer to be armed with a lucky name. The directors too might have wanted to play it safe, assuring the audience that the villain, however powerful, was going to be trounced.

Saxena, Ramesh, and his gang in *The Great Gambler* succeed in trapping Mr Nath, an Indian government servant, through the gambling victory of Jai. They force him to disclose the secret plan K2, which is actually wanted by Saxena for endangering the security of the country. Saxena plays a humming villain in this film, looking a bit comical in an odd vainglorious way and paving the way for the great Mogambo of *Mr. India* in the eighties. Ramesh, on the other hand, foreshadows the appearance of the terrorist villain, Dr Dang, of the next decade. Chopra is at his menacing best in many scenes, like when he follows Jai to Deepchand's house to get back to his custody the evidence of their underworld activities. He manages to get everyone tied up before fulfilling his mission. It is obvious that Ramesh doesn't seriously love Shabnam (Zeenat Aman) and uses her as his partner. *The Great Gambler* was followed in 1979 by two Amitabh films: *Jurmana* and *Manzil*, both having had nothing to do with villains. Glossed over as if they were aberrations in Amitabh filmography, *Kala Patthar* brought back the superstar image of Amitabh, having Prem Chopra at the center of action. *Jurmana* was released on May 1, *Manzil* on May 14, and *Kala Patthar* finally on August 24. Significantly, both *Jurmana*, a Hrishikesh Mukherjee film, and *Manzil*, a Basu Chatterjee film, bring out Amitabh's acting prowess when he doesn't have to fight with villains. But, they are not associated in any way with his superstar image. This clearly establishes the fact that without the presence of strong villains at the center of action, Amitabh Bachchan's credentials as a superstar, or anyone else's, for that matter, are likely to lack the boost.

As suggested before, the villains in the seventies had to tackle two (sometimes three) heroes most of the time. Look at only the above examples. *Kala Patthar* had Shashi Kapoor and Amitabh, *The Great Gambler* had Amitabh in a double role, and in *Muqaddar Ka Sikandar* the stage was shared by Vinod Khanna, not to mention the other films discussed already. Remember also that both Vinod Khanna and Shashi Kapoor costarred with Amitabh in more than one film in the seventies. In many cases the heroes, riding on the songs and screenplays written to their advantage, fought for someone else. They went after the villain and trounced him, having no agenda of their own. Their success, as a consequence, looks self-abortive and nugatory. The fierce battle, anyway, leaves the hero exhausted and he pays the price for accepting a persona not his own (*Don*). Amitabh Bachchan begins the decade as a reflective thoughtful person (*Zanjeer*), becomes a pensive lover (in *Sholay*), loses his woman, and dies (*Deewar*).

On the other hand the villain, receiving the wallop, appears in different names. He never changes his primeval role of subverting the system.

Bravo villains, carry on! You have made gods and superstars, after all.

4

The Eighties and After

*T*he decade of the eighties shows two major political events and a defi-nite turning-point in the presentation of villains in Bollywood cinema. It opens with Mrs Indira Gandhi's return to power, followed later by her tragic assassination in 1984, and the emergence of Rajiv Gandhi as the prime minister of the nation. Thereafter, it totters on and ends with the assassination of Rajiv Gandhi right at the beginning of the nineties. Homicides registered a 45 percent increase during 1985–95. Under-standably, the deteriorating relationship between the police and public was taken up in *Ardh Satya* (Half Truth), released in the year 1983. The Shah Commission's Interim Report II of April 26, 1978, said:

> Police officers behaved as though they are not accountable at all to any public authority. The decisions to arrest and release certain persons were [based] entirely on political considerations.... The Government must seriously consider the feasibility and desirability of insulating the police from the politics of the country and employing it scrupulously on duties for which alone it is by law intended.[1]

This led to the evolution of the politician-terrorist villain on the scene. The relationship between the police and executive became a subject of suspicion and concern for the public mind. It's, therefore, not a surprise that a number of films in the eighties—*Ardh Satya*, *Inquilab* (1984), *Andha Kanoon* (1983), *Shahenshah* (1988), and later *Ghayal* should address this issue. The villains are seen using law and politics for pursuing their agenda. In *Coolie* (1983), the villain Zaffar Khan contests an election. So does Rama Shetty in *Ardh Satya*. Many villains of the decade were political bigwigs, addressing public meetings.

Later, as the political scenario turned bleaker down the decade, the villains started operating as terrorists, both from within the country and from outside. *Ardh Satya* authentically documents the operation of the politician-villain, making way for the terrorist villains in *Karma* and in *Mr. India* (1987).

Aakrosh (Govind Nihalani's debut film as director), released in 1980, seeks to expose the vile system of judiciary wrecking individual happiness. The villainous operation in this film is carried out with political connivance. Written by the noted playwright Vijay Tendulkar, *Aakrosh* continues the trend of the offbeat films that were presented by Shyam Benegal and others in the previous decade. Watching Shyam Benegal from very close quarters as the cameraman of his films, Nihalani must have felt encouraged to document the trend of the time in his own style. *Aakrosh* shows successfully how from now on the protagonist is going to be pulverized by the villain within the deteriorating scenario of law and order. Nihalani's skill in showing an action-thriller on the screen, involving the judiciary and police administration, is felt for the first time by the viewers of Bollywood cinema.

Importantly, this subject is repeated by him later in *Ardh Satya* and *Drohkaal* (1994) in the decades of the eighties and nineties. More importantly, this underscores the fundamental motif in the villain parlor of Bollywood cinema of the next decades. That Nihalani realizes this at the beginning of the eighties, or maybe from sometime before, speaks commendably of his directorial talent. Of course, both Vijay Tendulkar and Nihalani himself, drew their inspiration from the Naxalite agitations of the previous decade and tribal exploitation in the rural sector of India.

Om Puri, playing Lahanya Bhiku in *Aakrosh*, does not utter a single word nearly throughout the film. He merely puts on a stunned look after his wife is raped. The blame is shifted on to him by the amorphous interrelation between law and justice. Bhaskar Kulkarni (Naseeruddin Shah), fighting the case on behalf of the victim, is frustrated by his client's inexplicable silence and his stubborn refusal to provide any clue about who the real offender is. The incestuous connivance between power and money, law and authority, are expressed symbolically through Bhiku's intriguing silence. The suppressed anger finds a strong visual expression within the four walls of the prison cell where the victim is lying, not anticipating justice, but awaiting a foredoomed end. The twitch of muscles on Om Puri's cheeks, and the way he changes side in the cell with his manacled hands and feet, provide a scathing commentary on the devilish system that laughs and roars in the background like any full-blooded villain in human form. The foreman of the working site, responsible for the rape, looks like a tiny representative of the entire corrupt system, as if the 10-headed mythological Ravana was reincarnated on the grim scenario of contemporary Indian society.

Standing beside the funeral pyre of his wife, Lahanya Bhiku notices the same foreman watching his pre-pubescent sister with lustful eyes. In order to prevent the fate awaiting her, Bhiku grabs an axe, which is, ironically, a laborer's tool in the forest for chopping trees in the logging operation. A similar axe might have been used by Bhiku's departed wife during her work in the forest. Before anyone can guess anything, Bhiku chops off his sister's head to forestall her catastrophic future, and by choosing this extreme action, sends a caveat to the legal system that sent him to prison. He's thus able to prevent at least one marginalized tribal girl, his sister, from becoming a victim to the systematic and perpetual process of exploitation.

When the film was released, much was talked about whether Bhiku's violent action was justified. Could it really be termed as a protest? Seen from another angle, one might also say that Bhiku's *aakrosh* (fury/ resentment), the fomenting anger within him, his depression and morbidity for not being able to do anything against the corrupt system, were clearly demonstrated in this violent act. Talking about *Sholay*, we had drawn a distinction between nihilistic violence and democratic violence. Hailed usually for belonging to the genre of parallel cinema, Govind Nihalani's *Aakrosh* seems to be upholding this view, that is, what *Sholay*, with its apparent gory violence, had shown before. It is significant that the so-called parallel cinema of both Shyam Benegal and Nihalani were creatively responding to the changing deterioration in the legal and social system of the seventies and eighties. By so doing, they vindicated in a different style and format what the mainstream cinema of the time was doing commercially. That this feature of Bollywood cinema, taken as a whole, has not too often been noticed, or spoken about, may be due to an esoteric preference for *parallel* or *art* cinema, as if someone should be in charge of maintaining the purity and cleanliness of a secluded fort from outside the city of pollution.

Aakrosh, right at the beginning of the decade, prognosticates the trend of villains and villainy the audience was expected to see in future. It is now easy for any villain to get an honest police officer trapped or transferred, often inciting him to commit suicide, as it happens in *Shahenshah* (1988). In *Aakhri Raasta*, released in the middle of the decade, the villain operates as a political leader. A few stray films of the decade, one or two, tentatively looked back to the villain as a smuggler, probably waiting for the big bang to strike. The same happened in the seventies also. It took three years for *Zanjeer* (1973) to announce the mood of the decade. Remarkably, *Ardh Satya*, like *Zanjeer*, followed the same pattern, appearing in 1983, and keeping the schedule tight. This is because the villains, more than the heroes, behaved according to time, communicating forcibly to the changing social environment. The heroes didn't bother, since they were armed with songs and dances.

Ram Balram (1980) makes a tentative effort to look back to the seventies. Directed by Vijay Anand, it shows Ajit playing Seth Jagatpal, lame in one leg, like his predecessor Jivan in *Amar Akbar Anthony*. His buccaneering hunt for wealth makes him look diabolical to the two brothers, who are forced to do everything he wishes. Jagatpal kills his elder brother and pushes his wife into the river. Believing her to be dead, he takes charge of the property. Later, Jagatpal assumes the role of a surrogate father to the two brothers, Ram (Dharmendra) and Balram (Amitabh Bachchan). He teaches Ram to steal, but provides education for Balram, who becomes a police inspector, posted in Gaya. This is because the villain wants someone to protect him to run his smuggling business safely.

Jagatpal is a calculating villain. Later, he comes into contact with two other smugglers acting for him; Suleman Seth (Amjad Khan) and Chandan Singh (Prem Chopra). The ship sequence shows the menacing Jagatpal, shooting Tarabai (Helen) and forcing the police to give up chasing him on the sea. The characters of Seth Jagatpal, Suleman Seth, and Chandan Singh all look rightly poised to be transformed in future into Dangs and Mogambos, threatening the stability of the nation.

Dostana, released in 1980, and directed by Raj Khosla (famous for making crime movies) from a screenplay written by Salim–Javed, makes a distinct move in several areas so far as presenting the villain in the changed sociopolitical scenario of the eighties is concerned.

Prem Chopra plays Daga, while Amrish Puri, destined to play bigger roles later, operates as his acolyte. Pran plays a significant role, that of Tonny the informant, which is reminiscent of the one played by Om Prakash in *Zanjeer*. In *Dostana*, Pran calls up the police inspector to tell him that the car number MAX 4060 carries gold worth ₹1,000,000. Helen plays the vamp, determined to avenge the death of her sister. She works in conjunction with Tonny, whose family has been ruined by Daga. In *Dostana*, the villain is a master improviser. He shoots from inside his pocket, leaving everyone dumbfounded.

Dostana shows the bleak world of the eighties. The court cannot protect an individual, and it allows the criminal Balwant (Amrish Puri) to escape for want of evidence. Although Balwant is arrested by inspector Vijay Verma (Vijay–Amitabh is back again) at Malighat on October 16, his belligerent lawyer (Shatrughan Sinha) proves nonchalantly that the same day the criminal was under treatment in a hospital. This sets the tune of the decade that shows the triumph of villains on a number of occasions, frustrating the effort of the hero playing the role of a police inspector. Death in police lockup is also shown in *Dostana*, making it a document of the eighties. The court scenes are handled smartly in this film.

Hum Paanch (1980), directed by Bapu, and a remake of 1979 Kannada film *Paduvaaralli Pandavaru*, is another significant venture of the decade. One major point to say about this film is that the Mahabharata events are presented here most faithfully by Bapu. Yes, this indeed is the case of making overt references to the epic we were talking about in Chapter 1. The story of the five Pandavas, led by Lord Sri Krishna (Sanjeev Kumar in a memorable role), is told here in the modern context. The role of villain, a lecherous villain and one who has driven his own brother out of the house, robbing him of his claim to property, has been played by Amrish Puri. This is the time when Puri starts showing menace as a villain, and this possibility has been nicely exploited by Bapu. His foresight to spot the right villain at the beginning of the decade deserves mention.

Mithun Chakraborty, one of the Pandavas, serves the villain at the beginning, protecting him. Raj Babbar, aided by Naseeruddin Shah, sends the first caveat to the villain. Sanjeev Kumar, operating much like Sri Krishna, handles the situation cleverly when the Pandavas become rowdy, not willing to surrender to the police called in by the villain.

This incident sends a guide to what the decade is going to witness—the fact that the police and legal administration from now on are going to be used by lawbreakers. Mithun and his associates are advised by Sanjeev Kumar to surrender to the police. They do accordingly and come back after a few months with renewed energy, like the Pandavas after their exile. The entire film, even the final sequence, where the villain is vanquished, reminds one of the Mahabharata motif. The director's profound allegiance to the epic, having modern undertones, is outstanding.

In *Shaan*, Ramesh Sippy, the maker of *Sholay*, produces something truly menacing. Kulbhushan Kharbanda plays Shakaal in this film, sending a creepy sensation to the audience and preparing them to meet Dr Dang later. The audience sees a new tone of violence and hears a new rhetoric from the bald villain, sitting, and snapping at others from his chair in a technological paradise. This villain is different from Gabbar in the sense that he has mastered a good bit of technological knowledge and looks invincible by virtue of his innovative brain. He doesn't shoot to kill people, but presses a button fitted to his table. Jagmohan, Tiwari, Kumar—all are admonished by Shakaal in hysterical language for blunders committed by them.

Only Ramesh Sippy, the maker of *Sholay*, could present another appalling figure like Shakaal. He's not yet a terrorist, but terror personified. Nor is he a politician, but can become one any moment. Shakaal has a helicopter to chase his enemy running along a barren land. Helicopters here serve as symbols of pride and aggression of villains in the eighties, reminiscent of chariots in the epics. Ramesh Sippy, by way of a fortuitous coincidence, gives the lead again, just as he'd done before. The screenplay, like *Sholay*, is written by Salim–Javed. The same team works to respond to the changed scenario.

Another noticeable feature of this film is that the two heroes, the brothers (Amitabh Bachchan and Shashi Kapoor) of DSP Shiv Kumar, spend a lot of time in acts of purloining, like Jai and Veeru in *Sholay*. They're reform after the killing of their elder brother by Shakaal. Wild dogs chase the DSP as he tries to break away from Shakaal's death trap. The sequence is shown in detail in the earlier part of the film, suggesting the overall mood of gloom and desolation that magnifies the stature of Shakaal as a villain. Abdul, disabled, and a witness to the acts of smuggling, passes the information to Vijay and Ravi (Bachchan and Kapoor). He is brutally murdered. This sequence too is shown in detail to build the mood of trepidation. Any reader of this narrative may recall how often the heroes have taken the names of Vijay and Ravi in the seventies and eighties. The villains, being very powerful, didn't bother about names. The name Shakaal was used before on one occasion only; in *Don*, for example, to describe the bald Shetty, who cut the rope when JJ was escaping with his children. But he was a sidekick of the villain. The Shakaal of *Shaan* is different.

Rakesh (Shatrughan Sinha), who'd previously worked for Shakaal, joins the heroes for settling a score with the villain. That makes the number of people three the villain has to fight with. Added to this, the three-member team is further helped by Jagmohan, whom Shakaal had treated shabbily and banished. The job of the heroes in this film has little heroics about it. The frames, showing romance, have been trimmed drastically to focus on the villain and his activities. The changed political scenario hardly allows romance to thrive. Renu (Bindiya Goswami) is kept stranded on the spot of appointment for one hour and fifteen minutes before the hero (Shashi Kapoor) manages to arrive on the scene. She's fortunate not to have been abducted by the villain as Basanti was in *Sholay*. But Shakaal, as said before, is different, not bothering about flip diversions.

In *Kaalia* (1981), Amjad plays Sahani Seth. Amitabh, playing Kalia, voices the deteriorating trend of law and prison system of the time: *"Aaj ki duniya mein jurm kitna kamyab hai, aur kanoon kitna bebas"* ("In this world, injustice and oppression succeed, whereas justice fails to do its duty"). The villain succeeds in implicating the hero in a murder actually committed by him. He shows an awful presence of mind when he asks Abdul, his man, to drive the car, changing his previous decision to drive it himself. Abdul, planning to kill Sahani and become the leader of the gang, had placed a time bomb in the car. Abdul, asked abruptly to drive the car, sweats. "Why does he sweat like that in an air-conditioned car?" asks the villain. Later, Sahani shoots Abdul and shifts the crime to Kaalia, who, waiting to take on the villain at a spot arranged previously, is trapped into taking the rap. Sahani Seth's den is not a modern replica of Ravana's Lanka. It's better than that; more threatening than Shakaal's.

Nihalani, after *Aakrosh*, takes the issue of weak judiciary and shows the arrogance of a blistering politician-villain, out to destroy the hero

101

completely; his love and psychical stability—everything that makes up his existence. It shows the total helplessness of police administration before a villain who has joined politics for pursuing his agenda. In *Ardh Satya*, Govind Nihalani introduces the politician-villain. The thrust of the film is made clear at the beginning that shows Golchouki police station and its inspector Anant, played by Om Puri. The actor's close-ups, showing the twitch of muscles and veins, are used with great effect by Nihalani, similar to what he did in his debut film *Aakrosh*. But, Nihalani's greatest contribution is the villain Rama Shetty, played by Sadashiv Amrapurkar, making his maiden appearance. This sets the tune of the eighties, like it did in *Sholay* in the middle of the seventies.

Shetty is a macabre villain; ominously comic, reminding one of Kanhaiyalal of *Mother India*. The difference is in degree and intensity, responding to a decadent scenario. Shetty is a politician villain par excellence. He never forces anyone to do anything and yet gets everything done as he wishes. He fights the election of the corporation as an independent candidate, supported tacitly by the ruling party—a familiar scenario even now. Naseeruddin Shah plays a minor role, a man of the street, taken to boozing, after he has been sacked from job. It's revealed that he was once a police inspector and lost his job for being allegedly found in alcoholic stupor, a consequence brought upon him by those he wanted to punish. "*Chupchap naukri karta to kahan se kahan pahunch jata*" ("Had he done his job silently, he could go up the ladder"), says Haidar, giving money to the pie-eyed hobo. The figure haunts Anant as a specter.

Hyder Ali (Safi Imandar), a man who has tasted the sour fruit by experience, advises Anant to keep his cool and accept Rama Shetty as his friend: "*Rama Shetty ke saath sauda karo, baad mein tumhara hisab chukana*" ("Bargain with Rama Shetty at the moment; later you'll find time to call it even"). This is an acknowledgement of Shetty's towering stature as a villain, having influences in the corridors of power.

Anant can't check himself and restrain his anger, aimed at no one in particular, like the schoolteacher of *Nishant*. The corrupt system prevents him from arresting Rama Shetty. This is in spite of the fact that he has under his belt a dying man's declaration accusing Rama Shetty for burning the victim to death. An unseen hand not only releases Shetty's men arrested by Anant, but it reprimands him also for showing the temerity. Shetty, with macabre fun, applauds Anant for arresting his men. This is a new rhetoric of violence resorted to by the politician villain of the eighties.

Ardh Satya, intended to follow the tradition of parallel cinema framework places the hero in a realist framework and shows his sickening anguish for not being able to take on the villain. Anant is posted to see Shetty's security when he fights the election. That adds to Anant's anguish. Shetty waves at the crowd and is garlanded heavily as a neta. Watching Shetty and the crowd round him with quiet desperation, Anant later brandishes his rod at the people, asking them to keep off. It shows the huge depression of the hero, facing a politician-villain.

Thus, Shetty makes a raid on Anant's psyche, and becomes responsible for shattering his romance with Jyotsna (Smita Patil). In the eighties, the politician-terrorist villain succeeds in making inroads into the hero's existence as a human being, disrupting his happiness, mood, and psychical stability. Jyotsna, who accompanies a woman social activist to a factory, watches with dismay that workers, protesting against the management, are severely beaten by the police posted at the gate. Jyotsna reads in newspapers about gang rapes of women and lockup deaths. *"Mera pati policewala nahin hoga"* ("My husband will not be a policeman"), she says. But the police are not as corrupt as the newspaper men make them, adding spices to what they call a *story*—Anant defends. He hopes to be rewarded with a medal in an upcoming event for his bravery in catching a dacoit. This medal is denied to Anant. In sheer frustration, he beats a man in the lockup to death and is suspended from service. Hyder Ali advises him to meet Rama Shetty, who can reach the chief minister of the state. A little while before, we mentioned Kanhaiyalal to describe the essence of Sadashiv's villainy. Now, watch it.

Anant goes to Shetty, like a man holding a straw before being swept away by the current. Shetty, in return, wants to be served forever by Anant as a policeman. He needs someone to steer him out of troubles. Anant realizes that his position in future is going to be no better than a dog. Remember the insolence of Kanhaiyalal in *Mother India:"Sukhilala agar kutta bhi palenge toh…."* Similarly, Anant will be wedged in a gold chain, guarding Shetty's house. Furious, Anant strangles Rama Shetty. He goes back to the police station and tells Hyder: *"Sir, maine Rama Shetty ko mar diya."* The villain has the last smile while he dies.

The hero is going to experience death in life. This is how the villains of the eighties wreck havoc on everyone who challenges them. *Ardh Satya* is a surprise breakaway hit of Govind Nihalani.

In Bollywood film parlance, the presentation of villains has never failed in addressing the sociopolitical issues of the country. Thus, *Andha Kanoon* (1983) makes a critique of the blind operation of law in absence of having any humane intervention from the state or social institution. The upright jailor of *Kaalia* has disappeared. He's now replaced by someone who allows the three villains to move out of prison, kill a witness to their crime, and come back safely to the cell. Ironically, Pran, who'd played the jailor in *Kaalia*, now plays the villain, being the most powerful of the gang. R. K. Raghavan, the former director of the Central Bureau of Investigation (CBI) quotes from the fifth report of November 1980 of the National Police Commission (NPC) that was established by the new Janata government following the defeat of Indira Gandhi in the 1977 elections. Commenting on the poor state of police–public relations, the report said, "People now may not dread the police, but they certainly dread getting involved with it in any *capacity*."[2] No one, for example, was ready to give witness to the event of the wife's abduction in *Nishant*.

In *Inquilab*, the villains, following the trend of *Ardh Satya*, operate as politicians, representing a party called Garibo Ki Party, run by Shankar Narayan (Kader Khan) and Sitaram (Utpal Dutt). Amar (Amitabh Bachchan) can't find a job, and learns in an interview (as Shashi Kapoor does in *Deewar*) that the post has gone to another candidate recommended by a minister. Later, Shankar Narayan, appreciating Amar's grit and gusto, recommends him to the police force, hoping to get protection against their criminal activities. It's important to remember that both villains, being politicians, succeed in retaining their camouflage and are able to fool the hero for quite some time in the film. Soon Amar, as a reward of his service in which he'd vanquished the underworld criminal Anil Raj, is made the assistant police commissioner. Anil was employed by Shankar Narayan, the political head of Garibo Ki Party, to spread violence and panic in the state, and malign the government. The IG (Iftekhar), in a meeting with officers, mentions a CBI report pertaining to the conspiracy. This proves without doubt that Bollywood filmmakers, during the time, were familiar with many such reports. We've cited a few.

Let's mention another, again from R. K. Raghvan, who said that there was already strong evidence "available in many parts of the country of the growing nexus between some political parties and individuals with proven criminal records."[3] This gives credence to the fact that politician villains were becoming stronger during the time. This made the platform favorable for the terrorist villain to operate down the decade. In *Arjun* (1985), the political villains are shown again. Anupam Kher and Prem Chopra play the politicians—Shivkumar Chowgule and Din Dayal Trivedi. Sunny Deol plays Arjun and is used by the two politicians. Both use Arjun for their evil plans. Finally, Arjun realizes that he was fighting for a lost mission. Both villains in this film are unusually crafty. The gloomy scenario down the eighties echoes Deepa Gahlot's succinct statement, "By the eighties, films could not keep pace with the violence of everyday society—with the corruption, political skullduggery, and the seeds of terrorism."[4]

The danger of the country in the eighties is symbolically shown in *Mard* (1985), which places the narrative during the British Raj in India. Prem Chopra as Dr Harry, Bob Christo as Inspector Simon, and Kamal Kapoor as General Dyer strongly underline the gruesome activities of the villains. Directed by Manmohan Desai, this film shows the bleak and horrid nature of crime inflicted on the people of the country, and its native royal power, represented by Raja Azaad Singh (Dara Singh). After the capture of the Raja, his son Raju and wife (Nirupa Roy) meet with all kinds of miseries. Raju becomes separated from parents. The role of Danny, the son of General Dyer, is played by Dan Dhanoa, filling up the canvas of evil in this film. Chopra conveys through his smile and soft tune the menace of Harry, playing an active role in the capture of Azad Singh. Rani Durga later becomes a washerwoman, her misery running to extremes. There are scenes in the film that have been handled with agonizing pathos, particularly when Durga unknowingly tries to offer drinking water to the Raja from a pitcher. Danny sees it, and orders his men to drag her away from the spot. Conspiring with Dr Harry, Danny runs a camp where the native Indians are forced to give away their blood. This is a gory scene of huge magnitude and defines poignantly the nature of villainy in the eighties.

It is clear that Manmohan Desai, by using a story of the colonial past, wanted to impart a coeval message, like Shyam Benegal did in

Nishant. At least in this film, Desai wasn't using Amitabh Bachchan as a mere entertainer, though some stray scenes to that effect are still there in this film. Amitabh in the role of Raju runs a *tanga*, and has a wonder dog called Moti to help him out in crisis situations. Talking to statues is also there, like it was in *Amar Akbar Anthony*. But, the film's ruthless villainy looks so dark and gloomy that such stray scenes hardly stay in the mind of viewers.

The time was ripe for Dr Dang to straddle the screen. *Karma*, followed immediately by *Mr. India*, punctuates the image of the terrorist villain with awesome credibility. They are the movies of the decade so far as the villains' development is concerned. *Karma* is written, produced, and directed by Subhash Ghai, a man who unerringly read the sociopolitical scenario. By the middle of the decade the country was ripped by the menace of terrorism which, some felt, was the direct consequence of the Operation Blue Star carried out in Punjab by Mrs Gandhi. The recent happening in the red mosque of Islamabad has been described in newspapers as Pakistan's "Operation Blue Star." The Naxalite movement, having lost its previous venom, now looked like a mini rehearsal of a greater threat disturbing the stability of the nation. Rajiv Gandhi's handling of the situation was criticized by many. The technological hype, headed by secretarial administration, fizzled out. The menace of Tamil tigers of Sri Lanka went mounting up.

In *Karma*, Anupam Kher, a versatile actor, playing comic roles with equal flair (*Ram Lakhan* [1989] provides an example, among others), plays Dr Dang, the terrorist villain, with astounding brilliance. At the beginning, the Indian flag is seen fluttering at the top of a prison house. The camera tilts down to show the prisoners lined up for reading out their oaths in the large compound, conducted by the intrepid jailor Rana Viswa Pratap Singh, played by Dilip Kumar. Later, the photos of the leaders of the country are shown, those of Mahatma Gandhi, Jawaharlal, and Indira Gandhi. A song, praising the unity of the Hindu, Muslim, and Sikh communities, is heard on the soundtrack. Then, the face of Dr Dang is superimposed on the scenes of violence like bombing and gunfire. People scuttle about for panic. Dr Dang looks on with unperturbed face, as if nothing very serious has happened. This is a classic beginning of this genre of film. The national flag, the patriotic song, followed immediately by scenes of pogrom, suggest the gory mood of the film.

A cut to another scene shows Rana addressing the press about the threat and panic gripping the country. A guard demands bribe for allowing a prisoner to move out for collecting a bottle of blood for his brother dying in a hospital. A small, apparently insignificant detail, but it says a lot about the gloomy scenario. Michael Dang's first appearance in the film is as a prisoner, looking like a coxcomb. He's escorted to the cell by Rana, a believer in correcting criminals and reinstating them into the mainstream society. Dr Dang, chatting with Rana, strides up to his cell in style (like a political VIP). He asks mockingly, "How many of your children are now in this prison?" Later he says, showing his hatred for the Indians, *"Do do paise mein har hindustani bikta hai"* ("Every Indian is sold out for two paise only"). Entering his cell, Dang demands the walls to be painted and asks for privileges that suit a man of his status. Even Gabbar hadn't asked for that much. Probably he knew the time wasn't ripe.

Rana, unable to bear the insolence, slaps Dang. *"Dr Dang ko aaj paheli bar kisi ne thappad mara"* (For the first time today, someone has slapped Dr Dang"), hisses the villain, putting his spectacles back on. Dang uses his spectacles as a weapon in this film, a weapon that doesn't kill others but helps him get back his sense of dignity. The stylish and spruced villain of the sixties has now worked his way up the scale. The jail is raided. Dang escapes, killing many. The debris is shown in detail, suggesting the menace left by Rana's distinguished guest. It looks like the battlefield of Kurukshetra in the Mahabharata. Rana, representing the audience's perspective, moves around the gory sight, looking for his relations and others, dead or alive. Rukmini, Rana's wife, for whom the shock is too much to bear, loses her voice. After *Sholay*, the audience was yet to witness a scene of violence and disaster of this magnitude— funeral pyres burn; people wail; Rana vows to go after Dang.

Rana resigns from office and pleads with the authorities to hand him over three prisoners he knows—again, a *Sholay* motif. The number of adversaries taking on the villain now makes four, with Rana as the leader. They are: Vaiju Thakur (Jackie Shroff), Kheru (Naseeruddin Shah), and Johnny (Anil Kapoor). The three criminals, sentenced to life imprisonment, accompany Rana, known from now on as "Dadathakur." Soon, the scene shifts to the border area where Dang is ensconced in his den. Dang roars: *"Ek saal mein Hindustan ko tukre tukre kar dunga"* ("Within a year I'll tear off Hindustan into pieces"). In his castle beyond the border, Dang asks a new entrant to burst a coconut according to his custom. This is mandatory for anyone vowing to work with him. The man obeys. A bomb bursts and kills the man. Dang's flunkeys look on with terror. Dang says, *"Hindusthan ka C.I.D. tha."* He adjusts his spectacles and proceeds to the next business. Seth Tripathy joins Dang in the mission to terrorize and destroy India.

Toward the end of the film, Dang imprisons Rana's wife and his surviving grandson. Dadathakur manages to come out of imprisonment. Dang, on the pretext of treatment, makes him senseless. Later, the three heroes burst into Dang's den. Dang manages to get Vaiju wedged in shackles. With this ploy, he forces the other two to come out of their hiding. In a fit of mock surrender, a scene that will soon be repeated in *Mr. India*, Johnny throws himself at the feet of Dang, seeking his blessing. This gives others the time to retrieve their position and have Dang at gunpoint. Dang adjusts his spectacles.

This appallingly casual approach sends a creepy sensation to everyone watching the villain. Before getting killed, Dang runs along to get into his helicopter hovering overhead. He doesn't forget to say *"alvida"* (good bye) to Rana. This villain is *civilized and polite*. Unforunately, the adversaries of the villain are just too many to be tackled. Finally, cornered against a wall, Dang is surrounded by bullets that draw the map of India. Again, a positive message of violence, not nihilistic; something we argued about discussing *Sholay* and *Aakrosh*. Bollywood has hardly done anything otherwise. Subhash Ghai knows how to hook his audience. The upshot was that *Karma* earned the National Film Award from the president of India, mentioned as "the biggest award-winning hit of 1986."

Mogambo in *Mr. India* takes up the agenda of Dr Dang. The film is directed by Shekhar Kapoor, while the script is written by the famous duo, Salim–Javed of the seventies. Mogambo, out to destroy India, wants to grab the invisibility formula left by the departed scientist Dr Jagdish Verma, the father of Arun Verma (Anil Kapoor), the hero. One negative feature of the hero in this film is that after being thrown out of his house facing the sea by Mogambo's men, Arun becomes armed with the invisibility formula, intimidating the villain's men time and again. Still, to be fair, one should confess that at least in this film the hero fights his own battle. After all, he's forcefully driven out of the house where he looks after waifs and strays. The other point is that the magic watch of invisibility belongs to his father and he has every right, therefore, to have it and use it. So, this time, the hero has a personal agenda to fight for, though he looks pretty ordinary when compared to the mighty Mogambo.

Set in the garb of fantasy, *Mr. India* introduces some comic scenes that offset the gory subject of the film. On the other hand, the element of fantasy suits the presence of children in this film, and supplements Arun Verma's character, marked by innocence and simplicity. The eighties and after showed Sunny Deol, Anil Kapoor, and Jackie Shroff playing heroes in the changed scenario. By the mid-nineties, the space was further populated by Shah Rukh Khan, Ajay Devgan, Salman Khan, and others. Amitabh Bachchan, the superstar of the previous decade, was tried occasionally in between, but it couldn't make much of an impression. The ploy thereafter was to use Amitabh with the other heroes of the time, like he did previously also for an altogether different reason. Along with the heroes and changes in the sociopolitical scenario, the villains too changed. We will come back to this later.

The comic scenes add to the texture of *Mr. India*, ensuring box-office credentials. A food table is carried by invisible Arun Verma, now known as Mr. India. The starving people, waiting outside on the pavement, are delighted at this wondrous sight. "*Tum kaun ho?*" they ask. Mr. India says, "*Ek aisa hindustani jo janta hai ki jab bhookh lagti hai to kaisa lagta hai*" ("An Indian who knows what hunger feels like"). Before this, there's a funny sequence in which Teza, Mogambo's man, is fed by his darling, manipulated from behind by the invisible hero. The spoon whisks past Teza's ear instead of touching his lips. Teza, hugely disappointed, cringes, "*Darling, main kaan se khana nahin khata, kabhi nahi*" ("Oh, my darling, I never eat through my ears, never really")!

The villain Mogambo (Amrish Puri) is a menacing, towering figure in this film. His gait, laughter, looks—everything taken together—make him a worthy successor to Gabbar and Dang. He's also someone to give villainy a new definition in the decade—a grotesque figure, intimidating in an odd way. The film opens with a meeting of the higher police officials discussing a CBI report that speaks about a threat from outside to destabilize the country: "*Desh se bahar ki koi taakat*" ("Some power from out of the country"). After this, Mogambo is shown boarding down from his personal helicopter. His huge peals of laughter stun everyone.

Teza (Ajit Vachani) and Daga (Sharat Saxena) smuggle images of Indian gods and goddesses, made of gold, to Mr Walcott (Bob Christo) and in exchange get weapons from him. A business tycoon, Teza adulterates food with various indistinguishable items produced in his godown. Walcott has the sour knowledge later that Indian gods, especially the one called Bajrangbali (the monkey-god) beat wicked men with his mace. The sequence is hilarious and enriches the element of fantasy of the film. After coming to know from Calendar, the cook, that the golden image of Hanuman has been stolen by Daga and his men, Arun, now ensconced in his invisibility formula, runs to the spot. He plays his trick in punishing Daga and Walcott. The monkey-god is seen in action, and the bald Walcott, beaten by Hanuman's mace, snivels, "*Indian god marta hai.*" In a short while, Walcott also has the knowledge that the god laughs too. Daga and Walcott, joined by their men, are all seen lying on the carpet, and they are forced to say in chorus, *jai bajrangbali.* This is great fun, and entertainment of a high order.

Before this, Mr India was seen in action when Seema, who stays as a paying guest in Arun Verma's house, is in trouble for prying into Daga's affairs as Miss Hawa Hawai. Daga, wishing to whip Seema, raises his hunter. But, it's stopped in mid-air. All of a sudden, Daga is slapped by someone not seen around. Daga falls in a corner of the wall, capped with a brass plate on his head probably as a reward of his failed attempt. Daga manages to get up, and moves up to his hunter, groveling about. The fun of the scene mounts when Seema, in apparent appreciation of Daga's misery, asks him to crawl stealthily behind the hunter. Still, each occasion, the hunter slips away. Daga can't believe that his own hunter, having enjoyed so long his care, should betray him now when he needs it most. "*Ye mera hunter, mera apna hunter....*" Daga cringes in sheer desperation. By a strange turn of coincidence, the hunter coils up like a snake, followed by music used by a snake charmer. Horrified, Teza starts firing in air indiscriminately. The men start scampering round the room in panic.

This is all good, dexterously handled by the director. Still, one should remember that Mogambo's men, assembled here, are fighting an uneven battle. The hero enjoys the privilege of staying unseen and doing the tricks, as if he'd written his own script. One shouldn't forget that Mogambo, facing Arun Verma, makes life uncertain for him.

Arun Verma, without the invisibility aid, is a complete nitwit before Mogambo. Even when Arun manages to get hold of the magic watch in the final sequence, Mogambo, first taken by surprise, ferrets out the secret that Mr. India can be seen in red light.

This brings us to the final sequence of the film. Mogambo's den is a marvel of technological excellence. He has men working day and night in his laboratory to make and preserve missiles for destroying India any moment he wants. He's the godfather of all who wait on his orders. Mogambo checks from time to time how the missiles are working. That adds to his pride. Trying to get back at the invisible Mr India after he's punished his men, Mogambo fits bombs in the city, killing innocent people, and terminating the life of a beautiful little girl. The ghastly spectacle bears testimony to Mogambo's wrath, and shows what a terrorist villain in the eighties was capable of doing.

Mogambo's clownish megalomania is satiated. He knows that the invisibility formula, after all, does exist, and that one day he's going to have it. "People of India are all fools, ready to serve", Mogambo says, and roars into laughter, shaking like a volcano. It is this megalomaniac hysteria that is exploited by Arun Verma to his advantage just as the gods in mythologies did to trick the hard-working *asuras*. He falls at Mogambo's feet, cringing for mercy, and lifts the magic watch. Mogambo's men shoot around in search of their invisible enemy. Mogambo, first bewildered, but delighted later, asks his men to stop when he has a flickering glimpse of Mr India in red light. There's obviously some fun in it. But, that doesn't necessarily take away the ghastly nature of Mogambo's exploits in this film.

In the final encounter with the villain in his den where missiles are fitted to, Arun, now seen in red light, doesn't fight as Mr India but as a naïve "*hindustani.*" This is how Salim–Javed breaks the shell of fantasy. This is a small detail, but speaks highly of the excellence of the script and direction of *Mr. India*. The camera work is brilliantly done, like when it drizzles outside as Anil Verma and his trusted boy are in search of the magic watch in the abandoned house, or when the red light flickers, showing the real identity of Mr India. Add to it Sridevi's brilliant performance both as Seema and as Chaplin, apart from the dancer Miss Hawa Hawai. The hero being too ordinary, and given her film space, Sridevi carries the whole burden in this film. The element of romance is questionable, since Sridevi doesn't love Arun. She loves

Mr India, someone she hasn't seen. So, this romance, rather brief, is fraught with a sense of negation. Yet, Sridevi has managed to pull out a memorable performance. The children have all acted superbly. Then there's Satish Kaushik, playing the role of Calendar, the cook, to absolute perfection. Annu Kapoor as editor Gaitonde in a brief role is simply outstanding. The script, the direction, and everything taken together, makes *Mr. India* an unforgettable film of the eighties, having the claims of a classic.

Amrish Puri, playing Mogambo, gives a memorable performance, preparing the way for Isaq Khan in *The Hero: Love Story of a Spy*. Isaq is the ISI chief, and a menacing terrorist, operating from Pakistan and Canada, and looking for missile formula. It goes without saying that terrorist villains nowadays are armed with technological expertise, some even learning aviation so as to destroy the rhythm of civilization. Bollywood has used this to good commercial purpose. With Mogambo, the terrorist villain of the decade straddles the screen like a colossus, just as Gabbar did as a dacoit. The decade of the eighties, carrying some features of the previous decade at the beginning, ends in the nineties that opens on an ominous note—the assassination of Rajiv Gandhi on May 21, 1991, at Sriperumbudur of Tamil Nadu. Yes, this too was a terrorist attack on the country from outside India.

It is often said that in the eighties films couldn't keep pace with the violence of everyday life. As Deepa Gahlot says, Evil in society overtook evil in films. Still, there were many attempts in the decade to show the ugly faces of villains on the screen. *Arjun*, *Aakhri Raasta*, and *Shahensah* provide examples. Of these, *Aakhri Raasta*, directed by the famous Tamil director K. Bhagyaraja, and a remake of the 1984 Tamil film *Oru Kaidhiyin Diary* (*A Prisoner's Diary*, starring Kamal Haasan), uses the image of Sadashiv Amrapurkar as a politician villain, used already by Govind Nihalani in *Ardh Satya*.

Sadashiv plays Chaturvedi in *Aakhri Raasta*, repeating his previous feat. He slaps his assistant because he hasn't drawn his attention to David D'Costa's wife, Mary. David worships the leader like a god, and works for him. The couple approaches the leader to name their son. As soon as Chaturvedi sees the beautiful wife Mary (Jaya Prada), he becomes impatient to have her. Accordingly, the villain asks David to engineer an agitation in his favor that leads to David's arrest in police custody. Mary is summoned to meet the villain, and this turns out to be a prison cell for the hapless woman. In a closed room, Chaturvedi mimicks her curses: "Oh God, save me, save me … what a lewd villain you're, sending my husband to jail." Then, referring to Lord Krishna, who saved Draupadi in the Mahabharata, Chaturvedi mockingly says, that god appeared in the Mahabharata but "*iss Bharat mein nahin ayenge*" ("in today's India, that god won't appear"). The rape scene in *Aakhri Raasta* is presented in a macabre style, embellished by the imaginative and boisterous villain.

Mary leaves a suicide note, implicating Chaturvedi in the crime. But, the evidence is snatched away by the police inspector, Sahay (Dilip Tahil), and later burnt by Dr Verma (Bharat Kapoor) before David's eyes. The crafty inspector has David sign a blank paper, which is used as a confession given by David for murdering his wife for her floozy activities outside home. The politician villain is helped by administration and this provides a commentary on what was happening at the time. David goes to jail. In the final sequence, showing terrible pathos and irony, Chaturvedi, now relieved to see David shot by his son, a police inspector (Amitabh Bachchan in a double role), compares David to Ravana. Chaturvedi wishes to celebrate his death as people do in the Dussera festival. "*Hum utsav manaenge…. Bahut bada mujrim tha*" ("We'll celebrate … was a great criminal")—Chaturvedi says about David. Before dying, David rolls over on the ground and shoots Chaturvedi. *Aakhri Raasta*, by the way, was probably the last successful film of Amitabh, capturing his previous superstar image.

Ketan Mehta's *Mirch Masala* is a strong film of the eighties. Just when one felt that in the character of the villain Mogambo we had seen all the macabre features of a villain, Ketan Mehta presents another variation, worth viewing, in the figure of the local tax collector in colonial India, played by Naseeruddin Shah with great élan and intensity. *Mirch Masala*, so far as the villain's presentation is concerned, makes an important departure from *Mr. India*. The element of fantasy in Shekhar Kapoor's film is replaced by a realistic framework where the subedar, collecting tax from poor peasants on behalf of the British government, behaves arrogantly, inflicting tortures of all kinds on his victims, like tying them up to a heavy piece of log and whipping them mercilessly. The poor victim lies unconscious for days together, watched helplessly by his wife. The role of the helpless peasant is played by Paresh Rawal.

113

Mogambo wasn't lascivious, after all, and didn't care about women. One has to concede this redeeming feature to Mogambo, in spite of his being an outright terrorist. Possibly, a terrorist villain has no time for such diversions, unlike the villains of the seventies, who kept molls. So, the wanton subedar in Mehta's film is after Son Bai, a married woman of the village (played by Smita Patil), now alone, since her husband has got a job in the city. Interestingly, this takes up the familiar motif of the films of the fifties (*Mother India* and *Madhumati*, for examples), noted previously, when the villain was seen into action after the woman's husband or lover left the place. Another point of variation on *Mr. India* is that in Ketan Mehta's film, the villain is challenged by an organized group of women, all workers in a masala factory. The titles of the film are shown on the background of a heap of red mirchi, suggesting the theme of the film.

This feature also glaringly shows (too obviously perhaps) how Ketan Mehta's film looks back strongly to Shyam Benegal's film *Nishant*, and the other offbeat films of the seventies. Even the character of a schoolteacher, inciting the villagers to oppose the corrupt subedar, is shown in *Mirch Masala*, as it happened in *Nishant*. The schoolteacher, talking about organized insurgence against the villain, says at the beginning: "*Shuruaat ke liye ek hi kaafi hai.*" The *mukhiya*'s (the leader of the village, played by Suresh Oberoi) wife and brother later join others in putting up a fight against the cruel subedar. But the gloomy scenario of the eighties plays its role when the wife's resistance angers the *mukhiya*. He drags her from out in the street where she has been demonstrating with others and locks her up in a room of his house.

The sequence of the gramophone, once again like in *Ankur*, is used by the lewd subedar to rope in Son Bai. He too watches her (like the landlord of *Ankur*), washing clothes and bathing in a pond. In *Mirch Masala*, the gramophone is used as bait by the villain, lying comfortably in his armchair. One slight difference with Benegal's film is that a local man, doing the chores for the villain, breaks a record. This lapse enrages the villain to a boiling point, and he beats him mercilessly before the other villagers present on the spot, including the subedar. The gramophone has another purpose in the film. It raises the stature of the villain in the simple innocent minds of men, who have gathered around him to listen to the marvel. How's the music pouring out through the instrument—asks one. Where's the singer—another quizzes, cocking his eye at the round hollow instrument. The villain smiles, without divulging the secret, and with an obvious intention of capitalizing on the ignorance of his audience. This is a good piece of work by Ketan Mehta, making the use of gramophone in this film marginally different from the predecessor film.

And, mind you, "the smiling, smiling, damned villain" is blessed in this film to relax under the sky and amidst the mounds of the valley, a lush green ambience to whet his appetite. He always has an alfresco music, lunch, even sex inside his tent. Thus, the villain in *Mirch Masala* is absolutely his own self, offering us something unique and fresh at a time when Mogambo looked unassailable. The subedar looks uncannily relaxed, going completely gaga for Son Bai once he sees her bare shoulders and the hook of her bra. He behaves like one who's alfresco personified.

The occasional similarities with Shyam Benegal's films do not necessarily take away the merit of Mehta's film. On the other hand, *Mirch Masala* shows how Shyam Benegal remained a formidable source of inspiration to a group of Bollywood filmmakers. Maybe, he's so even now. Look at the cast of this film: Naseeruddin Shah, Smita Patil, and Om Puri and the band of actors and actresses (leaving another three or four not seen in Mehta's film) who ambled in and out of the frames of offbeat and commercial films with formidable ease and expertise. Om Puri plays the memorable role of Abu Mia, the guard of the masala factory. He speaks a lot more with his gestures and actions during the climax of the film. As a matter of fact, the entire group of women workers within the masala factory looks like a unit, playing the role of a chorus in the film. They form a community, getting ready for the penultimate moment in the film when they'll throw the dust of red mirchi at the villain's eyes, injuring him severely. *Mirch Masala* is not a very long film, making it look like a poetic drama.

Smita Patil's acting career, as known to all, was cut short because of cruel fate. Still, what she has left behind her on celluloid is enough to speak of her talent. When the villain tries to get hold of her before his tent, Son Bai slaps his face. The tax collector cannot believe the temerity of a woman who's staying in the village alone. The local barber has been shaving the villain's face. As soon as the villain spots Son Bai up the mound, ambling away from his tent, he's caught by libidinous impulse, leaves his seat, and goes up to her, face unshaven and foamy.

As Son Bai slaps the villain on his face the foam disappears, leaving the other side of his cheek foamy. For a moment, one has the impression that the clownish Mogambo is back. But, it's shattered when the villain orders his men to pursue Son Bai. She runs to Abu's masala factory. The wise and stubborn Abu closes the heavy entrance door on the face of the villain's henchmen, mentally ready to face the wrath of the lewd tax-collector.

The entire sequence has been built carefully by Ketan Mehta, since this makes the turning point of the film. After being slapped, the villain becomes enraged, and with that, mounts his sexual desire. The whole village is threatened with paying the *lagan* which, the tax collector says, according to his fictitious calculation, has long fallen due. He also tells the subedar that unless Son Bai is handed over to him from Abu's custody, he won't spare any woman of the village.

The villagers, headed by the subedar, decide on the handover. The villain operates with full venom, like anyone of his ilk in the turbulent hour of the eighties. Naseeruddin Shah manages to create a good deal of awe and panic in the mind of viewers. He uses his voice modulation and gestures imaginatively, occasionally nudging his bristling moustache to show his anger and devilish intention. Nearly a decade and half later, Naseeruddin uses these properties with different dimension in the film *Krrish*, especially when he chides an interrogator, saying: "*Kuch sawaal taqlif pahuchatey hain.*"

When the villagers, headed by the selfish subedar, reach the masala factory, a priest in the gathering tells Son Bai, "*sab maya hai*" ("everything is an illusion"). He means to say that Son Bai's body and flesh, wanted by the tax-collector for satiating his carnal desire, is merely an illusion in this transitory world. She should, therefore, sacrifice it for protecting the interest of the villagers. Many rape scenes were shown in the films of the eighties and nineties. Yet, none of these probably can match the arrogance of what the priest says here. The irony provides a scathing commentary on the numbness and selfish love of security of common people. This was shown in *Nishant* by Shyam Benegal when the schoolmaster's wife is abducted and raped by the villains. The important point is that this desensitized reaction of people speaks a lot about the crudity and height of violence the villains managed to inflict on society in the eighties and later. Even now, people react the same way, watching gory actions in the street committed by hooligans or terrorists. The present narrative of villains' development and their climbing the summit seems relevant from this point also: our getting numb to acts of violence of all kinds; sexual, financial, judiciary, and political—all adding enormously to the ordeal of day-to-day survival. The word violence, viewed from this angle, acquires a larger significance.

Mirch Masala ends on a positive note. Son Bai doesn't relent to the pressure of the villagers piloted by the villain; nor is she willing to relinquish her body to the subedar because it is maya. Abu dies, putting up a strong resistance. And, finally, the villain is punished. The weapon used is pretty simple: the powder of red mirchi. Why use guns and swords when a group of women is armed with mirch masala?

Shahenshah (1988) begins on a bleak note with the suicide of Mr Srivastav, a police inspector, well on his way to track down the criminals of the underworld. He's caught in a vile trap and loses his job. This sets the tone of the film. Designed to be a comeback film of Amitabh Bachchan after his brief stint in politics, this film is all centered around the impossible feats of the *shahenshah* (emperor), played by the great actor. This film doesn't naturally portray any great villain. Still, the atmosphere of the eighties, looking further bleak by the Bofors scandal, makes the villain look menacing. The villain J. K. Verma, a man of the underworld, is played by Amrish Puri. The film tries to bring back the politician villain, someone who wants to be a neta. Added to this, Prem Chopra plays Mathur, a corrupt bank manager. Both Verma and Mathur act together and use Julie (Aruna Irani), the dancer, to implicate Srivastav in the bank robbery. Puri looks more aggressive in this film than Chopra.

The way J. K. fights inside the court premises shows that this villain wants to make a mockery of the society that honors him as an eminent leader. Thus, J. K. is a creation of the society he's out to destroy. That's the principal point of irony in this film. J. K. stabs the newspaper editor at the printing premises and walks out unchallenged by the workers, present on the spot. This shows how violence shook everyone in the late eighties, something spelt out just a few paragraphs preceding this discussion.

It was probably most fitting to end the decade with *Agneepath*, only marginally away, actually a year to be precise, from the assassination of Rajiv Gandhi. Amitabh Bachchan was seen not just attending the

117

funeral of his friend, but he was with the royal family right since the tragedy shook them and the nation. Before this happens, Amitabh goes through the fire set by Kancha Cheena in *Agneepath*. Kancha is an awesome villain of the decade, being a combination of Gabbar and Dang. It is, therefore, in the fitness of things, that Mr Bachchan, who had by this time earned the distinction of taking on most of the mighty villains in the seventies, should have the last say on his adversaries. Meanwhile, he'd lost his space to Sunny Deol, Anil Kapoor, Jackie Shroff, and others. And now, for the last time probably, Amitabh wanted to go at a dangerous villain, taking once again his favorite name Vijay and his father's poetry behind him to get himself ignited to the task. While talking about the legendary Big B, one shouldn't forget Harivansh Rai Bachchan, a professor of English Literature in Allahabad University, and a poet. One has reasons to believe that this has always been a source of inspiration to Amitabh Bachchan both in his personal life and in his profession.

The hero in *Agneepath*, meaning "the path of fire," needs to be armed to the teeth before confronting Kancha Cheena in his den. He has another by his side—the grotesquely funny, but honest to the core, Krishnan Iyer M. A.— now selling coconuts on roads. This educated simpleton helps Vijay out at crisis situations, like when Vijay faces the villain in Mandwa village, his mother, wife, child, and sister all being in the custody of the villain. Thus, Amitabh's final encounter with the villain is punctuated by a past motif when the hero is helped by someone else, a feature of the seventies and eighties. In *Agneepath*, Iyer arrives on the scene of action a trifle late toward the end. He looks up, curses the heavens in sheer anguish, and throws the fire stick away in dismay. Although intended to be a film centering on Amitabh, Mithun Chakraborty gives a memorable performance, playing Iyer in *Agneepath*, which earned him the Filmfare Award for the best supporting actor. Amitabh Bachchan got the National Film Award for the best actor.

Ironically, Iyer's comic bonanza in the film slightly disturbs the rhythm of the narrative, focused on telling a gripping revenge story. There are moments in the film when one feels that Iyer's activities, such as his romance with Vijay's sister, Shiksha, are taking the attention away from both Vijay and Kancha—at least the gruesome aspect of the confrontation, which slides occasionally into melodrama

Kancha has goons to help him. But, when he faces Vijay in Mandwa village in the final sequence of the film, he has hardly anyone with him except the guards; since, by this time, Dinkar Rao, Usman Bhai, and Anna Shetty, who once worked with Kancha, are all dead. We will meet Kancha Cheena in more detail in a later chapter of this book, with the respect and attention he deserves, for anyone must give Kancha his *usul* (principle) he's particular about (*"apna usul kehata hai"*). Kancha has meticulously followed this principle in his life, whether he works in Mandwa or in Mumbai. A great exacting villain, Kancha reminds Vijay of this when he meets him at his seaside recluse.

As a matter of fact, Kancha appears late in the film, physically. He has no need, since he's always present in the mind of the audience even before he appears. That's one awesome feature of this villain who takes the cue from his predecessors, and transmits it to the later generation, adding his own chemistry. The *Agneepath* of 2012, starring Hrithik Roshan, Sanjay Dutt, and Rishi Kapoor, shows without doubt that the villain Kancha Cheena is stunningly resurrected in the changed scenario of the second decade of the present century. Karan Johar, the producer of the film, says that this film has something *special* for him, as the 1990 film was produced by his father Yash Johar. Mukul Anand directed the 1990 film.

The canvas of the villain's henchmen in 1990 is filled by Sharat Saxena, Bob Christo, Goga Kapoor, and Avtar Gill. Kancha is played by Danny Denzongpa, having a style of his own. The role of Vijay's mother is played by Rohini Hattangadi. This, of course, brings a change in the Vijay universe. It was probably time for Nirupa Roy to disappear from the scene. After all, the son was becoming older. Master Manjunath, already known for his role of Swamy in the 1987 television serial *Malgudi Days*, based on R. K. Narayan's story, has given a touching performance in the role of young Vijay. He had six international awards in his pocket before arriving on the set of *Agneepath*. The role of Vijay's father, a morally upright and kind-hearted schoolteacher, an important one in view of the film's perspective, is played by Alok Nath, making the character look rather anticipated.

Ghayal, written and directed by Rajkumar Santoshi, and produced by Dharmendra, is another remarkable film of 1990. It provides a powerful commentary on the deteriorating scenario of the time and helplessness of the police administration, spelt out by the Police Commissioner, Ashok Pradhan (Kulbhushan Kharbanda) to ACP D'Souza (Om Puri in a remarkable role). Like Kancha Cheena of *Agneepath*, the Balwant Rai dramatics of *Ghayal* is going to be reenacted in *Ghayal Returns* (forthcoming).

Like anyone in the anguished and confused scenario of the nineties, Ajay Mehra (Sunny Deol) is in search of his missing brother Ashok Mehra in Mumbai. The police know who the criminal is, but they can't reach him. Balwant is a social worker apparently, and donates ₹500,000 to a blind academy. He's a man of great stature, and yet hasn't joined politics. Still, he moves round the corridors of power. Sharat Saxena is once again in a familiar role, filling up the canvas of the villain's underworld business. His looks and gait supplement Balwant Rai's menacing stature in the film.

Ghayal shows Rajkumar Santoshi's expertise in telling the story of a film. It moves on without any impediment. Even the item number "Pyasi Jawani Hai," played by Disco Shanti, is well fitted to the story, since the brief diversion is related to the four absconders' taking on Captain Dekka (Sharat Saxena). *Ghayal* shows some memorable shots, like the close-up of the street lamp, ensuring the audience's sympathy for Ajay when he is alone with the dead body of his brother in the street. The close-up is shown twice in quick succession. Balwant appreciates Ajay's *josh* for accosting him twice before others, but kills his brother for showing temerity. One feature of this villain is that he plays tunes on the grand piano in high cringing notes when he's angry. Ashok, Ajay's brother, is killed after this. This is like Nero playing the violin, when people wail after losing their relations. Balwant's next move is to implicate Ajay in the killing of his brother and make a dent in his psyche by charging him with having an illicit relationship with Indu, his sister-in-law. He blames everyone; the police, the administration, Mohiley, his personal assistant, and even D'Souza. Balwant's excitement and dramatics are enough to make D'Souza suspect the *real* game behind the scene.

Prem Chopra comes back to the scene exactly in 1991 when Rajiv Gandhi is assassinated, with *Phool Bane Angaarey*. He plays Bishamber Prasad, a political villain, in this film. *Phool Bane Angaarey* shows the grim political scenario where political elections are manipulated. Rajnikant, playing inspector Ranjeet Singh, gets evidence of Bishamber's villainy, but soon he has to exit from the scene for his impertinence to challenge a political villain like Prasad. Significantly, political rivalry in this film ends with the killing of Dutta Babu. Ranjeet Singh gets evidence of Bishamber's direct involvement in the killing. He is prevented from acting by his superior officer Ravi Khanna (Dilip Tahil), showing the contemporary administrative connivance with political murders.

A major feature of this film is the treatment of its theme that moves on pretty straight without allowing any extra zing to the story. Rekha, playing Namrata, the widow of Ranjeet Singh, avenges herself on the sinister forces, much like what the hero does in *Agneepath*. Chopra, the veteran villain, plays his role with awesome menace, sending a spooky sensation to the audience. The crises in law and administration are most poignantly shown. It needs to be said that *Phool Bane Angaarey* is in contrast with *Agneepath*, where Gaitonde, the Police commissioner, is sympathetic to Vijay's agenda, and even helps him occasionally. In this sense, *Phool Bane Angaarey* supplements and completes the canvas of crime and violence that might have been left marginally incomplete in *Agneepath*. The film is directed by K. C. Bokadia. The deteriorating law and crime was also shown two years before *Phool Bane Abgaarey* in *Kanoon Ki Awaz* (1989) where Chopra played the role of Darshan Lall, a gangster, having control over the corridors of power. The film made it obvious that it was becoming increasingly difficult to hear the voice of law, in spite of having on the scene an honest public prosecutor. If she is not corrupt, accepting bribe, then her husband is. A lot of films down the eighties were concerned with the breakdown of law and the legal system.

Needless to say, the villains were garnering enormous strength in keeping with the deepening crises facing the country. The technological boom during Rajiv's time was wiped out by Bofors controversy. Rajiv Gandhi was defeated in the election, and the V. P. Singh government came to power. Leaders became busy checkmating one another. Political rivalries took precedence over national problems; issues of social justice, economic revival, and value-oriented politics took a back seat. Soon, the V. P. Singh government earned the distinction of being the first after Independence to be defeated on the floor of the Parliament. The villains had their hands full now. Paradise, or the dream of paradise, was shattered. Rajiv Gandhi, who was expected to come back to power through election, became a victim of terrorist politics. The early 1993 saw a Hindu–Muslim riot, following the destruction of Babri Masjid in Ayodhya. Rape cases which numbered 13,754 in 1995, according to an estimate, doubled during the same year. This is exactly the scenario the villains wanted to watch, much to their pride and satiation. The heroes became affected also and started behaving like villains.

Probably, we have missed noticing the upshot of the villains gathering enormous strength since the seventies. The result was seen in the emergence of multiple heroes as the scenario grew darker in the eighties and nineties. It was as if the villain, like the mighty Ravana with his ten heads, got himself split off in many forms and figures. The directors didn't know exactly which one of the heroes they should pair off with the menacing villains, benefiting from the blistering scenario. That also led to the disappearance of a single superstar from the scene, making the situation look confused and uncertain.

Javed Akhtar, who penned so many mighty villains in the past decades, said in an interview to Nasreen Munni Kabir: "Now, in 2001, we see the image of the hero and the villain is very confused. You can have a clear-cut hero and a clear-cut villain only if you are clear about the dos and don'ts."[5] What Javed Akhtar says suggests the unmistakable triumph of villains. The scenario reminds one of what the witches said at the beginning of Shakespeare's *Macbeth*: "Fair is foul, and foul is fair." With the arrival of Shah Rukh Khan on the scene, especially in films like *Baazigar* and *Darr*, both released in 1993, the process of confusion between the dos and don'ts started getting blurred. We'll come back to this point.

In *Baazigar*, Shah Rukh plays the role of a wizard criminal, out to destroy the family of the heroine, because her father had once wronged the hero's father. Assuming the name of Vicky Malhotra, Ajay (real name) seduces the heroine's sister and later kills her. The heroine too, though reasonably busy with making love with the hero, is in a different hunt, trying to retrieve clues and catch the unknown assailant of her sister. The film, up to this point, works like a crime movie, keeping the audience on the edge of their seats. The "*baazigar*" takes a number of personae and accomplishes his revenge; but, in the process, he too is killed like any villain of the previous decades. The film ends in a top angle shot that shows the tiny image of the mother, holding her dying son to her chest. The police officer, standing to the left of the frame, takes his hat off to guide the empathy of the audience in favor of a man who, for most part of the film, has behaved like a criminal.

It was left to veteran Yash Chopra to explore the hero–villain formula in *Darr*. Shah Rukh's quivering jittery voice admirably suits the role of a dejected lover, who does everything to ruin the happiness of a couple in the film, Sunil (Sunny Deol) and Kiron (Juhi Chawla). Rahul's (Shah Rukh) exploits in the film to have Kiron to himself by any means are no less menacing than what a confirmed villain would do in a similar situation. The voice-over at the beginning of the film pledges to tell the story of a Romeo and Juliet, although the present story that's going to be narrated in the film, it says, is distinguished by a sense of *darr*, a fear and panic, gripping the heroine.

With the release of *Dilwale Dulhania Le Jayenge*, and the years that followed, there was a belief in some corners that perhaps the story of villains in Bollywood cinema finally ended. The time for modern and multiplex cinema, many believed, had arrived, discounting action films altogether. The filmmakers concentrated on showing the protagonist. The villains bowed and made their exit like gentlemen. But, this is not true. Very soon, we are going to look closely at what was happening down the mid-nineties, and the beginning of the present century. But, first, let's watch the *dilwale* in action in order to do justice to what was happening at the time.

DDLJ begins in London, showing the anguish of an NRI for his motherland. The pigeons on foreign soil and homeland are not considered the same as a later scene in the film would testify. Amrish Puri plays the NRI father, Chaudhry Baldev Singh. *DDLJ* is basically a film on the conquest of love, like any Shakespeare's comedy. But, this hero too advances cautiously to fulfill his mission and discredits the bridegroom before all, especially his tough and would-be father-in-law, whom he'd once wronged at his store in London by shoplifting in the middle of night. What has not often been noticed is that this goody hero too hasn't completely gone beyond his traits shown in the two previous films. The father-in-law, unable to exactly connect the fellow with his London burglary, always watches him with suspicion and contempt.

While admitting the fact that the distinction between the good and the bad got blurred in the mid-nineties, one should also remember that it couldn't be completely eroded within the Indian system that is held firmly by its mythologies. It has to be remembered that the so-called confusion between the "dos and don'ts" hadn't anything to do permanently with our traditional faith in the good and the bad. After all, India is a land of myths and mythologies. So, in 1996, Danny Denzongpa, who had sharpened his skill as a villain in *Agneepath*, comes back as Katya, a ruthless gangster, in the film *Ghatak*. The film does send a lethal reminder of the nature of cruel villainy that ruled the seventies and eighties. At least in this film it is not a problem to identify the so-called "dos and don'ts." Both Kashi Nath (Sunny Deol) and Shambhu Nath (Amrish Puri), hailing from Banaras, represent traditional values of life. Kashi Nath represents the anger and virulence of life, though he stays calm at the beginning. The scene where the ailing father falls at the feet of Katya (Danny), seeking mercy for his son, watched by the silent crowd of the locality, is strongly reminiscent of what happened in Ramgad village of *Sholay*. The difference is that in the previous film it was one of the heroes playing a charade, whereas in *Ghatak* it's an old man genuinely overtaken with grief and anguish. The effect, therefore, is gloomier and heartrending. In *Ghatak*, the old man is put in chains, something that is perfectly in tune with the growing stature villains in the nineties. *Ghatak*, remember, is a Rajkumar Santoshi presentation. Katya, in some ways at least, is an iconic villain like some of his predecessors.

How can we forget *Drohkaal*, a hard-hitting cop saga of Govind Nihalani, the man, who had given us films like *Aakrosh* and *Ardh Satya*, punctuating the trend of villainy in the eighties? Released in 1994, *Drohkaal* is graced by Nihalani's imaginative camera handling—hazy lights, sharp focus, and extreme close-ups of both the protagonist and the villain, the last feature used so poignantly before. The lighting of *Drohkaal* has been consistently kept on a low key, suggesting the overall mood of terror and anguish of the film, like when Abhay Singh (Om Puri) and his wife Sumitra (Mita Vashisht) embrace one another, or when Abhay, unable to sleep at night, wakes his wife and makes his confession. And, mind you, *Drohkaal* shows one of the best scenes of rape not only in Bollywood cinema, but maybe, in world cinema also. Understandably, Mita, playing Sumitra in the rape scene, was given the Star Screen Award for Best Supporting Actress in 1996.

The film, intending to translate on celluloid the suffocating and increasing moments of horror and angst of the nineties, looks a bit different from either *Aakrosh*, or *Ardh Satya*, though it retains the same subject of cop-administration—something that was possibly Nihalani's forte. Making a subject look different each time, and handling it dexterously to comment on the changing sociopolitical scenario, makes Govind Nihalani a director of great commitment.

And, if it was Sadashiv Amrapurkar in *Ardh Satya*, now in *Drohkaal* it is Ashish Vidyarthi, playing Commander Bhadra, a totally different and aggressive villain. Nihalani's desire and ability to translate the changing social scenario must have motivated him to present a different villain each time. Ashish seems to be the calling card of this film. To tell the truth, neither Om Puri nor Naseeruddin Shah (dies early) was intended to carry the burden. They couldn't make the film look different, since both were known faces in their roles.

Watch the controlled aggression of Bhadra when he's beaten severely in the prison cell. Face bloodshot, he retorts, calling out the names of Abhay's wife and child. He's always menacing, but he never shouts. After Abhay's son is shot in the leg, Abhay becomes scared, and remains so till the end before he comes out of his shell of terror and concern for the family. The close-ups of the villain and the protagonist in every meeting at the villain's den, now out of prison, establishes the superiority of the commander of terrorists. It is always Ashish dictating the terms. Nihalani's unflinching dedication to show real-life violence without making any compromise with the usual kind of hero-worship, has given the viewers an authentic and convincing villain in the nineties, and probably in the years to come. The rape scene (may also be called a seduction scene) where Sumitra shoots Surinder (Annu Kapoor in an entirely different role) is the turning point in *Drohkaal*.

In the character of Bhikhu Mhatre in Ram Gopal Varma's *Satya* (1997), there is again an effort to revive the villain. But the underworld of *Satya* is so thinly populated that it's difficult to identify anyone to be truly menacing like Dang or Kancha. Let us remember the "Dev noir" films of the late fifties and early sixties, usually described as the golden era of Indian cinema. They did play a significant role in portraying the universal tendencies of the human mind plagued by evil desires. Toward the mid-nineties, the full significance of such early attempts strikes the viewers with appalling relevance, and asks one to interpret villainy in new terms.

Cut back to a familiar scene from *Sholay*. Killing and counter onslaughts are in full swing. Ahmed, the boy, is killed by Gabbar's men, and in retaliation, Gabbar's men are also gunned down by Jai and Veeru, the two small time crooks hired by the Thakur to catch Gabbar alive and kill him. In a memorable shot we watch Gabbar in a sadistic ruminative mood. An ant crawls on the reverse of Gabbar's palm. He merely looks on, showing no reaction. He realizes that now is the time to have real fun: tackling some *real* adversaries who are fit to take him on. This indicates that the crooks developed by the time of *Sholay* to take on the larger villain on the screen.

Gabbar's sadomasochism and cynical megalomania hiding the ambers of his savage discontent strongly foreshadows the psychical grooming and fomentation of the later heroes culminating in Rahul Mehra (Shah Rukh Khan) of *Darr*, the romantic psychological thriller discussed a while before, and many other recent films. The villain's resurrection in the latest scene of action and the possibility of his coming on to the center stage in many different ways and nuances seems to be a foregone conclusion. The idea of the so-called "dos and don'ts" has hardly anything to do with this inevitable development of the human psyche responding to a new environment. Probably, we might not exaggerate the simplistic notion of the dos and don'ts as it fails to explain the mysterious workings of the human mind in changing social circumstances—a feature that has been recorded on many occasions in films and popular literatures of the world.

The story, then, comes full circle. Interestingly, the decade of the eighties is marked by three major movies: *Ardh Satya* (1983), *Karma* (1986), and *Mr. India* (1987). Then, it ends with *Agneepath* and *Ghayal*. *Ardh Satya* sets the tune and rhetoric of the politician villain; *Karma* shows the terrorist villain in action, while *Mr. India*, coming down the decade, finishes the trend. Mogambo is noted by his peals of laughter, while Dang by his anti-smile. It is also noticeable that the most terrifying film of any decade usually appears in the middle, assimilating its features, as it happens with *Sholay* in the seventies and with *Karma* in the eighties. This shows a significant graph in the role played by villains in Bollywood cinema. *Ardh Satya*, coming in 1983, probably signals the ominous that is going to happen through the assassination of Mrs Gandhi in the next year; while the brief spell of promise during

Rajiv Gandhi's rule is questioned by Dang and Mogambo, sending a chilling forecast of the disaster that was going to happen yet again. After this, the heroes, utterly confused, started behaving like villains. But, this happened for a brief spell only, intersected by the appearance of confirmed villains on the scene.

What more could the villain ask for than see the hero, his eternal adversary, trapped in his image? It was quite worth the thrashing and losing the hand of the heroine.

Notes

1. Quoted by R. K. Raghavan, "The Indian Police," in *Transforming India: Social and Political Dynamics of Democracy*, Balveer Arora, Francin R. Frankel, Zoya Hasan, and Rajeev Bhargava (eds) (New Delhi: Oxford University Press, 2000), 292–310.
2. Ibid., 297. Raghavan says,

    > Two things are noteworthy about this Commission. Firstly, it was the first, and only, body to be appointed at the national level since Independence, to propose police reforms; and secondly, its recommendations had still not been implemented when Mrs. Gandhi and the Congress party returned to power in 1980.

    This is in spite of the fact that this Commission came into existence as a response to public outrage over the Emergency's excesses.
3. Ibid., 303. In another context, Raghavan says, "Failure to register complaints, impolite responses to requests for help in dealing with bullies, and blatant favoritism toward the more affluent of two contending parties, even if that party happens to be the aggressor, are common complaints against the police." One could easily relate Raghavan's diagnosis to Sunny Deol's emotional speech in the film *Indian* in a closed-door meeting of police officials where he wins over his agenda of arresting Shankar Singhania (Danny Denzongpa), the terrorist.
4. Deepa Gahlot, "Villains and Vamps," in *Bollywood Popular Indian Cinema*, L. M. Joshi (ed.) (Piccadilly, London: Dakini Books Ltd, 2001), 252–97, 211–12.

    Deepa's essay is hugely informative, as it was intended to be at that point of time. This is possibly the only full-length article written on the subject. This also shows that the villains and vamps at the turn of the century didn't lose their relevance, something that supports our contention expressed toward the end of the present chapter that the villains down the nineties didn't actually disappear from the scene.

5.   Nasreen Munni Kabir, *Bollywood—The Indian Cinema Story* (London: Channel Four Books), 91.

Part III

EMPIRE of EVIL and the EMPERORS

5

That Other Self: The Vamps

$\mathcal{W}$omen first. That's why we begin with the vamps—yes, those cruel women; yet not all that cruel, always. After all, they're born on the Indian soil, no matter how much they resemble outwardly Western dresses and manners.

Like the study of villains, charting social changes and developments over the decades, any detailed study of vamps is likely to make one aware of the changes that took place over the years in Bollywood cinema. It's commonly believed that vamps no longer operate in Bollywood films as they did in the past, since the heroines have now become objects of social desire; even models, for promoting the sales of company products. The idea is that the heroines have taken over the seductive function of the vamps of previous times. An overview of the nature and function of vamps in Bollywood cinema seems important in this discussion, because it runs parallel to what the villains did over the decades. Just as the hero took it over from the villain in the mid-nineties, similarly the heroine did it from the vamp down the seventies.

It's well-known that in the Bible that Satan, the first villain, operates through Eve, a woman, responsible for the banishment of Man from Paradise. In the Ramayana, we have the instance of Kaikeyi, responsible for sending Rama to forest. This leads to Sita's abduction, and Rama's encounter with Ravana. In many ways, the principal story of the epic hinges on the envy of Kaikeyi, whose role is much like the vamps of Bollywood cinema, though Kaikeyi is never known to be dancing to lusty tunes that might have been permissible in the age of the Ramayana. If Kaikeyi is cited (as often is the case) as having some ancestral source of inspiration to the vamps of our time, then this exception too needs to be remembered. No one, for example, expects Manorama of *Seeta Aur Geeta* (1972) fame to dance. Having a hump on her back, Kaikeyi, one guesses, was a repulsive woman, enjoying the role of ruining the peace of the royal family. Therefore, Kaikeyi stands as a model of the evil-minded widow, endowed with spite and twisted disposition, and out to destroy the family where she stays. This continues even now; in stories, films, and television serials.

Let's also look at the other face of the vamp. In India, the hissing serpent has been associated with women of enticing beauties. The idea of a woman as *nagin*, a serpent, has been again and again used in Bollywood cinema. *"Nagin hai tu, nagin,"* screams Prem Chopra at his wife (Bindu) in the film *Do Raaste* (1969). Sridevi plays the role of a reincarnated woman–serpent with Sunny Deol in the film *Nagin*. She takes her revenge on the ambitious snake-charmer, played by Anupam Kher. Rekha in *Mr. Natwarlal* seduces the gangsters and takes away their guns, while her dance performance is followed by music in the background, used by snake-charmers. The audience has responded to this idea with delight and awe, just as they've to the duel between the hero and the villain.

Alternatively, the vamp, in course of development, was also no longer the courtesan or *devdasi*, though the idea of dance and music has also been retained while showing the vamp on the screen. A *devdasi* was the consequence of religious superstition, used for satisfying the carnal desire of the nobility visiting temples. What started as an original indigenous tradition gradually ended up in getting Westernized, at least apparently. The vamps in skimpy clothes started dancing to music, as ritzy hotels sprang up in the seventies along with swimming pools and lawns, flanked with trees and flowers. The villains needed molls to entertain them. Dr Dang, the terrorist villain, is entertained by Sridevi in his den. This is an instance where the heroine, for a while, behaves like a vamp. So, a vamp is by and large someone who dances with a purpose. The indigenous feature was retained, while changes in the sociopolitical ambience turned the vamp into a moll, acclimatizing the western inputs.

The vamp doesn't always dance. In *C.I.D.*, Waheeda Rehman plays the vamp, luring inspector Shekhar. She is seen staying alone in a mansion, keeping contact over phone with the villain, and informing him about all that happens. The villain, operating from the heart of the city as a generous *seth*, instructs the vamp about her duties. The hero is seduced by her looks and gestures and, later, on instruction of the villain, she throws the hero out into the street. The entire operation is done by the vamp craftily. Much later in the film, she develops an attraction for the hero, which is a universal feature of a woman's psyche. In this case, the vamp actually helps the hero reach the villain's underground. Finally, during a hide-and-seek operation, the vamp is shot by the villain. This is usually the fate of vamps in Bollywood cinema.

Nadira is often credited with being the earliest sophisticated vamp in Bollywood cinema as early as the fifties, when girls were supposed to look demure and tender, doing positive roles. Later, Shashikala, Aruna Irani, and others took Nadira's mantle when time became more favorable. Nadira made her glitzy appearance in *Aan* (1952) with Dilip Kumar and in *Shri 420* (1955) with Raj Kapoor, the supreme entertainer. Nadira's arched eyebrows exude sensuality when she woos Raj Kapoor, mouthing the lusty number "Mud Mud Kena Dekh Mudmud Ke" that sent many hearts stuck to the throats. Later, Nadira appeared in such well-known hits as *Waris* (1954), *Dil Apna Aur Preet Parai*, and *Saagar* (1985). She won the Filmfare Award for the Best Supporting Actress for playing the role of an overbearing mother in the film *Julie* (1975). Nadira set the trend of the vamp playing a definitive role in a film, something that was later emulated creditably by the legendary Helen. *Josh* (2000), starred by Shah Rukh Khan and Aishwarya Rai, was Nadira's last appearance as an actress, though *Zohra Mahal*, released in 2001, showed the old woman for the last time on the screen. Nadira spelt out the dimensions that vamps later emulated in Bollywood films.

Dil Apna Aur Preet Parai is an excellent film, released in 1960. But before this, and as said before, Nadira had played the spiteful princess in the film *Aan*. Immediately, it was clear that this girl from Israel, playing the negative roles, had come to stay in the industry for some time, which eventually lasted till 50 years. Nadira's stunning performance in *Aan* as an untamed woman, never ready to accept Dilip Kumar's (a village boy) love till the end, might have later inspired many others. Rajashree, the princess in *Aan*, makes a raid on the hero's village for avenging the death of his brother. Zeenat Aman, in the seventies, playing the role of a similar princess opposite Dharmendra in *Dharam Veer* (1977) that deals with the story of two princes as brothers and their queen mother, might have found her inspiration from Nadira's role in *Aan*. Mehboob Khan, the director and producer of *Aan*, should be credited with for choosing a completely new face to play the lead role in his film. It is said that Nargis was Khan's first choice, but she wasn't much interested in playing a negative role. Nadira's shrill articulation and her anglicized sharp look made her an inevitable choice for playing the temptress, the vamp, opposite the chaste heroines of her time. Only Helen's anglicized look made her a worthy successor to Nadira, who hadn't the spring-like slim physique of Helen, enabling her to do the feats on the dance floor.

Dil Apna Aur Preet Parai is directed by Kishore Sahu, a director and storywriter of considerable merit and literary taste. This film, for example, tells the story so smartly without any fleshy and unnecessary interludes in between that it moves steadily on to its climax. Even the songs and dances, neatly harmonized with the main story, provide perfect entertainment without impinging on the narrative space. "Ajeeb Dastaan," the number sung by Lata Mangeshkar, went on to become a classic, and still remains so in the minds of music lovers of the nation. The point to notice is that Raj Kumar, Meena Kumari, and Nadira are all within the frame when this song is picturized. Till this moment, the vamp hadn't shown her spite for the heroine. She does so only when her position as the wife of Dr Sushil Verma gets jeopardized. This happens later in the Omar Khaiyam dance sequence that celebrates the silver jubilee year of Malhotra Hospital. During the dance recital, Dr Sushil Verma and Karuna, playing their roles, come too close to one another. It is only after this that the wife starts reacting sharply.

The villain and the vamp are nearly always discredited for playing negative roles. But in this film Nadira, playing Kusum, the rich girl from Kashmir valley, never shows her resentment before she detects the infidelity of her husband. The fact that the doctor and nurse Karuna had some meaningful exchanges between them before the doctor was taken to Kashmir by her mother to pay a previous debt, does not establish the claim of the heroine. Or, the doctor's sipping coffee with the nurse at 2 a.m. after an operation in the hospital cannot either negate the vamp's claim. Why did Sushil marry at all after telling his mother in the middle of the night that the marriage with Kusum wasn't possible? Why was the mother blind to what she saw in Simla—the goody and all-virtuous heroine? Who should pay for what she later finds to be her wrong choice and her ploy of taking her son to Kashmir? Kusum, after all, cannot be held responsible. These details from the film text go in favor of Kusum.

In *Dil Apna Aur Preet Parai*, the vamp's character has been imaginatively handled by Sahu, something that isn't usually done by many Bollywood filmmakers. There are many commendable shots and sequences in this film. The black and white photography, for example, has been superbly handled, making it a worthy successor to Satyajit Ray's experiment with neorealism in *Pather Panchali*, creating history. The shot of the tossing sea-waves, for example, symbolizing Karuna's oscillating mind, is brilliantly done. If this appears to be too ordinary, then the shot of the running wheel of the car when Sushil and Karuna are going to a distant town for professional obligation can be mentioned. Take again, the shot of the dangling lamp, swinging like a pendulum out in the verandah as a consequence of the wrath of the elements. All these are unforgettable. Giridhari, suffering from cancer, is a minor character. When Tun Tun arrives on the scene and carps about what she believes to be her husband's fake illness for lying in the comfortable bed of the hospital, Giridhari murmurs, "This is how every husband has to pay for choosing a grousy wife." This provides a commentary on the main plot. The hospital scenes are neatly handled. No bravado; no drama. Yet, every scene speaks. The operation scenes, likewise, are short and precise.

When Sushil becomes ill, Kusum, who'd left for Kashmir after being insulted at her husband's house, comes back, worried. She goes to the hospital and hears a comatosed Sushil utter Karuna's name, articulating his love for Karuna. This scene too deserves special mention as it contributes to the climax of the story that ends up in the accidental death of the vamp, and the equally fortuitous union of the hero with the heroine. The shocking and despicable experience of the vamp-wife in presence of the heroine at the hospital bed is too much to swallow. Boiling with venom and jealousy, and the agonizing knowledge of an end in her conjugal life, Kusum has Karuna sit by her in the car. She changes gear and accelerates the car at an inconceivable and suicidal speed, knowing that she too is going to die in the accident.

She does, washed away by the current. Karuna, alive, is later retrieved by Sushil.

Thus, Kusum has to make way for Karuna, like it happens in many films, up to the seventies. The story of the vamp after that, down the seventies, makes a different story. We are going to discuss later, at the bottom of this discussion, why it happened like that. Why is it that we notice a graph in the use of vamps in Bollywood cinema between the fifties, sixties, and the seventies, maybe a little beyond that? An effort is made in recent past to bring back the vamp of the sixties to a changed social environment. That does indeed show a third graph— something that has been called as the "revamped vamp" in Bollywood cinema. But, even this view needs to be corrected, like the original view itself. The story of vamps in Bollywood cinema hasn't been that simple and cannot be tied around easy generalizations. Let us pause for a while and look at another prolific woman of the fifties and sixties. The decade of sixties, needless to say, had shown the vamps to be truly venomous.

Lalita Pawar, apart from Shashikala, was another very important actress, playing the roles of overbearing mothers and wicked mothers-in-law in the films of the fifties and sixties. In *Dahej*, released in 1950, she tortures the wretched daughter-in-law, demanding dowry. In *Mr. and Mrs. 55* (1955), she doesn't allow her niece to get married to the person of her choice. Women crusading against women, subjecting them to huge torture, have been a recurrent feature of films in general, possibly reflecting the trend of Indian society. In towns and villages of India, it's seen even now. Also, it may not be typically an Indian phenomenon, since the Cinderella story filmed in 1950 by Walt Disney, shows Lady Tremaine, the evil stepmother as an archetypal personality. Stepfathers and stepmothers around the world are traditionally known to be wicked. Even mothers have proved to be overbearing and cruel, reflecting the possessive disposition of a lonely widow.

Junglee provides an example. Lalita Pawar plays the role of a fearful mother so stunningly that Deepa Gahlot says, "The several cruel mothers-in-law she played were a lark compared to this role."[1] True, but even this character has some underlying shades suggested toward the end of the film, and these bring her nearer to the typically Indian tradition. A "horrid mother," she's still gullible (like any villain), and is deceived by an employee of her company, now disguised as a doctor; someone who has fallen in love with her daughter, breaking the *parampara* (tradition) of the house. The doctor is called in for treatment of her supposedly diseased son, who has also fallen in love without the knowledge of the strong mother. Still, she too has some tender sentiments, revealed occasionally in spite of her efforts to hide them. Lalita plays her role admirably, hardly daunted by the scintillating "Yahoo" number that favors the hero and the heroine on the ice-capped Kashmir valley.

The horridness of the mother pushes the film forward. It is stated early in the film through a voice-over, describing her as a "*jwalamukhi,*" (volcano). She's seen standing on a flight of stairs, waiting for the arrival of her son Shekhar from abroad. In *Junglee*, a Subodh Mukherjee production, the main protagonist is the mother who gulps the existence of the ever boisterous Shammi Kapoor. It is around her that the stories of her son and daughter Mala (Shashikala) revolve. The mother is a stickler for discipline in the house, and holds on to two things in particular. One is her devotion to her dead husband, and the other is her defiant will to keep words and promises. Gifts, parted with once, are never taken back. When her son fights with the wrongdoer in the final sequence of the film, she doesn't allow anyone to intervene, saying that it's her son's fight and that he should slog it out alone. From time to time, she talks to the portrait of her husband and takes Rajkumari (Saira Banu) near the photo to seek her husband's blessing. When the doctor wants to record the temperature of Shekhar, pretending illness, the mother prevents him saying: "*Hum sirf apna thermometer dete hain*" ("We use our own thermometer"). This scene, where the harsh mother is deceived by all, draws the audience's empathy in Lalita's favor. She uses less dialog, more expression.

In *Professor* (1962), Lalita Pawar plays the crazy role of a woman, offering a good variation from the type of an arrogant and disdainful woman. She hates men but manages to fall in love with the hero, disguised as a codger. While it arouses hilarious fun among the audience, the pathos and frustration inherent in the fun cannot fail to appeal to sensitive minds. If one carefully looks at the closing frames of this film, one feels the subtle changes in Lalita's character; the anguish of a conceited and haughty woman, who had previously dressed herself with great panache to appear attractive to her hero whom she believed to be a lonely old man. Toward the end, she has to make way for someone else, as if it was all game, a film within a film. This is so unlike the usual exit of a vamp when she's either shot or forgotten, making way for the heroine. In *Professor*, the vamp's sacrifice is no less than that. Maybe, it's even more, since the woman is suddenly forced by circumstances to break the shell of her romantic trance. Even the great boisterous Shammi Kapoor looks pensive and apologetic, empathizing with the plight of his one-time lady love. The usual response of looking for only fun in the closing frames of *Professor* may not be justified. Lalita Pawar's ability to read a character's psyche with all its nuances and then render them dramatically, should be appreciated; a great actress; someone who deserves to be remembered by posterity. Bollywood certainly owes much to such unforgettable acting personalities.

Mention should be made of another well-known stepmother, deceptively vicious. In *Beta* (1992), Aruna Irani plays the stepmother with stunning menace. She manages to wreck the happiness of the family by making her husband a nonentity in the house, having him locked up in a room, and pretending to love her stepson, Anil Kapoor. She uses every ploy to earn the trust and confidence of her stepson, making him depend on her. She does everything to create a misunderstanding between Anil and Madhur Dixit (playing his wife). As a matter of fact, *Beta* shows the gruesome picture of a jealous and overbearing stepmother, like any villain, ruining the interest of the hero. In many ways, the stepmother of the film behaves like a serpent that hisses and stings everyone. But, this horrid woman too changes later when she realizes that her stepson takes more care of her than her own son. In this case also, the vamp's realization seems to be guided by the values of Indian tradition.

Occasionally, the villain uses the vamp not only for his personal entertainment, but also for taming someone else who looks to be a tough guy. In the film *Shahenshah*, police inspector Srivastav is ruined by falling into a trap set by the villain with the help of his woman. The villain sometimes feels proud to imitate the act of God and see him reflected for a while in a woman, as the Puranas often testify. Sometimes, the villain takes rest, watching how his web works, leaving the action to his female counterpart. The villain knows that he can have his will fulfilled through guile rather than through force. This is what happens in the film *Shahenshah*. The role of the seducer in the film is played by Aruna Irani, who had played many such roles along with Bindu, Lalita Pawar, and Sashikala in the previous decades.

With the use of color in the sixties, the vamps and heroines were looked upon as sex objects. Still, the time wasn't ripe for vamps to disappear from the scene. As a matter of fact, vamps became more seductive and alluring like any heroine of the time. They became stronger, along with their male counterparts—the villains. The dancer, at the beginning of the film *Dushman*, entertains the truck driver (Rajesh Khanna) and sleeps with him for the rest of the night. The villain knows when to use the vamp for his purpose. Having an exquisite woman by his side adds to the villain's confidence and raises his stature before others. This is what happens with Teza in *Zanjeer* in the early seventies.

Suzie, the cabaret dancer of *China Town*, discussed in a previous chapter, looks like Teza's Mona Darling of the *Zanjeer* fame. But, the fact is that Suzie is seriously in love with Mike, though Mike is always rude to her, never recognizing her love for him. Suzie knows about the underground operations of China Town, led by Joseph Wong and others. She dances in the hotel, entertains people with her songs and lusty dances, a job in which she's assisted by Mike. Suzie helps in the job and hoodwinks the police when there's a raid on the hotel. This makes Suzie's position quite interesting in this film.

On deeper speculation, it appears that Suzie is a professional cabaret dancer. She works as an aid of Wong, like any vamp. It is Suzie who first ferrets out the mystery of Shekhar's identity after he kills the dangerous Ching Lee in the shoe-shop of China Town. Pistol in hand, Suzie looks dangerous and authoritative in the scene. She's ready to wipe off anyone not friendly with the gangsters of China Town, led by the villain Joseph Wong. This establishes her identity as an underworld woman. It cannot be denied that Helen plays an important role in *China Town*, kitting her out with the claim of an actress.

In her personal life, Suzie is in love with the man who sings and dances with her on the hotel floor. But this man, Mike, is also a gangster, and Suzie has to abide by the underworld modus operandi. She cannot choose a life of her own like any other woman. Suzie never expresses her discontent about the life she leads. Her constraint and limitation of a vamp life, felt acutely, makes her character sparkling in the film. Nevertheless, Suzie's love for Mike is rewarded at the end of the film, unlike many cabaret dancers. Mike recognizes her love before he goes to jail for his criminal operations, leaving his mother and brother Shekhar behind him, and saying good luck for Shekhar's marriage with the girl he loves. Suzie, meanwhile, has to wait till Mike comes back from jail. That is the impression left by the film. Shekhar had worked for the police, risking his life, and impersonating Mike under instruction from the police inspector. *China Town*, from this point of view, looks like a forerunner of *Don*, discussed in a previous chapter.

Before assuming his role, Shekhar has the inspector promise that when the gangsters of China Town would be caught, he'd look into Mike's case with sympathy and consideration. The face of law being humane and benevolent in the early sixties, one hopes that Mike is soon going to come back from jail and accept Suzie as his life-partner, fulfilling the social pledge of marriage. This end of the vamp is in sharp contrast to what happens in some other films like *C.I.D.* and *Phool Aur Patthar* (1966), for examples. That's why *China Town* is an important film so far as the vamp-heroine is concerned. Just as the heroines later played vamps, similarly in this case the vamp seems to be retaliating against what may be called role-usurping. That's why if the villains, by virtue of their invincible strength, assumed the status of heroes, the heroes too in the late nineties started behaving like villains. Then, the villains, after a brief rest, came back. They are coming back now. The story has been one of role-playing. No one leaves his space permanently to others. That's the rule of the game. That's the way of life.

The case of Suzie being different, it supports our previous contention that the vamp's role may not always be restricted to that of a cabaret dancer. At the same time, the vamp's being a cabaret dancer doesn't necessarily take away her status as a woman. This is because these vamps are characteristically Indian versions of a Western tradition. Miniskirts, for example, became the fashion in the early sixties both in western countries, and occasionally in India too. Sharmila Tagore created sensation with her bikini-outfit in *An Evening in Paris* toward the late sixties.

A short note here may be added on Helen Richardson, who made a unique contribution to Bollywood mainstream cinema. Helen rocked the nation with her scintillating appearance in Shakti Samanta's *Howrah Bridge* (1958), and she finished the cycle with great character and dignity by playing a dramatic role again in Samanta's *Pagla Kahin Ka* in 1970. In this film, Helen plays a longer character role. That is Helen, an icon in the art of cabaret dance, exuding dignity and art, restraint and confidence. "Mera Nam Chin Chin Chu," "Mehbooba Mehbooba," "Piya Tu"—all saw her catapulted into lasting fame. Helen lent a new touch, respect, and rhythm to the cabaret, probably questioning the traditional derision and low estimate of a vamp. She wasn't bothered about what later became known as "item dance," though she did that too with equal relish, as in *Kalicharan*, for example. The sizzling dance numbers were all graced with a new interpretation and authenticity. Right through the fifties, sixties, and seventies, Helen became the golden-hearted vamp of Bollywood mainstream cinema. Her great achievement was recognized when she got the Filmfare Lifetime Achievement Award in 1998 and Padma Shri in 2009. She has been unique and different like the villains of the decades, playing occasionally the other self of the villain.

It should be remembered that the vamps in Bollywood cinema moved far away from the *devdasi* dancing girls of the south and the erotic *lavni* of Maharashtra. With Helen, Ganga never became *moili*, because she wasn't a belly-shaker but combined both sex and sensibility, articulating a personality of her own. This enabled her to get the respect and admiration of everyone in the industry.

Let's look at the cabaret for a while. It is basically a Western concept and was in vogue in Paris for the entertainment of artists, writers, and composers. This was happening since 1881, having a long story behind it. This association with the artistes made cabaret essentially different from the kitsch. The name of Moulin Rouge is often mentioned as a venue of the art of cancan that combined sex and satire. On the whole, cabaret was recognized as a form of entertainment that provided dance, song, comedy, and satire on the floors of ritzy restaurants and night clubs. It was popular in Nazi-occupied Germany also, as Christopher Isherwood's famous novel *Goodbye to Berlin* testifies.

Thus, from the beginning, cabaret, intended to be a form of entertainment, seems to have acquired a dimension and significance that kept it different from coarse pleasures, just as the *devdasi*s of India were associated initially with the temples of south as a form of ritual. With the advent of time and industrial progress, cabaret became popular, and later it became degenerated into item numbers in Bollywood cinema when the vamps had to quit from the scene. Their place was taken over by the heroines dressed in skimpy clothes.

Bollywood films have always given us super duper entertainment. The *aam admi*, the toiling masses of the country, have received their money's worth by witnessing a complex network of drama, suspense, dance, and music. These are followed by endless fights out in the street and at the *mehfil* of the villain's grotto, his lavishly decorated wine cell that turns in a flash into shards. This entertainment package is so densely worked out that the cabaret package also, graced by vamps, has stayed in tune with our tradition. We love calling Helen, Bindu, Aruna Irani, and others *desi* vamps, people we are able to empathize with. This feature too is in keeping with Bollywood's aim to please and entertain. And, in doing so, they haven't made any compromise with the kitsch and the low, at least not as long as the vamps were at the scenes of action. This point too has to be noticed.

Down the sixties, the end of the decade, there was some confusion about how the vamp, as long as she's a cabaret dancer, should be used in a film. We are talking about *Pagla Kahin Ka*. As a matter of fact, the beginning of this film, up to a considerable point, is occupied by the cabaret dancer—Jennie (Helen) and her love for Sujit (Shammi Kapoor) and their dear friend Shyam, played by Prem Chopra. The impression that stays longer is that Helen is the heroine of the film; while Prem Chopra, generally considered to be playing a villain's role, is a good and innocent guy. All three are seen singing and dancing together. Chopra plays the trumpet to accompany Sujit singing, and Jennie dancing to the lusty number. Asha Parekh, as Dr Shalini, has to wait for her arrival on the screen. Sujit and Jennie decide to marry and live together. Their plan irks Mack, who owns the hotel. Shyam, like any good guy, announces Sujit's marriage with Jennie on the dance-floor of the hotel. It is then that Mack abuses Jennie and Sujit, not liking their forthcoming marriage as it would affect his business. Shyam grows furious and hits Mack. Although Shyam had no intention to kill Mack, he dies. Sujit asks Shyam and Jennie to leave the scene while he stays put by the dead body, and is arrested.

After this turning point, Sujit plays a mad criminal at the court to avoid punishment. He's sent to an asylum for treatment, and this introduces the rollickingly funny interludes in the film, bringing in Asha Parekh on the scene as Dr Shalini. Shakti Samanta, as director of this film, couldn't avoid the temptation of using Shammi Kapoor, the boisterous hero of the decade, for fun and entertainment. Samanta was hardly innovative and preferred to go by what others had done before him, riding on the tide of box-office craze. He used Shammi Kapoor when he became a box-office godsend, and later used Amitabh Bachchan like that in *The Great Gambler*. While the gamble behind the *Gambler* film was a flop at the box-office, the inconsistencies of *Pagla Kahin Ka*, following the same cast of *Teesri Manzil* (Shammi, Asha Parekh, Chopra, and Helen), couldn't take the film anywhere nearer. The narrative flow of *Pagla Kahin Ka* suffers from terrible lack of probability in dealing with Chopra, Shammi, and Helen—all three being sufferers. The confusion arises when Asha Parekh is introduced in the film.

Inexplicably, Shyam starts behaving like a villain after Sujit's exit from the scene. He rapes Jennie and forces her to marry him. Meanwhile, in the asylum, Dr Shalini starts taking an active interest in Sujit, trying to know if he's really mad. She succeeds in her effort and learns all about Sujit's story. This establishes the heroine's claim for the hero, a bit unreasonably though, like it happened in the Nadira film. When Sujit leaves the asylum, Shalini feels upset and shaken. It becomes apparent that Jennie has to make way for Shalini in the story, though she has bumped in late into the film space. This upsets the rhythm of the script. Back from the asylum, Sujit goes straight back to his hotel and learns about Jennie's marriage with Shyam. Completely disillusioned, Sujit goes back to the asylum, now really mad. Jennie goes to the asylum to tell Sujit how Shyam had misused her. But Shalini doesn't allow her to meet Sujit. This is like the injustice the villains nearly always suffered from. A complete stranger, having no agenda of his own, pulverizes the villain. Barred from meeting Sujit, Jennie tells her story to Shalini, hoping that she would later narrate it to Sujit.

Finally, Sujit recovers when the lady doctor, risking her life, brings Shyam on to the scene, watched over by Sujit and the other senior doctors of the asylum. Shyam, sensing that Shalini knows about his crime of killing Mack, wants to remove her from the scene and drags her to the edge of the rock. Sujit gets back his senses and realizes that Shyam is a traitor. He runs to Shalini's rescue. Jennie, for no apparent reason, arrives on the scene, and during the scuffle, she's pushed violently by Shyam down the rock. The cabaret dancer, bearing her love for Sujit, but having no right to live after Shalini's arrival on the scene, dies.

This leaves the hero and the heroine together, without having any constraint. Still, Shalini refuses to go with Sujit. She pleads her disapproval by saying what sounds like a Bengali hit of 1959, *Deep Jele Jai* (*Let Me Light the Lamp*). Shalini says that she is a doctor, and that she has often had to act as a lover for curing her patients. In the Bengali film, the heroine's role was played by the versatile and glamorous Suchitra Sen. The difference is that Radha in the Bengali film became mad herself and the film ended on a tragic note. Shakti Samanta's film where the storyline is supplied by another Bengali, Ranjan Bose, ends on a happy note, making it neither a full-fledged romance nor a tragedy, but a tragic–comedy, maybe. The odd treatment of Helen in this film retaliates itself in the treatment of the heroine too. Denied by Shalini, Sujit moves out of the asylum, anguished; but making no fuss, or going mad again, as if he knew what was going to happen in the last moment. Shalini too doesn't react much. After a wee while, Sujit discovers Shalini in the backseat of his car, much to his incredulity and joy, something that Veeru, in a far more tightened scenario, would experience in *Sholay*, that is, in finding Hema Malini on the train puffing out of Ramgad.

Now, what sense does the cabaret dancer make in Shakti Samanta's film? Probably, none at all, except betraying confusion and uncertainty in using her and forcing someone to split his hair. What happens in *Pagla Kahin Ka* defines how the vamp was going to be used in the decades of the seventies and the eighties. The vamp from now on wouldn't be playing the roles of venomous women, except occasionally. She would be doing the item numbers on a majority of occasions. Why? Because the villains were going to become exceedingly stronger. Only an item number became handy in the changed circumstance to trouble the heroes. *Teesri Manzil*, a Nasir Hussain production, again shows this. Helen plays the role of a cabaret dancer, Ruby, and pines for her lover Rocky (Shammi Kapoor). Again, it is Asha Parekh ruining the interest of Helen.

After Asha Parekh, it is Meena Kumari—possibly an icon of the goody-innocent woman. In *Phool Aur Patthar* (again, 1966), directed by O. P. Ralhan, Shashikala plays the sophisticated vamp in a blonde wig, threatening the love interest of the virtuous heroine. Starred by

Dharmendra and Meena Kumari, the film argues about transforming stones into flowers, a goody intention, which is challenged by the vamp. She professes her love for Saka, a career-criminal, who had previously served her boss. There's in this film no scene showing the vamp's interest for the villain. Reeta, the vamp, goes all the way to meet Saka in his house and learns that Saka, trying to save a girl from fire, has severely burnt himself. She throws a tantrum when she realizes that Saka may desert her for this woman and breaks the mirror where she spruces herself up. She soon discovers her adversary, the widow Shanti (Meena Kumari). Here's a vamp who presents a strong contrast to the pure virtuous heroine, rescued by Saka from the house of her cruel in-laws. When the villain abducts Shanti to prevent Saka from joining mainstream society and earning honestly by himself, Reeta drags Shanti out, and throws her into the villain's den where she's about to be raped. Reeta does it to avenge herself on the heroine and fulfill her love. In *Phool Aur Patthar*, the vamp looks more menacing than the villain. As Reeta hisses in anger and jealousy, she does look like a serpent robbed of her mate.

In *Ittefaq* (1969), Miss Renu (Bindu), the sister of the murdered wife, shifts the crime on to the shoulder of the protagonist. She's not seen dancing at all in this film. Kindly note this. Inspector Salve identifies her on the evidence of a piece of pearl. The second crime, the murder of Jagmohan by his adulterous wife Rekha, is done by Nanda. The role of the villain in this film is played by two cruel women—Miss Renu and Rekha. The villain's absence on the scene forces the vamps to come on to the center stage of action. *Ittefaq* is directed by Yash Chopra, and it is one of the few Bollywood films having no song or dance in it. As a matter of fact, the film looks more like a play, put on the stage. It was a bold and worthy experiment of the late sixties.

A look at another vamp at the beginning of 1970 throws interesting light on what may be called as the vamp's farewell statement before she was going to be dubbed *only* as a cabaret dancer. It is as if the vamps were feeling anguished, sensing their disappearance from the scene. *Kati Patang*, a fabulous hit of 1970, was produced and directed by Shakti Samanta. Taking this time no risk of the story, Samanta rode on the popular novelist Gulshan Nanda, who also wrote the screenplay of the film. Samanta had previously worked with Nanda in the film *Sawan Ki Ghata* in 1966, after *Kaajal* (1965), directed by Ram Maheswari, which was nominated for the Filmfare Award for Best Story. Interestingly, *Khilona* (1970), also a work by Gulshan Nanda, and directed by Chander Vohra, received the Filmfare Best Movie Award. Anyway, in terms of money, *Kati Patang* brought good luck for Shakti Samanta.

Starred by Rajesh Khanna and Asha Parekh, the roles of the villain and vamp are shared by Prem Chopra and Bindu in this film. This provides an instance where the villain and vamp operate together, working in tandem. They plan and weave the net for wrecking the happiness of the heroine who leaves her home on the wedding night for joining someone she believes to be her lover. But, Kailash (Prem Chopra) is discovered by the heroine to be in arms with Shabnam (Bindu). Later, the heroine finds shelter away in a town in the house of a rich man who accepts her to be their daughter-in-law, known to be a widow but whom they've never seen. The widow, along with her child, has been traveling on the same train with Madhvi, the heroine (later Poonam). The train meets with an accident. Madhvi survives, but the widow dies. Before dying, she asks Madhvi to take her place and go to her in-law's house with the child. Later, the villain and the vamp chase after the heroine and start blackmailing her. The storyline is good, and this feature leaves much scope for Shabnam to plan and work out her love. There is Rajesh Khanna on the scene to be paired off with Madhvi/Poonam. So, Shabnam is safe. As a matter of fact, the film found success and earned credibility because of the presence of Prem Chopra and Bindu in strong roles. Not many vamps are lucky like Shabnam. Probably, Shakti Samanta, remembering his unjustified treatment of Helen in a previous film, was now determined to present a strong credible woman on the scene. It's the villain who tries to kill the father-in-law of the house by mixing poison in his milk. The blame is shifted on to Poonam, the supposed daughter-in-law of the house. Following a bizarre turn of events, the villain and his female partner, who now bears his child, try to take control of the house and usurp the role of the heroine.

Kati Patang, showing the vamp in action, occupies a distinctive position in Bollywood cinema so far as showing a strong vamp on the screen is concerned. It assimilates the tension and restlessness of the previous decade and throws issues wide open for the seventies, known usually as the decade of villains. The vamp looks more venomous and cruel than her male partner, who is yet to become stronger.

Kati Patang suggests two important consequences in the narrative concerning the vamp. First, she becomes pregnant in this film; second, she wants to take charge of the house and grab the property. Usually the vamps, especially when they accompany the underworld dons, scarcely become pregnant, and they don't want to stay confined within the four walls of a house. While the second motif goes with the trend of the Pran–Shammi Kapoor starred films of the sixties when the property issue inspired the villain's love, the first feature makes a distinct move to bring the vamp back within the fold of Indian tradition. According to this trend, the vamp, being a descendant of the courtesan, appears to be suffering occasionally from the anguish of suppressed love and motherhood. Rekha provides an example of this in the film *Muqaddar Ka Sikandar* in the seventies. She dances to entertain others, though she loves Sikandar and dies pining for her love. In comparison, Bindu in *Kati Patang* is a tough woman, taking on the heroine. Unlike the other vamps, she has an identity of her own, and accompanies the villain to everything he does. Bindu plays her role to perfection, occupying a good amount of film space. The dance number "Mera Naam Hai Shabnam" in *Kati Patang* makes an unforgettable statement on cabaret as a popular art form. Yet, this feature of the vamp, as suggested before, didn't continue in the decade and after.

Note the difference in the role of the vamp played by Bindu a year before the mid-nineties when she isn't accompanied by a strong powerful villain. Bindu, playing the role of a bad woman, disturbs the happiness of a family held together by mutual affection in the film *Hum Aapke Hai Kaun*, a popular hit of 1994. The previous venom of the vamp is gone. There's also no Prem Chopra on this occasion to support her. To make matters worse for the vamp, she's now slapped for trying to undo the good. This was the time when both the villain and the vamp took to the backstage due to the arrival of what may be called the NRI films. However, down the mid-nineties, women started playing stronger roles, carrying the burden all alone, as Kajol did in *Gupt* (1997). The trend was felt when the same Kajol, exactly in the mid-nineties (*Dilwale Dulhania Le Jayenge*), was seen touring unknown lands all alone after she got separated from her friends. Rekha's *Phool Bane Angaray* was a 1991 film, but Rekha in this film was playing the role of a protagonist, taking on a politician villain. This film has been mentioned already.

After *Kati Patang*, Teza's "Mona Darling" became famous, still remembered by many. This vamp is a direct development of the turbulent hour of the seventies when lockouts in factories and labor unrest became regular occurrences. The villain, as a consequence, grew stronger. Consequently, the vamp takes far less part in the action compared to what she had done before. Teza employs her in the party scene to win over Vijay, the uncompromising honest police officer, whom he considers to be a threat to his smuggling business. This is in keeping with what we said before—that the villain often uses the vamp to spread his net while he skulks around, watching how his plan works. Mona's target in the scene is Vijay. She offers him drink, pretends familiarity with him, while the act of seduction is watched and enjoyed by Teza from distance. Toward the end of the film, Teza looks after her safe exit before Vijay and Sher Khan break into his den. The vamp in *Zanjeer* entertains the villain at the swimming pool. In course of a chin-wag with her, Teza confesses his previous crime to her, the way he took charge of the gang by killing his one-time boss.

Teza's frequent address of her as Mona Darling gives him the pride that she's someone on his side, someone from the other sex to take care of him. In *Sholay*, Helen entertains Amjad with her dance only once, like the item numbers of these days. She's not seen any more in the film. With the arrival of Gabbar, the scenario became further bleak. The villain, gaining awesome stature, didn't need the vamp, not even to the extent as Teza did. The same Ajit, in the film *Kalicharan*, takes no notice of Helen, where she's referred to only as a dancer. An exception to this is the Mahesh Bhatt film *Lahu Ke Do Rang*, released in 1979. Helen plays Suzie in this film, opposite Vinod Khanna. She becomes pregnant in Hong Kong, and is later deserted by Khanna. Not exactly a vamp like she was in *China Town*, having the same name Suzie, Helen plays a slightly bigger role in *Lahu Ke Do Rang*, fetching her Filmfare Best Supporting Actress Award. Down the seventies, Salim Khan, coscripting with Javed Akhtar, helped Helen get some roles. Realizing that vamps, in any form, weren't the demand of the hour, Helen formally retired from movies in 1983, appearing in some guest roles thereafter.

Bindu, too, played a bigger role in *Imtihan* (1974), a year after *Zanjeer*. In this film again, she has to make way for Tanuja. Helped by Rakesh (Ranjeet), Bindu retaliates against the injustice by falsely implicating Pramod, the hero (Vinod Khanna), in sexually harassing her. Still, she doesn't look as authentic as she did either in *Kati Patang* or in *Phool Aur Patthar*. Interestingly, in both the last significant films of Helen and Bindu, Vinod Khanna, the star of the decade of seventies, played the hero.

Vinod Khanna began with films like *Purab Aur Paschim* (1970), *Mera Gaon Mera Desh* (1971) (dacoit Jabbar Singh), and soon rose to huge fame with films like *Parvarish, Amar Akbar Anthony*, and others at the end of the decade. In a majority of films, Vinod shared the stage with Amitabh Bachchan with equal charisma and flamboyance. Still, stardom is something elusive, and ordained by circumstances, though the person concerned has to stay focused. Vinod didn't. At the height of his career, Vinod, hearing a spiritual call from within, announced his retirement from films, left Mumbai, and joined his spiritual guru, Rajnish. He accompanied his guru to the USA, and it is reported that there he did such hard chores like gardening, plumbing, and cooking. However, the star within hadn't deserted him. His comeback film *Insaaf* (1987), directed by Mukul Anand, was also an instant hit during a very critical time of his career. That speaks highly of this star. Vinod Khanna had a successful career in politics too after he joined the Bhartiya Janata Party (BJP) in 1997, winning the election twice and becoming a union minister. In 1999, Vinod received the Filmfare Lifetime Achievement Award. It was in the fitness of things that both Helen and Bindu should have Vinod Khanna as the hero of the films in which they honorably shared the platforms.

The vamp in Bollywood films, therefore, has fallen in love, in spite of her being a cabaret dancer. In doing so, the vamp threatens the interest of the heroine, like the villain does of the heroes in the sixties. That's the point to notice here. The difference is that in the sixties, the villains returned to their folds. The vamps didn't. The usual notion of the vamp as a seductive cabaret dancer is essentially a Westernized concept, and may not be always correct so far as Bollywood vamps are concerned. This view needs to be modified by our instinctive reliance on the indigenous tradition. Indian tolerance and act of absorption has been like that of a sponge. The intake process, being less stirring, shows assimilation.

The move to take over the role of vamps started with Zeenat Aman down the seventies when the vamps, sharing the stage with stronger villains, became only dancers. Zeenat, having the chic and seductive looks, added by certain oomph and the carefree, "follow-me" style, hooked the audience when she played Rupa in Raj Kapoor's *Satyam Shivam Sundaram* (1978). She was soon followed by Parveen Babi, who added innocence to the oomph, making the vamp look redundant. Asked what made them carry on like sex-bombs, Babi proudly said that both Zeenat and she had full-fledged roles to play right from the start of their career. Bracketing Helen and Bindu as essentially cabaret dancers, Babi said that they didn't know what acting was all about when they stepped into the industry.

As seen before, both Helen and Bindu had bagged prestigious awards, playing some important character roles. The citations above are enough to prove that. Babi's claim suggests two things. First, the vamp is more than a cabaret dancer, something we have been suggesting so far. Second, it shows the audacious and haughty way in which these heroines were determined to see the ouster of previous vamps. Babi, however, feels that it is better knowledge of acting that separates Zeenat and her from their predecessors. This is not true.

When awesome villains like Gabbar, Din Dayal, the Lion, Rama Shetty, Dang, and others weren't seen around on the screen, a strong stepmother within home was needed to do the villain's job in *Beta*. Zeenat herself plays a negative role in *The Great Gambler* and pays the penalty. This is because she is accompanied by Prem Chopra in this film and has to stay with him nearly always. Zeenat, playing Shabnam, can hardly make love with Vijay, the police inspector she adores, and cuts a sorry figure in the role because she's never lucky to sing the famous number "Mera Naam Hai Shabnam." While the name of the role she played reminded Bindu of *Kati Patang*, the ouster of the stronger predecessor in the *Gambler* was still a far cry.

Doing the item numbers like Shilpa Shetty, Urmila Matondakar, even Aisharya Rai down the decades also hasn't anything to do substantially with the previous vamps. This feature has often been mentioned, wrongly perhaps, as the "revamped vamp." On the other hand, in *Jism* (2003) we really watch a revamped vamp, taking charge of the narrative. This is because, by the turn of the present century, women were seen taking far more initiative than men in various walks of life. They were becoming independent personalities right since mid-nineties, as suggested earlier. A comparison between *The Great Gambler* and *Jism* sufficiently testifies what a vamp can achieve alone in the absence of a strong villain in the advanced scenario of recent years. Let's pack up this discussion by looking at this extraordinary event of our time.

Ironically, both Zeenat and Babi were later overtaken by the fiery bombshell Bipasha Basu, exuding greater oomph that oozes into the mind, blocking the heart altogether. That's exactly what happens to Kabir, played by John Abraham in *Jism*. Ah, yes, that's it. Now more than ever seems it rich to die, watching the "revamped vamp" as she strides away from us; stopping, looking from behind, ambling away, and shuffling, before the shell explodes. The audience claps and whistles, enjoying the pitiable condition of the hero. These viewers, like the groundlings of The Globe Theatre in Shakespeare's time, have never failed to applaud the rollicking package of entertainment provided by Bollywood filmmakers, like they have lately at Sanjay Dutt and Rishi Kapoor, the two outstanding villains of *Agneepath* in 2012.

Sonia (Bipasha Basu) plays the temptress in *Jism*, convincing Kabir to kill her husband, a millionaire. Finally, she gets the will of property altered in her name. The film is a thriller, and the job of storytelling has been done with élan without adding any extra zing to the story. One great feature of this film is that the first half shows Bipasha as a vulnerable woman, not happy in her marriage with Rohit Khanna (Gulshan Grover). In the second half, Bipasha's complete volte-face takes one by surprise. She sends men to kill Kabir, wishing to wipe him off the scene because he'd threatened her that he'd confess his crime to the police. The avenging woman, her teeth clenched, shoots Kabir. He too kills her. Bipasha, playing a completely negative role which any other actress might not have dared to accept, appears with great panache in every frame of this film, winning the nomination of the Best Villain Award by Filmfare. She also won the Best Villain Award, given by Bollywood Movie Award judges. *Jism* is a Pooja Bhatt film, and the story is written by Mahesh Bhatt, her illustrious father. Amit Saxena makes his debut as the director of the film. John Abraham too makes his debut appearance, playing the alcoholic lawyer.

Mind you, Bipasha, as late as in 2003, gets the best villain award, for playing a cruel and venomous vamp in *Jism*. This feat should make one rethink about the villain and the vamp's disappearance from the scene. The more justifiable assessment of this singularly important phenomenon would be to concentrate on the changes and developments of the dark pit of desires of men and women shown in Bollywood cinema as a replica of life.

Bipasha Basu plays the villain as the vamp in *Jism*—the two selves merging into one. She has no need to dance on a cabaret floor, being a rich merchant's wife. She isn't also doing any item number in this film. Possibly, Zeenat and Babi couldn't be better paid in their own coins.

Note

1. Deepa Gahlot, "Villains and Vamps," in *Bollywood Popular Indian Cinema*, L. M. Joshi (ed.) (Piccadilly, London: Dakini Books Ltd, 2001).

6

The Empire of Evil: Villains' Henchmen

*T*he villains in Bollywood cinema built up their empires of evil, drawing active support from their henchmen who carry out the orders faithfully like soldiers fighting in the battlefield. Countless examples from films show that the arch-villain can be approached only after these whacky, arrogant, and fierce henchmen have been defeated and vanquished by those breaking into the villains' den. After the belligerent hero has won over these powerful henchmen, he finds the King of Evil ensconced on his throne, acknowledging the effort of the intruder. Thus, one cannot forget the likes of Shetty, Bob Christo, Mukesh Rishi, Sharat Saxena, and others who stood like rocks, protecting their masters. While talking about villains, it would be unjustified to forget these henchmen contributing their mite to the empires of evil. How can one, for example, forget Mr Walcot or Daga in *Mr. India* or the big bald baddie in the film *Don*? Even the devil has to be given his due for taking the pains to build his well-protected fort, like a spider does its net. This chapter makes a humble effort to do this much-needed job that hasn't been tried with the focus it deserves. Some of these henchmen are no less awesome than the monarchs of evil themselves. Think of M. B. Shetty, for example, who speaks less, rarely indeed, since he's always the action master.

M. B. Shetty

Often touted as the greatest Bollywood villain ever, Shetty made his debut in 1962 with the film *Neeli Aankhen*, opening the door for the legendary Helen. His last film *Black Cobra* was released in 1981. Between this, Shetty made a huge impression in Bollywood cinema both as a fight-composer and actor, playing the vicious bad man. Known often as *takla Shetty*, this man has always protected the villain's fort with dogged tenacity. One great characteristic of Shetty as an actor playing the villain's henchman is his dark podgy face, a pair of earrings, and bald head. This sends a creepy sensation to viewers, and their dislike for the queer bad man goes on mounting. This as well makes a fearful impact on the goody heroines in films who shriek in terror as soon as they spot his face around them. Mala Sinha in the Shetty-dominated film *Night in London* does exactly the same. This is in spite of the fact that the heroine, also a part of the underworld, has seen Shetty more than once. This is the fearful Shetty-impact. The bald baddie arouses hatred every time he appears on the screen. This has probably made Shetty a celebrated bad guy in countless Bollywood movies.

In *Night in London*, Shetty plays a bigger role and occupies the frames for a long time. In spite of the romance between Biswajit and Mala Sinha that passes through a series of upheavals and misgivings in this film, it is Shetty's frequent appearances that keep the viewers glued to their seats. The turning points of the romance depend heavily on what Shetty does and says in the film. If in the sixties, seventies, and eighties, Shetty's presence became inevitable at the height of the popularity of action genre films, *Night in London* probably showed the way. A memorable exception is that Shetty does speak a lot in this film, threatening the heroine, because he's running madly after diamonds. When he manages to have Mala Sinha captive under him, he wants to know the secret of the diamonds. Mala refuses; angry and adamant. What Shetty does after this becomes terribly agonizing for Mala, driving her nearly mad. Shetty sits before a sophisticated electrical device in the other room and operates its knob, showing Mala a whirlwind of visuals till she reaches a point in making the confession. The whole operation looks like a forerunner of the lie-detector test, used by investigating officers now. Interestingly, Shetty's activity in this film predicts the arrival of the fiercer and technically knowledgeable villain Shakaal on the scene at the beginning of the eighties (*Shaan*). Remember that two years before the release of *Shaan*, Shetty had played Shaakal, a fierce gangster of the underworld in *Don*.

That many such things have gone unnoticed is no surprise, since neither the villains nor their henchmen have so far received the focus and attention they deserve. Just think how Shetty's bald and bulky presence became inevitable in the Dharmendra-starred high action dramas both to highlight the virile power of the hero and the villain's fearful presence on the scene. Shetty contributed to the popularity of the action genre films of the seventies and eighties, and quite often, these films ended up making "tiger" Shetty's fights nearly mandatory.

Behold Shetty on the deck of the ship, talking to Mala Sinha in the film *Night in London*. "Where are the diamonds?" Shetty asks for the last time, reminding Mala that the police anyway will find her and that it is only he who can save her from disaster. Mala, who is in search of her father from the clutches of the underworld criminals, still refuses, boiling in anger. Shetty brings his hand up his nose, nudging it with his finger. A whole world of effects is achieved, expressing his disgust and ironic disapproval of the heroine. If somebody is prepared to face danger, Shetty is helpless—that's his message. Within the film, the deck scene works admirably.

Shetty speaks occasionally in *Night in London*, quite unlike of him, as *Don* and many other films show. This is because his roles rarely demand him to speak. He has no emotions to convey. Why should he speak? Words are hardly necessary for Shetty. A fight master, Shetty's actions speak more about him, hugely making up for the lack of articulation. Remember Iago, Shakespeare's masterly portrayal of evil, also didn't speak after the cataclysmic events toward the end of the play. One wonders if the concept behind evil is inherently fraught with the power of visuals and suggestions than all the songs and love-prattles of the hero and the heroine—goodie-goodies' talks on morality and moral behavior. Evil looks personified and rides on visuals, while the good relies on talks. If one cares to go back to the genesis, then both good and evil would appear synonymous, inseparable from one another. Let's again remember the numericals 6 and 9 as explained in *Aakhri Raasta*. That may be why the antiheroes in the mid-nineties and early years of the present century as well as in the "Dev noir" films long before became popular, catering to people's imagination. The audience was instinctively aware of the possibility at the back of their mind, but couldn't connect it with experience. With Shetty, evil begins like a perception when one sees him. When the action begins, the perception, anticipated previously, turns into experience. That's why speech becomes redundant.

In *Kismet* (1968), a Biswajeet–Babita starrer that followed the year after, Shetty is again seen in action, confirming his relevance to Bollywood commercials as a bad sinister guy. *Kismet* was encouraged by the success of *Night in London*. It was directed by Manmohan Desai, the man who was to present the action movies in the seventies, playing a pivotal role in the emergence of Amitabh Bachchan as the superstar of the decade. With *Kismet*, Shetty's position got secured. If one takes Shetty out of the frames of these two movies, one realizes the importance of Shetty as a bald baddie. *Kismet*, importantly, was a little ahead of its time, because it showed at the beginning how a terrorist organization was out to destabilize the nation by resorting to a series of bomb blasts, killing innocent men. Both *Night in London* and *Kismet*, one should remember, were released during the late sixties when the Pran–Shammi Kapoor pair was going great guns. The presence of Shetty in the two films had a lot to do in making them popular against the Shammi-wave. In *Kismet*, Shetty is seen into action early in the film when, helped by a moll of the organization, he manages to kill an investigating official.

Later also, it is Shetty who sees through the deception of the hero and the heroine in the famous dance number "Kajra Mohabbat Wala" (Shamshad Begum lending her voice for the last time to an O. P. Nayyar composition along with Asha Bhosle), and runs after them for retrieving the microdot kept in Vicky's (Biswajeet) guitar by Gonj, owner of a musical store, now killed by Scorpion and his men, the underworld organization. Shetty plays the role of Joe, a deadly member of the organization, doing most of the damage. The other members of the organization look quite common and ordinary beside Shetty. As for Scorpion, the leader of the gang, the audience comes to know his identity as Roma's (Babita) father toward the end of the film.

We were talking about Shetty's unflinching loyalty as a henchman. When Lopez, the right-hand man of Scorpion, feels that the Chief's filial affection for his daughter is going to affect and ruin them all, Shetty as Joe airs an important caveat: "*Chief organization ke liye hota hai, organization Chief ke liye nahin*" ("A Chief exists for the organization, not the other way round"). This may be read as a symbolic reminder of Shetty's absolute dedication to the roles he played in Bollywood cinema.

It is equally difficult to forget Shetty in *Don* where, aided by the deteriorating law and order situation of the seventies, he talks much less and does more. Once, he manages to escape through the window after a fight with Amitabh. Later, within the police van he looks most ugly and sinister among the other gangsters. No one, even Narang for that matter, can match Shetty's looks and gestures. It is Shetty who cuts the rope in the air to prevent the escape of Pran and his lost (found captive a little before) children. This is a Shetty speciality. His villainy is ruthless.

If Ranjeet as a villain (in *Laawaris* [1981] and *Karan Arjun*, for examples) has his own dynamics, Shetty too has his own style of conveying the chilling menace. As a matter of fact, Shetty is more calculating and fearful than Ranjeet. Ranjeet is a lascivious villain; Shetty shows no such weakness. He is never emotive and doesn't care for women. The impact Shetty leaves on his viewers is more disquieting and creepy.

Director Rohit Shetty is the son of M. B. Shetty. Rohit's upcoming flick *Bol Bachchan*, recreating the Anthony Gonsalves magic of Manmohan Desai's 1977 blockbuster, hit the theaters on July 6 of this year.

Jeevan

Jeevan appeared in the role of Narada in the film *Bhakta Dhruva* in 1947, and then again in *Gopal Krishna* in 1979. Symbolically speaking, this mythological role of Narada, creating troubles for others, set the trend of Jeevan's persona. Coming down to the secular level, Jeevan turned this to playing the baddie with more venom.

Most often, Jeevan is the maternal uncle, misleading his sister and nephew to disastrous consequences. In *Takkar* (1980), for example, starring Sanjeev Kumar, Jeetendra, and Zeenat Aman, Jeevan plays the typically wicked *mamaji*. *Takkar* was directed by K. Bapaiah. Ranjeet plays an ally to Jeevan in this film, like he did in *Laawaris*. A stepmother and her brother seek to ruin the life of the son.

Jeevan appeared in several Dev Anand films also. Still, it was Manmohan Desai who used Jeevan's villainous intention with unerring commercial insight. The year 1977, for example, proved crucial for Jeevan so far as his masterly portrayal of the villain is concerned. In *Chacha Bhatija*, directed by Desai, Jeevan plays Laxmidas, while Roopesh Kumar plays Kiran, both entering into a conspiracy for ruining the happiness of Teza's family. The role of Teza's brother Shankar is played by Dharmendra. Everything was running well for the family. But, things turn ugly when Teza remarries after the demise of his previous wife Sita. Sonia, the new bride, enters the family, along with her brother Laxmidas. Jeevan starts holding the key of the story after this, contributing to an otherwise stale family drama. As said before, Jeevan's natural flair in playing the role of a maternal uncle, bringing down the Narada trappings within the muddy squalor of the modern world, makes his agenda of taking over Teza's property look quite convincing. Conspiring with Roopesh, and earning the trust of Teza, Jeevan manages to have Shankar driven out of the house. This film depends heavily on the ugly role played by Jeevan.

Dharam Veer, a film of 1977 by Manmohan Desai, shows Jeevan at the center of action. He plays the maternal uncle, Satpal Singh, being the brother of Queen Meenakshi. Like in *Takkar*, Ranjeet plays an ally to Jeevan, this time his son and therefore an active member of the conspiracy within the palace. Utterly shaken by a prophecy that his nephew will be his killer (the Kamsa–Devaki motif being apparent), Satpal attempts to destroy the baby soon after it is born. Meenakshi gives birth to twins. Satpal swaps his son with his sister's. This leads to a chaos due to the secret intervention of Satpal's wife. In the mythology also, Kamsa's wife was a pious woman.

Ranjeet, as usual, shows his lecherous motif when he sees Roopa (Neetu Singh), the gypsy girl. Later, he joins his father in the conspiracy of creating a misunderstanding between Veer (Jeetendra) and Dharam (Dharmendra). Jeevan tackles Dharmendra in the film *Takkar*. But, Desai sets the trend in *Dharam Veer*. Much of the interest of *Dharam Veer* depends on the role played by Jeevan, sabotaging the interest of the palace. He also ruins the peace of Pran, who plays Jwala Singh in this film, the father of Veer and Dharam, staying outside the palace. Pran, by this time, had already switched over to playing character roles.

The experience of *Dharam Veer* leaves Jeevan geared up to take on Pran in the frolicking entertainment of the decade—*Amar Akbar Anthony*. It should be mentioned in passing that all three films of Desai discussed here were the biggest hits of the year 1977. One could say that the seventies, in spite of the *Sholay* fever in the middle of the decade, was hooked by Desai magic, Jeevan contributing actively to the spell. Desai, by this time, had immense faith in Jeevan, and *Amar Akbar Anthony*, the much celebrated blockbuster of the seventies, opens with Robert Seth's (Jeevan) betrayal of Kishenlal (Pran). Kishen comes out of jail after taking on his shoulders the blame of a fatal hit-and-run accident, committed actually by Robert, his boss. The sequence in Robert's hall in his residence that shows the ugly face of Robert is deeply poignant and sets the tune of the film. Desai is a master in creating pathos and then working it out elaborately within the film text to impart his message of universal love and fraternity. This feature largely contributed to the popularity and large-scale appeal of his films among the masses. To achieve the effect, Desai makes the pendulum moving between the moods of despair and hope in the frames, like when Kishen's children get lost along with his wife who goes blind, and who later gets her eyesight back. Jeevan plays a convincing baddie, contributing substantially to this underlying Desai message. Robert is a gold smuggler in this film, and the menace of the dark underworld for highlighting the optimistic notes is entirely carried out by Jeevan.

Jeevan's quaint and macabre mannerisms remind one of the old Kanhaiyalal. As an actor, Jeevan seems to be sharing the traits of the old master. Jeevan, for example, can't be a Shetty, but he's what he's, lending immense support to Manmohan Desai like he did to several Dev Anand films. That is why in the film *Bandhan*, discussed earlier, where Jeevan shares the frames with Kanhaiyalal, Jeevan plays his role with greater malice and venom, being unusually haughty. Probably he had to push the gear up to offset the presence of Kanhaiyalal in the film. This feature should be noted, because it speaks a lot about Jeevan as an actor and his wonderful contribution to Bollywood cinema.

Kiran Kumar

Kiran Kumar, son of Jeevan, shows what his father might do in the changed environment of the nineties if he continued as an actor. Yes, Kiran Kumar, a student of the Film and Television Institute of Pune watched his father from very close quarters since boyhood.

The deteriorating law and order situation of the nineties after the assassination of Rajiv Gandhi and the overtaking wings of evil enveloping the society, gave Bollywood a greater and authentic evil personality through Kiran Kumar. Now, the villain raved and stomped the stage of action far more atrociously than behaving like a cunning baddie as he did previously. He needs no camouflage at all. In the changed circumstance, a villain like Kiran, for example, wouldn't plead with his driver in so many words for taking his crime like Jeevan, but would just order it.

Kiran Kumar reads this situation perfectly and starts behaving arrogantly in *Tezaab* (1988), playing Lotiya Pathan, a dangerous criminal of the underworld. His performances as Pasha in *Khuda Gawah* (1992) and as Shamser in *Sapoot* (1996) are also worth remembering. In both, Kiran plays his role with great macho brilliance. Hailing from a Kashmiri royal family and having a robust physique helped Kiron in giving his roles a fearful authenticity to the viewers.

How can one forget, for example, Lotiya of the *Tezaab* fame? Without Kiran Kumar's presence in the film, much of the heroic exploits of Anil Kapoor and his romance with Madhuri Dixit would be lost. *Tezaab*, one should remember, saw Anil catapulted to stardom after his goody-goody appearance in *Mr. India* in the previous year. In *Tezaab*, Anil settles down to behaving like his own self, and he's paired off admirably by Kiran Kumar on nearly equal terms. It should be pointed out in this context that Anupam Kher, playing Shyamlal, the wicked father of Madhuri in this film, articulates his villainy on a lower scale, which he repeats the next year in *Ram Lakhan*. So, the burden is left to Kiran, and he does it with remarkable gusto.

Remember Kiran's contribution to *Khuda Gawah*, intended to bring back Amitabh into the nineties after his glitzy appearance in *Agneepath*. Danny Denzongpa is there, but he's not the villain in this film. The burden, therefore, is taken by Kiran, playing Pasha, a fierce Pathan. He takes on Badshah Khan, an Afghan Pathan, who has killed his brother Habibullah in India so that he can marry Benazir. This girl also is out to avenge the death of her father. In the end, Pasha has to take on everyone alone. What is noticeable in this scenario of revenge and rivalry is that the story doesn't hinge on a very sound cause against Pasha, who later becomes a drug lord in this film. Pasha too has a cause of his own to take on Badshah Khan. This is an important point to be noticed in this film. Willy-nilly, Bollywood has often conceded a cause to speak for a bad guy, a point mentioned elsewhere in this story of the villains. Kiran Kumar's presence in this film truly sets off Amitabh Bachchan, restoring, and adding to his previous image.

In *Sapoot*, starring Sunil Shetty and Akshay Kumar, Kiran Kumar shares the stage of action with Mukesh Rishi. Kiran plays Shamser, while Mukesh the role of Tezeswar. Both belong to the intimidating underworld, and they kill Kader Khan, who plays the role of Singhania, another don of the underworld. *Sapoot* is full of action, and Kiran plays his role with great authority. The turbulent hour of the nineties has been translated on celluloid in *Sapoot*, and Kiran makes it believable by his awesome get-up. Probably, Shetty's disappearance from the scene has been made up with by the presence of both Mukesh Rishi and Kiran Kumar. Physically and temperamentally, they have something in common with their predecessor—M. B. Shetty. The only thing is that unlike Shetty, both roar on the frames, uttering haughty dialogs. The changed scenario of the nineties makes this believable.

Mukesh Rishi

Taking the cue from Kiran Kumar, it is relevant to say a few words on Mukesh Rishi. Talking about the baddies of Bollywood cinema, we cannot forget Mukesh. And, what a role does he play as Wasim Khan, the dreaded terrorist, pursuing his agenda from within the prison cell in the film *Indian*! This certainly looks forward to the more gory and macho brilliance of Sanjay Dutt in this year's first blockbuster, *Agneepath* (2012). Mukesh in *Indian* is rightly paired off against Sunny Deol, also noted for his virile strength and ability. Sunny Deol plays the role of DCP Rajshekhar Azad in this film. Within the solitary prison cell and mocked by Azad when an attempt to spread terror in the country by killing the Imam has failed, Mukesh looks dangerous and awful. One should remember in this context that Mukesh had played a completely different role in *Sarfarosh* where he fights against the terrorist agenda as Inspector Saleem, helping the hero Aamir Khan (ACP Ajay Singh Rathod). Both roles are played with equal flair and conviction. This speaks a lot about this actor, who has played many big roles in films of the nineties and the present decade where villains have been pursuing their sinister agenda of spreading communal violence.

It wouldn't be any exaggeration to say that without Mukesh Rishi, many such films wouldn't appear as blood-curdling as they do now. Even Sunny Deol's heroic macho feats would have lost much of its charm and brilliance.

Gabbar Singh and Dang might have boasted of breaking out of their cells in jail. The four walls of any jail were insufficient to hold these predatory villains for a longer period of time. But Wasim Khan, much to his awesome credit, makes no attempt to move out of his cell in the jail. The confinement itself boosts him to spring into action, sending instruction outside to terrorize the country. This is more terrible. A close ally of the brain behind the organization, Shankar Singhania (Danny Denzongpa), an industrialist, someone who's much respected by the society and protected by Rajshekhar Azad's father-in-law—DGP Suryapratap Singh (Raj Babbar in a breezy role)—Wasim Khan turns his prison cell into a palace of activity. Rishi's violent image as an international terrorist grows larger when one remembers that Suryapratap dies early in this film, shot by his dutiful son-in-law, DCP Azad. Danny Denzongpa is, of course, there throughout the film, but he stays aloof, wearing his mask before all. So, the responsibility of carrying out the terrorist agenda is left to Mukesh Rishi. If one looks at the film from this perspective, then Rishi's power and height as a henchman adding to the villain's empire can be properly appreciated.

In *Garv: Pride and Honour*, a 2004 film, starring Salman Khan, Amrish Puri, and Arbaaz Khan, Mukesh Rishi occupies the center stage throughout the film, playing the unforgettable Zafar Supari. All the first three are honest and brave cops. Amrish Puri plays a positive role in this film. So, Zafar Supari takes charge of confronting ACP Arjun Ranawat (Salman Khan) and his friend Hyder Ali, who is like a second heart to Arjun. Amrish Puri leaves the scene early, and Hyder is killed in an open confrontation with Zafar. The underworld-political nexus is shown powerfully in this film. Before getting killed, Hyder is falsely implicated to be a traitor to the country, suffering ironically the same predicament that Mukesh Rishi had to go through in the film *Sarfarosh*. Shivaji Satam and Govind Namdeo play their roles with conviction to suggest the nexus between the politicians and the underworld.

The violent character of Zafar Supari in *Garv* is Mukesh Rishi's outstanding contribution to Bollywood cinema. Likewise, the

towering menace of terrorism in *Indian* is translated on celluloid by
Wasim Khan, not by Shankar Singhania.

Sharat Saxena

One cannot forget either Daga, Mogambo's henchman in *Mr. India*,
or Captain Dekka, Amrish Puri's trusted man in *Ghayal*. Both roles
are played by Sharat Saxena, an indispensable man of Bollywood villain
parlor, who has added creditably to what may be called the villains'
charisma. Amrish Puri's freakish get-up in *Mr. India* and his popular
refrain "*Mogambo khush hua*," followed by hysterical laughter, is most
fittingly supported and made credible by Sharat Saxena, noted for his
butch exploits. Even before Mogambo is seen in the film, his men
start doing things on his behalf, like terrorizing the city and running
the godown, where adulteration of food grains is made to perfection.
People are seen milling about in panic in the streets. Daga is Mogambo's right-hand trusted man to carry out his evil orders and plays a
pivotal role in evicting Anil Kapoor and the orphans from out of the
house near the sea beach. Sharat Saxena is as faithful as M. B. Shetty
would have been under the circumstances.

But this powerful henchman of Mogambo is helpless too and goes
crazy facing Anil Kapoor, armed with the magic watch. Still, it is Daga,
who ferrets out the mystery behind the dancer Hawa Hawai (Sridevi)
once he catches sight of the dancer's feet under the curtain. But,
Sharat Saxena's acting ability is seen in the hunter sequence where he
registers a variety of moods—hope, desperation, anger—all following
one another. The scene becomes so much enjoyable mainly because of
Saxena's acting skill; especially where he, crawling on all fours, looks
at his favorite hunter, trusted over the years, with dubious eyes. That
shows the transformation of a much-feared henchman into a clown,
a very ordinary man, invested with an inexplicable megalomaniac
feat. More importantly, even while playing this role, Sharat Saxena
is indirectly commenting on his master, Mogambo's clownish mannerisms and macabre humor. The two become inseparably connected
in this scene of confusion and awe, tinged with fun. Sharat Saxena is
always a real henchman of the villain, too faithful to ignore his master's
quaint humor. That too is a service to Mogambo. Can anyone think

of another instance where a henchman so suggestively and dutifully complements his master?

The truth is that this scene of bedlam in *Mr. India* has never been seen from Sharat Saxena's point-of-view, but always from the perspective of the hero's triumph. Yet this *is* the scene where, apart from Daga, the bald Walcot (an international smuggler) too contributes a lot.

Now, look at Captain Dekka of *Ghayal*. Here too, Amrish Puri, playing Balwant Rai, is Saxena's master. Interestingly, this film too shows Puri's panic-stricken and nearly hysterical anxiety for safety once Ajay Mehra, seeking revenge, escapes jail along with the other hardcore convicts. By this time, Dekka, guarding Balwant's godown, has been killed by Ajay. He knows well that Balwant's most trusted and powerful man, Dekka should be eliminated first. That's why Ajay calls up Balwant in the middle of night to say that he has killed Dekka, and set fire to Balwan't godown, storing crores of rupees. This unnerves Balwant. Later, he sits before his piano and jabs fiercely at the black and white keys to produce a range of wild notes that symbolize the raging storm of his mind. Balwan't antics are noted by ACP Joe Dsouza. Om Puri's portrayal of this role nicely communicates his amused reaction to Balwant's fury. In absence of Dekka, Brahmachari, Balwant's personal assistant, does the job of obliquely commenting on his master's moments of trepidation. He starts closing the shutters of the windows to prevent Ajay's rowdy entry into the room and bullets flying in from outside. Later, Brahmachari asks Dsouza which side he should look out, guarding Balwant.

Brahmachari, like many other minor characters of Bollywood cinema, paints the fringe of the commercial canvas with great sense of purpose, like Annu Kapoor does as the editor (Mr Gaitonde) in *Mr. India*. Brahmachari's apparently facetious query and gesture highlight Balwant's nervous state of mind, apart from relieving the tension. If we appreciate the Porter's *wise* tattle in *Macbeth*, that of the Gravedigger in *Hamlet*, and Touchstone's courtship of Audrey in *As You Like It* (forgetting for a while the malice of the court), then the Dagas, the Brahmacharis, or the editors should also impress us in nearly the same way. The occasional comic membranes don't hide the underlying terror. Actually they burst as the narrative unfolds itself, showing the macabre stuff.

This feature of Bollywood cinema looks unparalleled in the history of world celluloid. It's sad that such minor details have so far gone unnoticed, primarily because we believe to have done our duty once we have explored the glamor of the heroes and heroines within and out of the film text. That no doubt is an important job. But there are others too, crying positively for our attention.

Before dying, Dekka too has his share of entertainment in the godown. Sharat Saxena is believable in all such mundane affairs just as he springs into action as smartly when Ajay and the convicts attack the godown. Similarly, in *Krrish*, Saxena plays his role with equal conviction both as a companion to the evil scientist and also as a guide to the hero for a good cause. Remember also in this context how Saxena plays his role in *Agneepath* of 1990, serving Kancha Cheena and also dying for the sake of the villain's odd humor. Sharat Saxena, like others of his ilk, is still making good contributions to Bollywood cinema. He has been playing some comedy roles in between other than the baddies. Saxena played Kichaka in the popular television serial *Mahabharat*.

Bob Christo

Bob is no more with us. One cannot see him again playing the *gora* henchman as he did in the eighties and nineties in Bollywood cinema. His famous cringe "*Indian god maarta hai*" in *Mr. India* is still memorable. Bob, by birth an Australian, played the memorable role of Walcot in *Mr. India*; someone, who smuggles golden Indian gods and gives in exchange weapons to Mogambo and his henchmen. The hilarious sequence showing the titillating dance of Miss Hawa Hawai (Sridevi in skimpy clothes) is embellished further by Walcot's presence in the scene. Bob's bald head and white skin suited him the roles he played. His presence had nearly always ensured international hand behind the terrorist agenda shown in the films of the eighties. The action–thriller of 1986, *Kala Dhanda Gorey Log*, directed by Sanjay Khan, is a typical reminder of the roles Bob Christo played in Bollywood cinema. A civil engineer by profession, Bob came to meet Parveen Babi in Mumbai for a personal reason. We don't know what it was. But we do know that he didn't go back, both for us and for the sake of Bollywood cinema.

Bob Christo got his first break as a villain magician in the film *Abdullah* (1980), directed by Sanjay Khan. Much of the action of the film revolves round Bob's prophecy made to Addullah that he was going to be killed by the Hindu boy Krishna he was rearing up just as it happened in the Mahabharata. A pious man, Abdullah later kills the magician. Bob showed promise as an actor in his first appearance. Apart from the Hindi films, Bob also acted in Tamil, Telegu, and Malayalam films. But he's more widely known for playing the typecast role of a villain's henchman, that of a British officer in pre-Independence related Hindi movies. In *Dushman*, Bob plays Sadashiv's aid with great conviction. Before this, he played with astounding brilliance the role of Simon in *Mard*, the story of the film being set in pre-Independent India. As a matter of fact, such films wouldn't have been possible without Bob's presence.

In *Mard*, Bob is in league with Kamal Kapoor (General Dyer) and Prem Chopra, playing Harry. Colonial oppression reaches its height in this film, and Bob's presence makes the theme suffocatingly convincing. Simon, the British Inspector is behind the capture of the Raja, and the film takes off from here. In *Disco Dancer*, a 1982 film, Bob plays the role of an international hit man, causing fear among the viewers.

In *Fateh* (1991) Bob plays the role of an arms dealer, probably taking the cue from *Mr. India*. The spread of terrorism in the previous decade and its dire consequences in the next makes Bob's role very convincing, probably more than it did in *Mr. India*. Starring Sanjay Dutt and Suresh Oberoi, *Fateh* is an action movie, and it moves on like a thriller after the death of the handicapped Anand. Interestingly, Paresh Rawal, who had a small stint as a baddie (Bhanu Nath) in the film *Ram Lakhan*, plays the role of Samrat, a drug mafia, in this film. Bob joins hands with Paresh, the man responsible for Anand's death.

The bald Bob Christo made an unforgettable impression in Bollywood cinema as a *gora* henchman, leaving a substantial contribution to the *empire of evil*.

Roopesh Kumar

Roopesh Kumar was already a name in the sixties. Still, his reputation as a bad man became secured after the famous *Seeta Aur Geeta*, where he plays the dangerous whip-master (Ranjeet), beating innocent Seeta (Hema Malini) mercilessly and betraying often his lecherous intention for her. Seeta is turned into a mute slave of the house. Ranjeet's villainy in this film becomes the center of action. Later Geeta, Seeta's twin, and a look-like, is mistaken to be Seeta after she leaves the house. Ranjeet comes back after his brief disappearance and takes charge of the house. But, Geeta is different: strong and stubborn. She teaches Ranjeet a lesson by paying him back in his own coin. Roopesh, bewildered for some time, ferrets out the mystery with the help of police, like Pran did in the film *Ram Aur Shyam*. *Seeta Aur Geeta* seems to have been modeled on the predecessor film that had told the story of male twins and look-alikes. The point is that Roopesh Kumar's villainy in this film and his cruel treatment of Seeta makes him a worthy successor of Pran, a major villain of Bollywood cinema.

In *The Great Gambler*, Roopesh shares the stage of action with Utpal Dutt and Prem Chopra. Still, Roopesh manages to show his relevance as Sethi, the baddie. In *Aadmi Aur Insaan* (1969), a Yash Chopra film, starring Dharmendra, Saira Banu, Feroze Khan, and Mumtaz, Roopesh Kumar, a cousin of Mumtaz in real life, plays the role of Abdul Rashid. The other films where Roopesh and Mumtaz have acted together are *Nagin*, *Maa Aur Mamta* (1970), *Dharkan* (1972), *Bandhan*, etc.

In *Dharkan*, Roopesh plays the major role of a drunkard villain and that of a killer of Deepak for the sake of usurping his property. Later Roopesh, actually Kewal Sharma, the killer of Deepak, arrives at Anandapuri, and takes over the business and the estate. He also marries Rekha (Mumtaz) and starts living a lecherous life. Helen plays Laajwanti in this film; Bindu the role of a prostitute. Deepak is reborn as Dobby D. Prasad, and finally the real villain is exposed. *Dharkan* has a good story to tell and much of the interest of the film relies heavily on the arrival of Roopesh Kumar on the scene of action. Roopesh Kumar has played baddie in many other films, like *Hum Paanch*, *Zakhmi Aurat* (1988), *Mujrim* (1989, directed by Umesh Mehra), *Paappi Devataa* (1995), and so on. However brief his appearances, like it was on many occasions, Roopesh Kumar has proved again and again that he too has something to add to the villain's domain.

The list goes endless. One should say with humility that the inexhaustible resources of Bollywood cinema and its villains do hardly allow a quick once-over. There are many other henchmen who have added in some way or other to the villains' empire right through the forties till now. There are Madan Puri (the underworld don in *Deewar*), Kamal Kapoor (*Don*, for example), Pinchoo Kapoor, Om Shivpuri (the mastermind of the underworld in *Don*, again), and so on. Goga Kapoor plays a crucial role in the 1990 *Agneepath* as Kancha Cheena's henchman in tarnishing the image of the school-master, and driving out his family in utter humiliation from Mandwa village. The film couldn't have taken off in the true sense without him. Tinnu Anand plays the role of a chorus in guiding the audience response to the tragic death of the schoolmaster and his family's eviction. What has not been noticed is that even here both Tinnu and Goga are obversely related to one another, one doing good, and the other bad. The result is that both help in channelizing the emotions of the audience. The *Agneepath* of 1990, often hailed as a classic (not without reasons), left a layer of suggestions and motifs underneath the events.

Finally, there is Gulshan Grover, playing the henchman and villain in many films, and receiving the Filmfare Best Villain Award for the film *Sir* in 1994. In *Sir* Gulshan plays Chhapan Tikli, a ganglord, taking on another gangster, Paresh Rawal. *Sir* is a Mahesh Bhatt film. The hero is Amar Verma (Naseeruddin Shah), a goody college teacher. However, the main subject is the confrontation between the two ganglords and its effect on others. In *Mohra* (1994), Gulshan plays the role of Tyson, being an associate of the main villain Naseeruddin Shah, playing Mr Zindal in this film, and staying undetected till the end of the film.

We should pay our gratitude to all these men, embellishing the canvas of evil in Bollywood cinema and bringing the good in sharper focus.

7

Those Dreadful Men

*L*et's have a beginning at the beginning. Many actors have essayed villains in Bollywood cinema in some capacity or other. The villains discussed here are so rich in their dimensions that any account of them is bound to be incomplete. The actors playing the mighty personalities of Bollywood cinema are certainly going to be remembered along with our heroes and heroines. One-time romantic hero Raj Babbar occasionally switched over to playing the roles of villains. The film *Indian*, where he plays Sunny Deol's father-in-law, provides an example. Bollywood has presented a bevy of stars over the decades to boast of. And, mind you, one meets with this rich abundance in spite of the fact that these people stood marooned by the image they created for themselves, and fought bravely against the limitations imposed on them, especially during the fifties and sixties.

The richness of actors in Bollywood cinema is shown by the men playing villains, one taking over from the other as the decades rolled on. First it was Yakub and then it was Kanhaiyalal. Then, Pran came on the scene, and he was soon followed by Ajit, Amjad, Prem Chopra, Ranjeet, Sadhashiv Amrapurkar, Amrish Puri, and so on. Pran was an old-timer, playing the role of villains in the fifties and sixties; then came Amjad Khan at a very crucial phase. He made such a lasting image playing Gabbar Singh in *Sholay* that many thought of using him again more or less in the same image. But, Amjad himself couldn't beat his previous feat. Movie awards for villains weren't introduced at the time, and it wasn't much of a vogue to award someone playing a dacoit or a bad man by the government. People have been instinctively drawn to the world of the so-called glamor of actors and actresses. Magazines talk about the latest gossip in "tinsel" town, making the hype, which, nowadays, is also part of the show and business. Thus, Amjad Khan receives an award for the best supporting actor for playing a good role in *Yarana* (1985), though none for playing Mongal Singh in *Parvarish*. Similarly, Prem Chopra hasn't been recognized for playing the memorable role of Harry in the film *Mard*, though he got the Filmfare Award for playing a treacherous friend in *Do Anjaane* (1976).

The Indian tradition of distinguishing between the good and the bad is so much a foregone conclusion that those playing sinister roles are seldom recognized. Remember Pran was booed whenever he walked down the streets of Bombay. We've been swayed so much by an actor's persona that we can't distinguish it from the person playing it. This shouldn't be, however, considered a drawback or blemish, since popular arts thrive, as Bollywood cinema has over the years, when it is helped by a little gullibility of the public.

Whether honored or booed, these lion-hearted men went on playing villains from one decade to another, keeping the show alive and vibrant. After Emergency, Pran left the show, as it became dominated by politician villains in the next decade. Amrish Puri later took over to play the terrorist villain according to the changes in the sociopolitical scenario. Down the seventies, Ranjeet played villains more authentically, showing his own dynamics. The film space was densely packed by *bad* men right from the beginning.

Interestingly, all of these actors showed the phases of transition in the sociopolitical scenario faithfully, as if the names were enough to suggest the mood of a decade. There has been abundance in the other genres of acting also, those playing the comic roles, for example. If it is Johnny Walker at a certain point of time, then it is Johnny Lever the next, intercepted in the middle by Asit Sen, Satish Shah, Annu Kapoor, and others. Finally, of course, the heroes, entertaining the audience: Raj Kapoor, Dilip Kumar, Rajesh Khanna, Shammi Kapoor Amitabh, Anil Kapoor, Shah Rukh, Salman, Amir Khan, and so on. It's a little unfortunate though that the heroes always hogged the headlines of film journals and magazines, not the villains. Only recently have they been mentioned in reviews and blurbs. Importantly, this too may be the consequence of the overall squalor of our time, the way we are now intimidated by terrorists and scams of all kinds. Anything related to popular art quickly responds to changes and developments in the sociopolitical scenario.

The following pages make a humble effort to remember some of the unsung *heroes* of Bollywood cinema. One cannot do any justice to the versatility of these acting personalities, nor can it be exhaustive by any account. Since we dealt with Kanhaiyalal playing the notorious Lala in a previous chapter of this book, let's begin this study with Ajit.

Ajit Khan

Ajit is the screen name of Hamid Ali Khan. This great actor, noted for his excellent dialog delivery, passed away in 1998 due to a cardiac arrest. The lion's heart ("*Sara sheher mujhe lion ke naam se janta hai*"—film *Kalicharan*) stopped beating all of a sudden, though the man and his works continue to move us. Prem Chopra and Ajit, appearing together in films like *Jugnu* (1973), *Chhupa Rustam* (1973), and *Ram Balram*, shared a common passion of reciting Urdu *shairi* in and outside the sets. Like Chopra, Ajit too was an amiable man, who loved making jokes and laughing with all he came in contact with.

This feature of making himself appear pleasing made Ajit speak with a nasal drawl in films, giving it a comical touch. Within the film text, it sent chills to those who heard him, especially his henchmen. Many of them were Christians, like Robert, Peter, Michael, and so on. Ajit's golden period in playing villains was the seventies. In the mid-seventies alone, Ajit played the grotesquely macabre villain in over 57 films. Before playing the villain, Ajit had made his niche as an actor, playing the second lead in films, like in *Mughal-e-Azam* (1960) and *Naya Daur*. As mentioned before, Ajit's possibility of playing the villain in future was suggested by *Naya Daur*, where he betrays his friend, the hero.

From *Zanjeer* on, Ajit didn't look back. This film showed that a new villain was on the scene to use and exploit the sociopolitical uncertainties of the time. In keeping with the trend, Ajit played the smuggler villain with great élan. It should be noted that *Zanjeer* not only set the ball rolling for Amitabh Bachchan, the superstar of the decade, but it also signaled the shaping of a new villain who could be unusually calm and arrogant while facing the hero. Ajit's casual way of replenishing the glass of whisky for himself and his adversary was something new at the time.

In *Kalicharan*, playing Din Dayal, Ajit shows how a whole world of effects could be achivevd by doing restrained acting before the camera. No fuss, no excitement: only eyes and voice. He does so in the oddest of occasions when, to his utter disbelief, he discovers his adversary to be still alive although he'd sent him to the graveyard. Ajit actually faces a look-alike of the hero (Shatrughan Sinha) who rants before him. Din Dayal plays his role with dignity and composure. Later, he finds out the mystery, like all villains do, not excluding even a completely recent villain like Arjun Rampal in *Om Shanti Om*. But, in *Kalicharan*, it's not the case of reincarnation. It is, on the other hand, the case of a look-alike that brings a criminal and a goon on the scene. This has been a familiar scenario.

Ajit's great capacity to perform and his lion-hearted zeal to stick to his job is best seen in *Des Pardes* (1978), where Ajit shares the frames along with Amjad and Prem Chopra. Still Ajit, playing Gurnam in this film, a Navketan production, gives a gritty performance. It isn't easy to carry the stamp of authority and stomp when an actor in his time is surrounded by such greats as Pran, Prem Chopra, Amjad Khan, and later Amrish Puri. Ajit's performance as Seth Chandulal in *Gangster* is awe-inspiring. He rapes a tribal girl with the menace that perfectly goes with the mayhem of the legal system prevalent during the nineties. He's genuinely puzzled with the good intentions of his younger son. Is he his son's father, really? It was possibly a bit difficult for a villain of the seventies and eighties to get himself acclimatized to the sociopolitical degeneration of the nineties. After all, Ajit had started his innings with promise in the fifties, though he'd appeared in many other roles before that. By the nineties, Ajit became a veteran guy in the profession. Still, Ajit had no problems, since he had found his inspiration in Mona Darling. That kept him glued to his task. Every successful man is said to have a woman behind him.

Pran Krishan Sikand

Pran played the major villains in the fifties and sixties till there came a period when, with the change of time, he decided to play character roles.

The film *Upkaar* (1967) is often cited as a turning point in his career, though in *Andha Kanoon* Pran again plays the villain. *Zanjeer*, *Dharam Veer*, and *Don* show how well Pran excelled in his new persona.

In *Munimji* (1955) and *Chori Chori* (1956), both released in the mid-fifties, Pran is seen as the savior of preserving evil. *Madhumati* shows Pran as a dangerous, lecherous villain, having a gun in hand, probably being an inspiration to Prem Chopra, and later Ranjeet. He plays the role with ease and confidence, often using sneers and smirks. In *Madhumati*, Pran intimidates by a special style of walking into the frame. This is true about his first appearance in the film as well as his hiding behind the tree when he watches Madhu, waiting to meet the hero.

A large part of the sixties, till Nehru's death in 1964, was dominated by hopes generated by the previous decade. Playing a powerful villain in *Ram Aur Shyam* that coincides with Mrs Indira Gandhi's victory and promise for reviving the economy, Pran still manages to look threatening. In the end, he shows his repentance and becomes united with his wife. This is, as we said before, in conformity with villains returning to their folds in the sixties. So, Pran had to play his role according to the restrictions imposed on him by the sociopolitical environment of the time. Still, Pran transcended the limitations by using his voice and gestures. The whipping scene at the in-laws' house is an example. Similarly, Pran looks enormously threatening in the godown scene where he forces Ram to sign the property in his favor. Raising his eyebrows or making a flinch in movement, Pran shows his anger and displeasure effortlessly. Remember his performance in films where he operates as a feigned lover, thwarting the interest of the hero, Shammi Kapoor.

In *Jis Desh Mein Ganga Behti Hai*, discussed before, Pran plays Raka with appalling ebullience, especially towards the end of the film. To convey the proper emotion wasn't easy, because Raka is skeptical about following Raju's advice of laying down arms. At the same time, he knows that it is the end of the game, since the dacoits are being surrounded by the police. He is afraid of going to the gallows and, being a breaker of law, he doesn't have any faith in the system. Nor can he hope, at that phase of social transition, that anyone is going to bail him out and destroy the evidence of his criminal activities, as it happens again and again in the eighties (*Akhri Raasta*). Second, Raka is alienated from the gang, since others have decided to give up and surrender. This inconclusive state of mind gives Raka the apoplexy, and Pran brilliantly conveys this by a mere smirk of his lips.

Going out in characters is sometimes a useful preparation of actors rather than getting confined to rehearsal rooms and studios. Technical help and other niceties weren't much available when Pran was playing his roles. But, he weighed every emotion succinctly and conveyed them accordingly. Out in the world, an actor may perceive his role, feeling as if he were some other than himself. Charleston Heston, for example, looked upon himself as a cavalryman, and he was so adept at his role that people didn't realize he was acting. Simply walking as someone else brings an actor nearer to the role he's playing.

In *Zanjeer*, Pran plays Sher Khan, a man of the underworld. He speaks throughout the film in a different jerky voice, making every articulation very self-assuring and confident, so unlike that of *Madhu-mati*, for example. The fact that Sher Khan never takes back his words is suggested by Pran's articulation in this film. This is great achievement; the Pran magic, to be fair enough, occasionally takes the audience empathy away from the hero (Amitabh Bachchan). Watch any scene occupied by both Sher Khan and Vijay. It's Khan, who envelops the frame, winning much of the kudos. Who can forget Pran's superb lip sync and dance to the tune "Yaari Hai Imaan Mera" that became an instant hit though it wasn't from the lips of the hero. In *Don*, Pran takes his cue from *Zanjeer*.

Pran played villains very strongly in the sixties. *Madhumati*, discussed in a previous chapter, showed the possibility. His golden period as the menacing villain was films in which he paired with Shammi Kapoor. Pran troubled the other heroes also, like Jay Mukherjee, in *Love in Tokyo* (1966) and Dilip Kumar in *Dil Diya Dard Liya* (1966), where Pran plays the dangerous Ramesh, bearing jealousy and hatred for Shankar (Dilip Kumar) and putting a kibosh to his love for Roopa, Ramesh's sister. The scene where he throws Shankar off the cliff shows Pran at his menacing best. Pran works out every emotion meticulously.

Like it happened in the Shammi films, Pran's claim as a suitor on a foreign land is denied in *Love in Tokyo*. Although Asha's (Asha Parekh) uncle wants Asha to marry Pran, Asha goes away with Ashok. This motif is taken in *An Evening in Paris*. In *Love in Tokyo*, Pran shows his anger with vehemence in the scene where he chases Ashok with his car and runs him down. This scene, showing Pran's awesome hatred as a villain, can be compared to when he beats the innocent Ram in the film *Ram Aur Shyam*. Add to this list *Bluff Master* and *Brahmachari*, one from the early sixties, and another from down the decade. It cannot be denied that Pran was a smart debonair villain of his class, having the looks of a hero. This sets him apart from some of his contemporaries, and later Ranjeet, because Ranjeet too shares Pran's overruling passion, switching over to hectic actions. But, there the similarity ends. Ranjeet and others couldn't claim the hand of the heroine like Pran did. And, this ability puts him in a distinctive place in the sixties where he ruins the possibility of the hero again and again by running after the heroine. Pran plays villain with authority and conviction, using his charms and, on many occasions he is able to dupe the audience by making them believe that his is a rightful claim.

Pran could say with relish, "*Well, guy, if you're a bluff-master, then let me love too and have my share.*"

Amjad Khan

"*Tumne suna maine kya kaha?*" Gabbar says to Jai in *Sholay* with a mocking politeness. Yet, it spits (Gabbar does spit often) on all polite expressions of the world. At this moment, Gabbar is on top, having his adversaries trapped in Ramgad village. He has ridden into the village to avenge the insult of Kalia and his men who were sent back by Thakur Baldev without giving them food grains. Gabbar heard from Kalia that there were two gunmen responsible for their disgraceful exit. He sees before him one, cowering. Where's the other one? Gabbar wants the two men to apologize to him before the villagers so that they don't again show the temerity of refusing his men. Thakur and the villagers must serve him as before. Amjad's sinister smile shows his pride and satisfaction, and the drop-a-pin quietness of the scene adds to his stature.

Amjad, as everyone knows, was a new entrant to the glamor world. The scene that shows the villain of the decade for the first time in the valley is memorable. The camera shows his feet stomping about; then it rolls up to show the person. The valley around is silent with panic, since they know that Gabbar is in a furious mood. It is then that Gabbar speaks; actually he rants that ricochet off the valley. Amjad draws all the attention, using the camera space brilliantly. His voice matches with his gait and appearance. This sets the tone of the film, all that *Sholay* was about. Before this, we saw enough of the heroes, engaged in acts of purloining. This is another instance of how much this film is dominated by the villain, nearly swallowing the rollicking heroes.

"*Pura mitti mein.*" Gabbar abuses Kalia and others later in the scene for tarnishing his image as a terror to the villagers. He delivers the word "*pura*" in a style of his own, lengthening the sound, and lacing it with a jerk. Amjad had perceived his role well, and he knew what was wanted of him in the situation. By and large, *Sholay* is not just the film of the decade; it's also the film of the century. Everything sailed through Amjad Khan, who made his maiden appearance as momentous and distinguished as anyone playing the hero for the first time. *Sholay*, after all, was Amjad's first major billing, though he'd made several appearances in films before this. *Sholay*, reportedly, was titled earlier *Angaaray*. Much of the *angaar* (fire) had to be released by Amjad himself, and *Sholay* can rightly be described as an instance of Amjad's volcanic eruption. A great actor, astounding and brilliant. Surprisingly, Amjad gets the Filmfare Award for playing the best supporting actor in *Sholay*. Many excellent villains of previous decades missed the award because it was instituted since 1992 for playing the best negative roles.

There was a time in Bollywood when Marlon Brando was occasionally mentioned in connection with Dev Anand's style of acting. Brando was known to be a follower of "method" acting. Incidentally, Brando is Prem Chopra's favorite actor, Dilip Kumar being the other one. It is difficult to identify with precision the exact points of difference between "method" acting and "English" acting, since "English" acting is not known to have been a consciously developed system. In the thirties, all three famous books of Stanislavsky were published. They were used for framing theories about acting technique. Still, it'd be incredulous to believe that an actor first reads a book on acting and then goes to the set to demonstrate what he's learnt. Brian Bates suggests that non-method actors are not likely to follow any rigid system. Bates finds Marlon Brando's idea of walking past a telephone booth and observing what the author is doing with his elbows disconcerting. Bates quotes Brando saying:

I could sit all day in the Optimo Cigar Store telephone booth on 42nd Street and just watch the people pass by.... Human behavior has always fascinated me. Actors have to know how much spit you've got in your mouth and where the weight of your elbows is.[1]

What Brando says about observing people out in the street makes a good option for any budding actor. Many Bollywood actors, in some moments of their lives, are likely to have done this. Those, playing villains, must have taken their inspiration from people they saw around them or read about in magazines and newspapers. Amjad's absolutely natural and convincing performance in *Sholay* bears testimony to the fact that he'd read his role in the script, in books, and out in the street—in real-life situations. Interestingly, Amjad's name for playing Gabbar Singh was suggested to the Sippy brothers by Salim Khan. Amjad prepared himself for playing the fierce dacoit's role by reading diligently *Abhishapth Chambal*, a well-documented book on Chambal dacoits written by Tarun Kumar Bhaduri, actress Jaya Bhadhuri's father. The preparation that went behind is important to remember in the present context. Mention should also be made of another popular line mouthed by Amjad in *Sholay*, "*Arre o Samba, kitne aadmi the?*"

In *Des Pardes*, Amjad looks a fierce villain on a foreign land, though he works actually as Ajit's henchman. Later, Amjad played character roles too, like he did in *Laawaris* and *Yarana*, making his presence felt very strongly. By doing so, Amjad followed both Pran and Amrish Puri. After *Sholay*, Amjad again takes on Sanjeev Kumar, this time on a chessboard, in Satyajit Ray's *Shatranj Ke Khiladi* (1977).

Amjad was the son of the legendary actor Jayant and was a theater actor before he came to films. In view of our examples of his acting in *Sholay*, Amjad's training as a man of the stage acquires greater significance. Three years after *Sholay*, in *Muqaddar Ka Sikandar*, Amjad played the role of Dilawar with memorable gusto. He passed away early, at the age of 51 in 1992.

Amrish Puri

Amrish Puri failed a screen test in 1954 for becoming a Bollywood hero at the age of 22 (born 1932). That turned out to be a great failure, since we would have missed otherwise an actor of distinguished cult who spelt out over-the-top villainy in new terms. Amrish Puri benefited from the degenerating social scenario of the eighties and nineties. Associated with the theater movement of the sixties, especially with such noted playwrights as Satyadev Dubey and Girish Karnad, Amrish Puri found his niche as an actor of enormous possibilities, behaving before the camera with great assurance. His performances at the Prithvi theater were much talked about, bringing him the Sangeet Natak Academy Award in 1979. Amrish Puri's failure to become a hero on screen made him symbolically suited to take arms against the heroes with greater gusto and retaliate against a previous disappointment in personal life. Madan Puri, who essayed villains in Bollywood cinema, was his elder brother.

With Puri, evil was let loose. He was seen in *Ram Balram* and *Dostana*, grooming as a villain, and before that in *Nishant*. He begins looking far more sinister down the eighties, as the muddy ambience of the hour suited the political-terrorist villain. His versatility as an actor is shown by his marvelous rendering of some character roles in *Virasat* (1997), *Chachi 420*, and the NRI father in *Dilwale Dulhania Le Jayenge*. Still, he played the diabolical Thakur in *Karan Arjun* down the nineties with incredible flair and competence, sharing the platform with Ranjeet. How well Puri switched over to playing different roles!

Amrish Puri possessed a sonorous in-depth voice which he used brilliantly (stage experience becoming handy), playing the fiendish militant Isaq Khan in the film *The Hero: Love Story of a Spy* or the abnormal sexist in *Koyla* (1997), not to speak of the outrageous Mogambo in *Mr. India*. Talking about the last, one should note how Puri changes his voice in this film to conform to the narrative's fantasy mode. It's no longer the familiar in-depth tone, but a mixture of orotund grandiloquence and waggish banality that sounds striking because of the pitch in which the volcanic laughs and speeches are delivered. The famous refrain "*Mogambo khush hua*," delivered in different pitches, altering the time of articulation, is a proof of Puri's ability to use his voice in accordance with the demands of the narrative. This is astounding brilliance.

When Mogambo's men start firing indiscriminately in *Mr. India*, Mogambo, for a moment, catches a fleeting glimpse of his adversary in red light. This turns out to be an end of Mr India operating unseen, and brings in Arun Verma, the yokel-hero, on the scene. Arun is forced to make a fight of his own in the final sequence of the film. As the wayward gunfire creates panic and disruption in the grandiloquent courtroom of Mogambo, Puri shows his physical agility by swooping down on the floor, and doing a somersault. He yells, "Stop! Stop! Stop!" This brilliantly conveys the villain's desperation and determination to get hold of his enemy at any cost. With Amrish Puri every role is a challenge, and he plays it merrily, gravely, sadistically, and menacingly, as the occasions demand. In *The Hero: Love Story of a Spy*, Puri uses his voice modulation with astounding effect in the carriage scene where he confronts the hero. Playing Isaq Khan, the terrorist villain, who's on hunt for the atomic formula, Puri envelops the entire film space no matter where he's operating from, be it Pakistan, the border of India, or Canada. His tenacity, perseverance, and faith in his agenda of terror are all writ on the face. Riding on the blessings of the time, Puri becomes indistinguishable from the character he plays in this movie.

Or watch, for that matter, the Chief Minister (CM) of Mumbai, giving interview on television. Dressed in dhoti-kurta, a scarf round his neck, the Chief Minister (Amrish Puri) in *Nayak: The Real Hero* (2001) looks frightfully convincing. He knows what he's up to, wrecking the happiness of people through the camouflage of social welfare measures. Talking to the journalist (Anil Kapoor), the CM doesn't follow the word *tankha*, but responds to the word *salary*, though he has a disliking of the English language. As the interviewer goes on asking a series of unpleasant questions, Puri signals him to stop and goes down for the glass of water kept on a stool. This too is brilliantly done, perfectly in tune with the situation. Acting is always nourished by details, and Amrish Puri was a master of using them, bringing in improvisations.

There's another. During the interview, the belligerent minister throws a challenge at the young interviewer, inviting him to assume his office for a day. Puri snaps his fingers; once, twice, thrice, throwing the challenge. This is also an instance of great acting. The Constitution, the CM assures, has provision for it. The scene speaks beyond the frame, embellished by Amrish Puri's star persona. He knows how gestures, apparently insignificant, should be handled before the camera with stunning effect.

In films like *Andha Kanoon, Shahenshah*, and *Ganga Jamuna Saraswati* (1988), Amrish Puri plays the villain with equal flair and roundedness, taking on the great Amitabh Bachchan again and again.

These two, significantly, haven't appeared in many films. Prem Chopra, on the other hand, has taken on the superstar more frequently. It is, however, a little sad that Puri, although nominated for the Filmfare Best Villain Award on at least four occasions, never managed to reach the final round. He got, however, the Filmfare Award as the best supporting actor more than once.

Prem Chopra

In the film *Aanchal* (1980), directed by Anil Ganguly, Rajesh Khanna (playing Shambhu) proudly tells his friend Jagan (played by Prem Chopra): *"Prem Chopra naam hai mera."* The cue was supplied by Chopra himself in *Bobby*, a Raj Kapoor film, released in 1973: *"Prem naam hai mera ... Prem Chopra."* Chopra says that this one-liner "went on to become so popular that on every traffic signal I had little beggar children surrounding my car, and repeating that line." Chopra agreed to play a small role in *Bobby* in recognition of his friendship with the legendary Raj Kapoor. It is also, by the way, one among his favorite films. This shows that Chopra loves to play a variety of roles, long or short, and yet he makes an impact on the audience.

Chopra is still very popular as a man, though on the screen he has managed to earn the hatred of viewers. After the success of *Teesri Manzil* and *Upkaar*, Chopra started getting an unending series of offers for playing the role of the villain. He left his job with the *Times of India*. That was the turning point for both Prem Chopra and Bollywood cinema. It's difficult now to separate the two, like when one fails to draw a line in the water of the ocean. Playing the villain, Chopra developed a style of his own as the decades rolled on. Soon, he became a cold-blooded menacing villain, a characteristically lascivious villain, like the one he played in *Daag* way back in 1973 as Dheeraj Kapoor. A well-read man, Prem Chopra has been honored both within the country and abroad.

By the seventies Rajesh Khanna had reached stardom, and down the decade Chopra also became famous. That Khanna should see himself as Prem Chopra may be viewed as a tribute to the actor who essayed villains in Bollywood cinema for most part of his career. Recently, Chopra has started taking comic and character roles. In *Aanchal*,

Khanna believes Chopra to be his friend in the above scene. In reality, Chopra puts up a camouflage and is out to ruin the happiness of the hero and his family.

Before looking back to *Aanchal*, let us remember the shy young man of Raj Khosla's famous *Do Raaste* (1969); usually known to be a "classic" (Raj Khosla's interview with Lothar Lutze, March 21, 1980). In this film, which describes the tension between traditional and western values, represented by Navendu and Birjuprasad (Chopra), Prem Chopra initially appears as one dedicated to family tradition. As the narrative moves on Chopra changes and deserts his family, provoked by his wife (Bindu). In both halves of the film, Chopra plays his role with conviction, posing a threat to the stability of the family. Using his fingers on his lips or with left hand nudging his tie, Chopra expresses his dilemma, like when his wife keeps his salary to her custody without giving it to the elder brother Navendu. At the same time, Chopra's connivance with his wife in doing the damage to the family is too clear. The underlying ambivalence of the character is brought out convincingly.

Chopra is known to have a special liking for characters having different shades and significance. Released towards the end of the sixties, and a year before the decade of seventies, *Do Raaste* is conditioned by the tremors of excitement when the opposition was acquiring teeth, and discontent within the Congress party was coming on to the surface. It was difficult to cling to traditional values. Chopra's acting conveys the dilemma of the time.

In *Aanchal*, Chopra looks distinctly poised to play the sinister villain in future. In another film of the year, *Doli*, for example, Chopra plays the lascivious villain. Once again Rajesh Khanna is the hero of the film. Chopra's eyes speak a lot in *Doli*, though he's not yet as menacing as he looks in the seventies and eighties. The villain is allowed to return to his fold. The same eyes sparkle with venom in *Trishul* (1978), where Chopra plays the bad man in the most favorable decade of villains. From the beginning, he's jealous of his boss and wants to become the second man in the company. His looks and movement in the birthday party of his boss's daughter show his mind. Chopra, playing Balwant Roy, withdraws himself from the crowd in order to overhear his boss. Balwant speaks no dialog; his gestures reveal his intention.

It's Balwant, again, who calls up Babli and tells her softly that it'd be foolish to report to the police. Chopra emits most venom when he sounds gentle. He is not a believer in rant and rave, making him different from the other actors essaying villains. When Vijay (Amitabh) meets Balwant in the underground concourse, he slaps him to answer to a previous insult. But, he doesn't stop. More slaps follow; since interest to the principal injury, Balwant reminds, has accrued: "*Thappar ke jawab, thappar ke sud.*" That's the Chopra dynamics: unforgettable. No hysterical outburst, but action; plain and simple, and yet it puts one to terrible shame, rousing self-indignation. One wonders if Chopra, as an actor, has something in common with Sadashiv Amrapurkar, who played the politician villain so successfully. *Dostana* suggests this inner chemistry.

In *Dostana*, Chopra plays the main villain Daga, leaving Amrish Puri hover in the background. He confronts the heroes, calmly, and with restraint. Aided by the sociopolitical mess of the early eighties, Daga, the smuggler, operates cunningly, causing a rift in the relationship between the heroes. To a large extent his plan succeeds, enabling Daga get the help of the lawyer hero, Ravi (Shatrughan Sinha). Chopra uses his cool calculating villainy with awesome monstrosity in this film. Inspector Shinde gives false evidence. So does Baldev Singh, the convict. Contemporary weakness in the judiciary helps the villain immensely. Having Sheetal, Ravi, and Vijay bound in his den, Chopra steals the show as Daga. When he says "*accha,*" hearing that Sheetal should be spared of the whip, Chopra is seen at his best. He uses his chin and lower lip with great effect, making each riposte sound soft; but that's enough to send a creepy sensation to those hearing him. Everyone remembers the murmuring threats of Chopra in a low bass voice. Chopra adds to it a certain humor that evenly balances his blood curdling mannerisms. The Chopra dynamics is a unique contribution to cold-blooded villainy in Bollywood cinema, unmatched till now. Danny Denzongpa often tried this, partly in *Agneepath* (1990), and more consciously in *Indian*, where he plays Shankar Singhania, a terrorist in camouflage. But Danny, a good actor for other reasons, lacks the mellifluous villainy of Prem Chopra.

"Bloody Indians," Chopra blurts, playing the blood-sucking villain in *Mard*. Playing this role might have been difficult, since the actor had to psychically transport himself to the British period when some natives played traitors. But the film shows that the trust Manmohan Desai had reposed on Chopra gave him rich dividends. The acts of simulation in the mirror scene, where Chopra shares the frame with Amitabh Bachchan, have earned the distinction of legendary acting. It's great to watch the two behave against one another from both sides of the mirror that doesn't exist at all. There's no dialog, only gestures. This is mimicry at its best, under the intoxication of *bhang*, made from Indian hemps. A whole range of emotions has been conveyed by the actors involved in the scene: surprise, stupidity, self-pity, anger, frustration, incredulity—everything following in quick succession. It's fun on the one hand and awakening to one's world on the other. Within the film reality, however, the hero isn't drunk, wanting to escape, whereas the villain, much to his disadvantage, has been forcibly put on a higher dose of *bhang*. If posterity remembers Amitabh Bachchan, it cannot forget Prem Chopra also.

Chopra continues to play the bad man in *Udaan* (1997), where he shares the dark platform with Danny Denzongpa and Dilip Tahil, troubling Rekha again, like he'd done in *Phool Bane Angaarey* (1991). As said before in a previous chapter, Chopra plays the villain down the nineties, providing commentary on the deteriorating law and legal system. His performance as Bishamber Prasad in *Phool Bane Angaarey* is a testimony of how he plays the villain with menacing relish. Chopra too considers this performance as one among his best.

It's difficult to say any last word on this great veteran actor of Bollywood cinema, for Chopra still continues in great guns, unlike others of his ilk. *Agent Vinod* rocked the theater halls on March 23, 2012. Chopra plays a ruthless villain (having also other shades in the character) in this film, running the drug trade in the Mediterranean. Directed by Sriram Raghavan and produced by Saif Ali Khan, the film hasn't found much success due to the absence of a good storyline. Chopra too dies early in the film. There're others on the queue—*Mr Tikdambaaz* and *Yaara O Yaara*—both set to release this year. That's indeed a surprise package. Maybe, it's no surprise also, since Prem Chopra shoots from inside the hole of his coat pocket, like he does in *Dostana* (discussed earlier), taking everyone unaware. Another Chopra dynamics! It is Prem Chopra who can say with pride, "*Main woh balaa hoon jo sheeshay se patthar ko tod de*" (*Souten*, 1983). Unforgettable, and one of the great lines uttered by any villain in Bollywood cinema.

Ranjeet

As an actor playing bad roles, Ranjeet has his own dynamics. He demonstrates this even when there're other villains on the scene. As years rolled on, Ranjeet's significance as a villain became more and more obvious. In *Bandhe Haath* (1973), Ranjeet had shown his dynamics facing Amitabh and ruining his interest, a feat he went on to repeat in many later films, in *Laawaris*, for example. *Bandhe Haath* showed his shaping as a villain. Remember the two fight scenes in the film, one taking place before the eyes of the Seth, and the other in Ranjeet's den. Shammu (Amitabh), now playing Deepak, stumbles into the villain's den when he's pursued by police. Ranjeet plays his role with ease, thwarting the interest of the lovers, and aspiring after the girl of the Seth, and in the process her property.

As the sociopolitical scenario became gloomy and the judiciary faltered, Ranjeet acquired greater confidence and power as a villain. Thus, in *Muqaddar Ka Sikandar*, *Laawaris*, and *Yaarana*, Ranjeet became his own self. One thing that distinguishes Ranjeet as a villain is that he plays his role ruthlessly without caring to put on a camouflage. He lacks, for example, Chopra's tact and finesse, but can be a real menace when guided into action by others. This continues till *Laawaris*. By mid-nineties, Ranjeet becomes a real threat to others in his own capacity. Another feature that distinguishes Ranjeet is that he doesn't betray any concern to be a clever manipulator, and in this sense, Ranjeet more resembles Amjad of *Des Pardes*, in particular, rather than Prem Chopra of *Dostana*, or Amrish Puri of *Ghayal*, for examples. He's what he's and can't be anyone else. In this sense, Ranjeet is a full-blooded aggressive villain. He's a bit coltish, but effective.

Muqaddar Ka Sikandar is possibly the turning point. Ranjeet shares the stage with Amjad and uses him for his purpose after watching him involved in a brawl from over the bridge. When both Amjad and Ranjeet come in touch with one another, what we have is ruthless villainy that takes no heed of niceties. Ranjeet brings his car to Amjad, allowing him to escape. He plays an important role in leading Zohra to poison herself, and informs Amjad of the incident. Later, he abducts Sikandar's sister; the film, thereafter, turns into its gory end. Ranjeet's villainy in this film provides a commentary on the system that has to sacrifice a man like Sikandar. Remarkably, the world of evil in this film is composed by an alliance between Amjad and Ranjeet. This provides a commentary on Ranjeet's villainy. He's someone who needs another of his ilk to become really venomous.

As the decades rolled on into the eighties and nineties, Ranjeet acquired greater strength, operating alone. Thus, he plays a bigger role in *Laawaris*, occupying the center stage. It's actually Mahinder (Ranjeet) who employs Hira to their farm. By doing so, Ranjeet becomes responsible for everything that later happens in the film. Mahinder is the son of Ranvir (Amjad Khan in a good role), who'd abandoned Vidya (Rakhee) when she was carrying his child. In the film, Mahinder is a lecherous villain, misdirected by Lala (Jivan). Ranjeet beats Ram Singh to satisfy his carnal desire with his sister. As the girl pleads for the life of his brother, now beaten by Mohinder's men, Ranjeet manages to get the approval of the girl and walks away with her. This is villainy and rape at its best. Later, Mohinder shifts the blame to Hira with the help of lawyer Kailash (Satyen Kappu). That completes the sequence of villainy, ugly and cruel. Ranjeet's uncanny villainy is seen again when he promises to eschew evil path and continues as before. The Ranjeet dynamics, as said before, is devoid of repentance. He isn't someone to operate in the sixties, deserving to be killed.

Karan Arjun, released a year before *Dilwale Dulhaniya Le Jayenge*, is a strong reminder of Ranjeet's black villainy. He plays the villain with such monstrosity that he's applauded by his senior partner Durjan Singh (Amrish Puri). When Durjan and his men are terrorized in the film by Vijay and Ajay, the reincarnations of Arjun and Karan from a previous life, both Puri and Ranjeet find the situation tough and agonizing. Both brothers were killed by Durjan's marauding sons. So, how could they appear now in their old appearances? This was a million dollar question. Ranjeet, playing Saxena in the film, Durjan's business partner, tries to unravel the mystery by using his daughter Sonia (Kajol) as bait. Vijay, Sonia's lover, is trapped. Sonia is imprisoned in the *haveli* for forcing a marriage with Durjan's son. Saxena, apparently, changes his mind, and pretends to help his daughter in her confinement. He asks his daughter to move out and meet her lover. The plan works for the villains. Durjan Singh is all joy. Saxena says, looking at Vijay, and the shocked Sonia: "*Log sher ka shikaar karne ke liye bakri ka istemal karte hain, maine apni beti ka kiya hai*" ("People use a goat as bait to hunt a tiger; I've my own daughter"). Durjan, all joy, admits that he'd so long

185

known himself to be a nasty treacherous villain. From now on, he's ready to accept Saxena as his superior. This is enough to suggest the diabolical villainy of Ranjeet. Saxena's cruel treatment of his daughter remains a sinister reminder that villains, although taking backstage in the middle of nineties, weren't going out of frames.

They all did this, in films after films, where the end was predictable. It's difficult to think of any other similar instances in world cinema. If the scenario of Bollywood films shows a variegated spectacle, a major portion of it is occupied by those who get the thrashing. They receive the blows, bleed, and die for the sake of enhancing the pleasure of the audience. Still, we don't love these people and wish them succeed in their *grand* efforts.

Dear readers, just pause to reflect if this is not more savage than all the offenses committed by the villains. Aren't they *more sinned against than sinning?*

Note

1. Brian Bates. *The Way of the Actor* (Boston: Shambala, 1988), 113. Marlon Brando is phenomenally known as an observer of men and details of behavior which, he thought, reveals a person's inner secrets. This is, of course, nothing particularly extraordinary. The point is that Brando followed it consciously, and executed it on the sets with unerring verisimilitude. To me, Brando is an ideal example of the Aristotelian notion of imitation in the field of performing arts. Readers interested to know more about Marlon Brando can turn to an excellent book by D. Thomas, *Brando: Portrait of the Rebel as an Artist* (London: W. H. Allen, 1973). It sketches Brando's memorable moments as well as those he'd like to forget, and reminds one of James Joyce's candid portrayal of himself in *A Portrait of the Artist as a Young Man*. Brando too had a lean period before *The Godfather*. Brando once said that when one has a successful acting career it looks like a soft easy job, but when one is unsuccessful, it looks worse than having a skin disease.

8

The Unforgettable Baddies

Shekhar, the antihero

The villains, over the years, have played many memorable roles. There might be a few more than those discussed here. Speaking about the baddies, these certainly have stayed in the minds of viewers over the past decades. Shekhar, played by Ashok Kumar in *Kismet* in pre-Independence cinema, is one such character.

Shekhar, the memorable antihero, shook the screen in 1943. As said before, antiheroes seems to have a special place in our hearts, because they take us both by surprise and pleasure, unlike the hardcore villains. This is why the "Dev noir" films, discussed previously, became instant hits. Dev went on playing the antihero for quite some time, and created his distinctive image of a screen idol that made him very popular among the masses during his time. Dev evolved a type of acting that suited his temperament. The antihero, viewed from this point of view, lies somewhere between the good and the bad, making him easily accessible to common human knowledge and experience. He's someone who, trapped by the mysterious rule of life, assumes the traits of a villain, maybe against his will, or according to some hidden inclinations of the mind, shared by many. This makes the show engrossing, making it a perfect imitation of life. The antihero offers a contrast to the good guys, singing and dancing. There may be something in us that loves to be bamboozled.

It's no surprise therefore that Shekhar (Ashok Kumar) should carry the film *Kismet* alone on his shoulders, making the film a huge success at box-office. It was a smash hit, having enjoyed a run of more than three years in Calcutta. The concept of the antihero was introduced by Gyan Mukherjee, the director of this film. It was made by those who later launched the famous Filmistan studio in Bombay. Shekhar is a pickpocket in this film, estranged from his relations. Mukherjee uses the lost-and-found theme, and by doing so, he makes a significant impact on films of the later decades.

Indrajeet, a rich man, and Shekhar's father, plays the villain in this film. Shekhar steals the necklace of Indrajeet's wife, wanting to raise funds for the treatment of Rani (Mumtaj Shanti) whom he loves. The greed of Rani's father (P. F. Pithawala) makes the girl disabled. This part of the film looks quite dark, aided by realist photography and having an expressionist undertone. Shekhar meets Rani and discusses their future plans. There are moments in this film (like in *Jaal*) when the empathy of the audience goes in favor of the antihero. But, Shekhar reminds one most poignantly of the contemporary social scenario where a young man becomes a pickpocket, a kind of hobo (later played by Raj Kapoor) in a world that takes no heed of those living outside mainstream society. Shekhar's love of Rani partly redeems his character and turns him into a hero, though his deeds attract occasional disapproval. The conflict and confusion of the antihero have been nicely communicated by Ashok Kumar. The actor's performance makes a critique of the society, though he never betrays any awareness of it. Here lies the strength of the classic portrayal of this character.

The overall realistic presentation of the film made it very popular in those days, making it look different from the other films. The sequence of the puffs of smoke, allowing Shekhar to escape after the robbery, has been handled imaginatively by the director. The smoke also suggests the symbolical disappearance of all that was previously shown in the film. Shekhar becomes restored and united with his rich father. Ashok Kumar's performance in *Kismet* might have inspired Vijay Anand to cast him in *Jewel Thief* in the post-Independence era.

Lala Sukhiram

The *Amrita Bazaar Patrika* of January 2, 1901, wrote that the moneylenders, "at least the Marwari adventurers are the products of British rule in this country." The *Kesari* of February 18, 1902 observed:

No doubt, the moneylenders have increased in number under British rule; but this is because British rule has killed indigenous industries. When national industries have become extinct, and when about forty-five crores of rupees are every year drained away to England, is it to be wondered at that the various classes of the Indian population should have no alternative open to them, but to feed upon one another?[1]

Although a span of 56 years passed between the time this was written and the sinister operation of Lala Sukhiram in *Mother India* (forgetting *Aurat* for a while), it goes without saying that Lala's exploits in the film are conditioned by a large legacy. Lala Sukhiram, another memorable villain of the late fifties, has to be understood against this background. Mehboob Khan rightly felt the pulse of the country when he brought back the moneylender villain of *Aurat* of the pre-Independence era in *Mother India*.

It's on this strength of a vast legacy that Lala threatens Birju and his mother that with the help of police, he can at any moment take over the land tilled by them. The sight of the golden crops heaped on the floor adds pathos to this haughty utterance. After Shamu loses his hands, Lala reminds him with a sinister smile: "*Kal panchayat mein toh zameen likhni padegi.*" Both police and panchayat act in connivance under Lala's instruction. Lala Sukhiram can easily murder one's sleep, and force a loving and conscientious husband leave his family for good.

Lala, looking like a wolf, puts relentless pressures on Radha to have her by any means. Kanhaiyalal plays a heinous role, something that any mother in villages may talk about while putting her child to sleep at night, like what they will do in the seventies by mentioning Gabbar Singh (Gabbar's proud testimony). No one dares to meet Lala, far from talking to him.

What are Lala's looks? He's a fox personified: having the heart of a beast, the brain of a fox, and the claws of a lion. Nargis, playing the epic role of a brave fighting mother, looms before our mind because she's confronted by a powerful villain. Along with the mother's archetypal image, Lala Sukhiram has become an iconic figure in Bollywood cinema. If you want to remember the mother, you can't forget Lala. One exists for the sake of the other, bound by a gravity of reciprocity and repulsion. Lala ambles in when he's least expected, because he's on the sly, like a snake, waiting to slither in any moment, as he does in the famous flood scene of *Mother India*, holding a lantern in hand. A widower, Lala's carnal desire makes him, by and large, a macabre figure.

When Radha, at the height of her suffering, goes to Lala's house, asking for food (*"mujhe khana de, Lala"*), the scene looks unbearable and ghastly in the context of the idealist fifties. There's no other film of the decade where the villain looks so dreadful. In answer to Radha, Lala says: *"Samajh gaya, rani, samajh gaya ... Sukhilala agar kutta bhi palega to uske gale mein sone ki zanjeer pahna dega."* This is outrageous villainy and crosses the limits of all decorum and decency one would expect from a man talking to a woman. Lala manages to reach the height of incivility. Such atrocious desire to put a gold chain round a woman's neck sounds more sinister and cantankerous than all the rants of the villains in the seventies and eighties. Lala Sukhiram looks lethal in all the frames he appears in *Mother India*.

Mr Kumar, Shekhar, and Gajendra

"If I'm a villain, you're also, my dear, a bluff-master. So, let's call it even, and enjoy the world." This witty riposte might be expected of the suave-looking Pran of the sixties, vying for the hand of the heroine. The fact that the confirmed bluff-master (Shammi Kapoor) still wins our heart is a sad reminder that the villains have hardly been taken care of by the script writers of Bollywood cinema. Indeed, Mr Kumar (Pran) looks so sleek, glossy, and well-heeled in *Bluff Master* that he fully deserves the hand of the heroine, Seema (Saira Banu). Besides, the villain has come back from London, while Ashok (Shammi Kapoor) the hero, lives in a slum. Being a trickster, the hero tells others that he stays in Taj Mahal hotel. So, it is sad that Kumar cannot walk away with the heroine in this film.

Kumar is a memorable villain of the sixties, thwarting the love interest of the hero. He's distinguished not by his rant, though Pran hardly did that as an actor playing the villain. This makes Kumar a different villain, out to expose the hero's misdeeds so that the heroine finds him attractive. Kumar never falters while exposing the hero's masquerades before all. Early in the film, Ashok bluffs a storekeeper and manages to walk away with a packet of butter. He gets hold of a camera from another shop owner in the disguise of another person. Ashok's act of pinching makes the ground strong for Kumar and turns the battle easier for this chic and snappy villain. Probably, Prem Chopra was an ideal successor to Pran, sharing and acclimatizing some of the traits of his predecessor to his own benefit.

Kumar operates like a fox, taking no chance. Never for a moment does he become overconfident in handling his adversary. At the same time, he can become arrogant and aggressive, like when he shoots the heroine's uncle and walks off with the money. Ram Kumar was chosen by Seema's father to be her future husband. Still after coming back from London, Kumar suffers the humiliation of accosting a bluff master.

Pran's rendering of Kumar keeps the audience engaged more than the hero's acts of pinching and masquerades. Shammi Kapoor, aided by the script, is always an invincible guy, especially in the sixties. In *Bluff Master*, his masquerades, carried out with the special Shammi flamboyance, help him win the heart of the audience.

Pran's prospect as a lover is no better in *An Evening in Paris*, though he's stationed in Paris to woo the heroine. Shammi Kapoor, aided by the Rafi numbers, follows the heroine. Remember the famous "Akele, Akele" number, sung by Mohammed Rafi. Still, Shekhar (Pran) confronts Sam (Shammi) with reasonable confidence and it becomes obvious from the beginning that Sam is no comparison to Shekhar, who tackles not only the hero, but also the fierce duo Jack and Jaggu. K. N. Singh, playing Jack in this film, looks menacing and that makes Shekhar's job difficult. Singh was always the sophisticated villain since the days of *Baghban*, looking suave and smart, using his eyebrows to optimum effect. So, Shekhar's encounter with Jack in this film holds much of the interest of the audience. Finally, Shekhar succeeds in wiping Jack off from the scene.

Gajendra is another powerful villain in *Ram Aur Shyam*. Released in the same year as *An Evening in Paris*, Gajendra is a coeval partner of Shekhar. Gajendra dominates the film space authentically till Shyam, the clever guy, appears on the scene. But Shyam is an outsider whereas Gajendra has all the rights to stay in the house. Gradually, he solves the mystery of the twin brothers, and exposes Shyam before all for assuming a false identity, like Kumar had done before him.

Teza, the smuggler villain

The smuggling menace of the seventies opens with Teza with astounding monstrosity. One disconcerting feature of this villain, played by Ajit with remarkable self-assurance, is that he stays calm in all circumstances. This becomes a distinguishing feature of villains who succeed him in the next decade also. Teza earns the distinction of showing to others what a villain is capable of doing in a favoutable environment. He might have taken his inspiration from another before him, Seth Dharamdas of *C.I.D.* Like Dharamdas, Teza too keeps a girl whom he lovingly calls "Mona Darling." Both Teza and Mona have become famous in Bollywood since *Zanjeer*. Yet, Teza is not someone to waste his time in meaningless romance, setting an example to a completely different kind of villain like Gabbar after him. Teza needs Mona to egg him on to his underworld activities but doesn't mind losing her any moment. This makes his character both awesome and unpredictable.

Teza shoots the boss and his wife to gain mastery over the whole gang, and later confesses his crime to Mona. The early seventies, with its deepening economic crisis and frustration, helps Teza operate with confidence in a free-for-all situation. A predominant feature of the seventies was that the smugglers, just as it happened in real-life situations, fought one another to gain control of the smuggling kingdom. After *Zanjeer*, *Deewar* continued the trend.

Teza, however, fears one in the police. It's Vijay. But Teza knows that so long as Vijay is working within the system, his hands are tied. Besides, Teza is known in society as a generous person, someone influential and respectable. Teza is a bootlegger and smuggles illicit liquor and drugs, killing many. It's due to him that Om Prakash, now a hobo, had lost his son. Since then, this man is after Teza, keeping information about his underworld activities, which he passes on to the police inspector, Vijay.

As a villain, Teza is nourished by society—its squalor, poverty, and disillusionment. *Zanjeer* truly exposes the world of smugglers and bootleggers of which Teza is the ruling monarch. Watch his composure when Vijay breaks into his den. As Teza pours whisky into his glass, his wrist shows the gold-band with the emblem of the horse—something that Vijay has been running madly after to locate and identify. He remembers the emblem, though not the man wearing it, since it is associated with the killing of his parents. Now, Vijay identifies their killer. Still, Teza makes a brave fight, alone, while Vijay is aided by Sher Khan, a man of the underworld. Teza remains a powerful villain of the seventies, inspiring awe and cruelty. When the decade finished, it was found that Teza wasn't overshadowed by the greater menace—Gabbar Singh. It is so even now.

Rama Shetty

The character of Rama Shetty in Govind Nihalani's *Ardh Satya* makes a critique of the early eighties when police weren't allowed to function. When they did, they shielded the real offender and punished the innocent, even beating someone to death in lockups. Sunny Deol, in a closed-door meeting with police officials, strongly criticizes this in the film *Indian*. In *Ardh Satya*, Rama Shetty dies, strangled by Anant, but he lives on symbolically, wrecking the psychical stability of the hero. The very fact that the hero throttles him all of a sudden shows his smoldering hatred for the villain and his disillusioned approach to life that makes no sense to him, forcing him to forget his girl, Jyotsna. Many villains were killed in the seventies and eighties, but *Ardh Satya* shows a singular instance where the killing of the villain leaves the hero hopeless and wretched. It is as if Rama Shetty wanted to be killed by the hero so that he could have the last smile. This feature makes Rama Shetty a period villain of the eighties; someone, we can't forget.

Both Shyam Benegal, by virtue of his offbeat films, and Govind Nihalani, his team-mate as a trusted cameraman in the seventies, were responsible in setting the tune of films that introduced men playing the strong villains on the screen. Shyam Benegal gave us Amrish Puri and Kulbhushan Kharbanda (*Shaan*), both of whom later attained iconic stature. Nihalani gave us two outstanding villains: Sadashiv Amrapurkar and Ashish Vidyarthi (*Drohkaal*). Rama Shetty occupies a significant position in *Ardh Satya*. In many ways, it is Shetty's film. He doesn't rant, but has his desire fulfilled. He contests the municipal election with the support of the ruling party. He's a *pukka* politician villain. There may be, as indeed there are, many politician villains; but Rama Shetty is unique. Campaigning for vote, Shetty manages to have the hero by his side, getting him to serve him. He knows the hero dislikes him. But Shetty enjoys his presence for exactly this reason. Anant hisses.

When Anant arrests Shetty's men, Shetty calmly says: "*theek kiya, apne apki duty ki.*" Now, the same police officer should do another duty of releasing Shetty's men. This is Rama Shetty. No rhetorical outburst, no anger. A simple statement, delivered with a sense of calm authority. He applauds the hero for doing something according to law and now asks him to go again by law, that is, law as Shetty understands it.

"*Kanoon ki ijazzat to honi hi chaiye,*" Shetty says. It was his men who'd attacked a constable on duty. Added to this, Shetty's own house (a typical *kothi*, actually) is a den of gambling. Police comes and goes; many officers too. They see people gamble inside, and play cards, but look amusedly at them as if they are selling wares in the market. A politician villain, Shetty is a great talker and knows how to pull strings for his benefit.

When Shetty's men create panic in a slum, teasing a girl, her brother goes to the police station to lodge a complaint. He whines his displeasure, saying, "*Chakku, chhura leke ghoomte hain… isse pehle ye sab itna nahin tha; par ab baat bahut badh gayi hai, saab.*" This statement gives testimony to the evil operation of hooligans during the eighties and later. Rama Shetty, wishing to honor law in his grotesque fashion, burns the complainant alive. Rama Shetty, as said before, is never trounced in this film; at least not in the sense that other villains are.

Shetty manages to become a friend of the poor and the starved. The hoarding up the truck, during his political campaign, says, "*Garibi ki roti, Rama Shetty.*" This is how the politician villain, having enormous influence in the corridors of power, operated in the eighties. Anant, tormented psychically by Shetty's arrogance, gets further piqued when he's not rewarded for arresting a Naxalite rebel. He beats a man to death in the police lockup. That ruins his prospect and his romance too. It's not the reward; it is actually Shetty, who stings the hero's mind. Anant is suspended from service. Haidar, his well-meaning colleague, advises him to meet Shetty.

When Anant goes to Shetty, seeking his intervention in the order of suspension, Shetty says, "*Sochna nahin, aaram se jina hai na tumko?*" Shetty's treatment of a police officer is very polite and considerate. Anant had previously beaten his son in the lockup, but the villain hadn't shown temper. Even now, he's in no mood to retaliate against Anant's previous insolence. He merely says, *"Mere bete ko peeta, peeta na? Lekin jo kiya, kanoon ke liye kiya, barabar hai"* ("You'd beaten my son, didn't you? Yet, whatever you did, you did for law. It's okay"). Shetty can do his job now. But, can Anant, being in the police, serve him till the end of his life? Thus, Shetty leads the hero to the edge of the cliff. Anant strangles Shetty, and jumps off the cliff, symbolically. Sadashiv Amrapurkar plays his role with authority and competence. Like Teza and Gabbar, Rama Shetty remains the villain of the decade along with Dr Dang and Mogambo.

Dr Dang

Subhash Ghai's *Karma* shows the emergence of the terrorist villain and remains a major film of the decade. Anupam Kher, playing Dr Dang, gives a stunning performance in the role. Like his predecessor Gabbar Singh, no prison can hold Dang in confinement longer than he wishes. He breaks out of the jail, killing many in the process. Dr Michael Dang is a typical creation of the mid-eighties, aided by the degeneration in the legal system. It was now a heyday for hooligans to whom the sky was the limit. Terrorism, by this time, had become an international phenomenon. There were two successive attempts on the life of Rajiv Gandhi. The Bofors deal gave a handle to opposition politics. The economy improved for a while, aided by the technological boom, but soon fizzled out. This was the ideal time for Dang to take control of the situation. The presence of a jailor, dedicated to his profession, makes no difference to Dr Dang, an atrocious terrorist villain.

Dang keeps a red tower in his den and smuggles weapons of the latest variety. This was the time when weapons were believed to be supplied by foreign agencies, out to disturb the peace of the country. Dr Dang boastfully says that ever since India got her independence he has been dreaming of destroying the country. He manages to kidnap the jailor's wife and have all his henchmen under control. Actually, it's not the jailor who turns the situation in favor of his team. It's Anil Kapoor, whose presence of mind turns the tide against Dang in the final sequence of the film. But, to achieve that, the hero has to fall at the feet of Dr Dang and take advantage of his complacence.

The jailor can't dare accosting Dang alone at the border. He takes as many as three men, and they're no heroes in the usual sense. They're all criminals, suffering life-term imprisonment in jail. In *Sholay*, there were two. Now there are three.

The villain's agenda is clear, and that of the jailor's too can be understood. But what about the other three? Being criminals, they've no agenda of their own against Dang. The bleak scenario of this film doesn't allow any romance to thrive in the charred hills. One hero dies (Naseeruddin Shah), carrying on the *Sholay* motif.

The supremacy of villains in the mid-seventies and the whole of the eighties are shown by the fact that the heroes are now social offenders, serving jail punishments, probably sending a signal for what is going to happen in the mid-nineties when the hero will usurp the job of villains. If in *Sholay* the heroes are ordinary pilferers, in *Karma* they're confirmed criminals. In fact, after *Karma*, the trend of the so-called hero was finished.

Mogambo

It's never possible to stare at Mogambo longer. Even Daga and Teza, Mogambo's sidekicks, don't. Arun Verma, the hero of *Mr. India* and an *aam hindustani*, looks like a moron before Mogambo. That's why Teza alone can trounce the hero when he is not armed with his father's magic wristwatch. Arun Verma, without this magic aid which he has inherited from his father, like someone getting the property as an heir, is pretty vulnerable. The scene before the sea beach is shown to suggest the gullibility of the hero, getting the merciless thrashing, and cringing like a ninny. It's also noticeable that Seema, the heroine, pays no heed to Arun Verma. On the other hand, she worships someone called the invisible Mr India. There's a touch of pathos and nullity in this romance, indicating its fragility. This is because the world is ruled by Mogambo.

The weakness of the romance also shows that the hero, behaving like an ordinary simpleton, can hardly be loved by a girl, far from taking on a mighty adversary. It also suggests that in the eighties the time of the superstar, unlike the previous decade, was gone, because the villains had grown awesome by this time. It was now the time of many different heroes like Anil Kapoor, Jackie Shroff, Sunny Deol, and others. The three Khans will be hogging the show in the nineties, and they will become distinguished by their muscles and macho excellence. As said before, the wipeout of any single superstar in the eighties makes one aware of how the villains grew stronger in the seventies, contributing to the need of a superstar for the time being. Within the decade itself, the hero felt frazzled, suggesting the ominous. Thus, Anil Kapoor, playing an ordinary hero in *Mr. India*, looked convincing in his role.

Watch Mogambo for a moment. His first entry into the frame shows him boarding down from a personal helicopter, suggesting that the villain has flown in from out of the country. He has arrived to check how his sinister activities are looked into by his men. The way Mogambo strides forward and away from us, accompanied by his volcanic peals of laughter, gives one the creeps. "*Mogambo khush hua.*" Yes, this Mogambo, this diabolical villain, becomes occasionally pleased to see his plan working well, but, occasionally. Apart from having an element of fun in it, this happy ejaculation has stayed in the mind of viewers. The fun element is the consequence of an exaggerated articulation that doesn't necessarily take away the accompanying menace. What a villain!

But, when is Mogambo pleased most? When his subordinates salute him, or when they succeed in killing innocent lives in the cities of India. Mogambo's greatest monstrosity as a villain is seen when a beautiful girl, an orphan, dies in the film due to the injury received from a bomb explosion. The presence of children not only supplements the fantasy element of *Mr. India* but it also shows the villain on an exaggerated scale. Mogambo, played brilliantly by Amrish Puri, is a proof of Bollywood's range of inventiveness. There can be many Arun Vermas, but there can't be another Mogambo.

Shekhar Kapoor's *Mr. India* is a classic film of the eighties. We have spelt out the reasons elsewhere in this villain story. Now, just one more point to add to what has gone before. Looks that we have been swayed a bit too much by the "*Mogambo khush hua*" refrain, wallowing in the fantasy and fun elements. Maybe, this time, the focus has been on the villain, but for a wrong reason altogether. *Mr. India* presented an unheroic hero and a fiendish outrageous villain to pair him off with. That the scale and the balance between the two have been maintained elusively and effortlessly speaks volumes about the directorial excellence of the film. The strength of the script and direction, aided by imaginative camera handling, and supported by brilliant acting from all, makes it a true successor to the all-time great *Sholay*. Both *Ardh Satya* and *Mr. India* are films of the eighties, because in both, villainy has been translated in new terms, verging on to black comedy and sinister fun. *Shahenshah* does it a little clumsily, simply because it wanted to show the superstar on an exaggerated scale, sidetracking the simpleton during daylight. That too is exaggerated comedy, having no other shade in it.

Kancha Cheena

We meet Kancha Cheena for the first time in *Agneepath* (1990)—the Mukul Anand film. We see him back again in the present day's terms in a totally different and mind-boggling height in Sanjay Dutt's boorish villainy in *Agneepath* (2012), directed by Karan Malhotra. When we had nearly written off the villains (wrongly perhaps), the stage of villainy in new *Agneepath* is shared by Rauf Lala to make further commentary on this hugely turbulent hour of rising prices, corruption, and scams of different kinds at the higher levels. Challenged by the equally awesome Lala, Kancha of this startlingly new version of *Agneepath* still manages to steal the show till the end, staying unforgettable in the minds of many, especially mothers in villages, towns, and cities, who might be murmuring his name for lulling their children to sleep, just as they used to during Gabbar Singh's time. We will look back to the new *Agneepath* at the end of this narrative. Meanwhile, let's look at the old Kancha Cheena, played by Danny Denzongpa.

The *Agneepath* of 1990 holds an important position in this discussion not only because it took the cue of the terrorist-politician villains of the eighties, but it also had something to say about how the villains were going to shape in the future. Kancha Cheena shows how his villainy is going to take within its fold nearly all, even an upright and honest schoolmaster like Dinanath Chauhan, living in a remote village of Maharashtra. Meeting Kancha is like entering a haunted house on the roadside. The spider net engulfs the visitor the moment the door screeches back, making agonizing cringes. As one tries to remove the web, he gets muffled by its unending stretch. This is what happens to Dinanath Chauhan in *Agneepath*.

Dinanath tries to bring electricity to a village called Mandwa and render service to the locality by teaching them moral principles of life. He tries to give lessons even to a prostitute but soon finds himself engulfed by the net we were talking about. This happens because the teacher unknowingly trespasses into the path of Kancha Cheena. Master Dinanath is lynched by the misled angry mob of Mandwa, which believes that the teacher has been sleeping in the room of the prostitute on the pretext of giving lessons. The charge is framed by Rao (Goga Kapoor) at the behest of the villain, Kancha.

Kancha wants to run his smuggling business from Mandwa, which is not far from the city of Mumbai. The banishment of Suhasini Chauhan, now a widow, from the village, accompanied by her son Vijay and daughter Siksha, makes a lasting impact on the agonized memory of the boy. He knows that his father is the victim of a conspiracy. Every look and gesture of Master Manjunath, who plays young Vijay in this film, confirms the depth of the wound the grown-up Vijay is going to bear in his psyche. This time the wound is deeper than the one Vijay bore in the film *Zanjeer*. Before Gaitonde, the Commissioner of police (played by Vikram Gokhale), asks anything, Vijay introduces himself, telling his name, the place he comes from, and his age till the hour of submitting his application. The truth is he spent his boyhood in the loving company of his father in village Mandwa, and he fondly remembers it. He remembers equally too how everyone in the village had shut his door on them after his innocent father fell into Kancha's trap. No one came to their help even for doing the last rites of his father. Vijay, the boy, carried a heavy cart all by himself, clenching his teeth, and doing the job with grit determination. This shot of the boy, pushing a cart on the uneven road of the village, comes back in the film several times. Kancha, mind you, is not yet physically present on the scene. This spells out what we call ubiquitous villainy in recent times. It is in this sense that *Agneepath* holds an important place in any study of Bollywood villains.

Without bothering to physically appear in the film at the beginning (he does only once to instruct Dinkar in Mandwa village) and still managing to hold the attention of viewers, Kancha probably suggests that villains from now on needn't always appear physically. On the other hand, he stays put in his beachfront residence, and invites the hero, his adversary, to meet him there for signing a deal between them. In *Deewar*, the hero was an underworld don, picked by Mulk Raj Dhabaria (Iftekhar) from the dockyard. That started the onset of Vijay's effort to go to the top and also his downfall. He had no score to settle on that occasion. In *Agneepath*, Vijay has a personal agenda. He wants to get back to Mandwa village and avenge the insult and humiliation of his father. Suhasini Chauhan, Vijay's mother, doesn't know this till her son dies on her lap in the final sequence of the film, bringing back the *Deewar* memory. So Vijay, reincarnated in the nineties, goes all the way to meet Kancha at his posh alfresco residence.

One critic, writing a book on Amitabh Bachchan, and spurred by the obvious intention of extolling the superstar's image (often for wrong reasons), says that Vijay in *Agneepath* is "a tired man," and that "the long dialogues ... are now short and guttural with incomplete phrases."[2] As a matter of fact, Vijay says too many words in this film. When he faces Kancha at his seaside residence, he knows he has finally got his man after a long wait of 25 years. He is both elated and cautious, because he has worked his way up the ladder to reach here. Needless to say, Vijay is also a bit perturbed, facing Kancha and, therefore, says less speech, at least on this occasion. One cannot also forget that Vijay had suffered minutes back a nasty bomb attack on his life and had to swim his way up the shore. He cannot curse the villain at this moment, since he wants to get Kancha's approval of working in Mandwa. Therefore, he speaks fewer words. It is possibly not correct to idealise Vijay's lack of speech at this moment of the film or elsewhere. This is not necessary also, since it offers an exaggerated and one-sided view of the film-text. Vijay is accosting Kancha Cheena and that too in his place. As a matter of fact, Vijay speaks throughout the film in a drawling, raspy voice in accordance with his stylish gait. He uses it before Kancha to his advantage. Besides, the "guttural" speech (though it wasn't received well by Amitabh fans) is an attempt to hide the wound borne by him within the film text, having little to do beyond it, as it probably shouldn't. The irony is that it hides quite a bit, making the speech appear slightly exaggerated.

The truth is that during the long intervening years (25, mind you), Vijay has never for a moment forgotten the humiliation of his father in Mandwa village. The shot of young Vijay, swearing to Nathu (Tinu

Anand) that one day he'd come back to the village to revenge on the wrong done to his family has been shown twice in the film. The contentions that Amitabh is a tired man, "*not of his struggles* with his fate but with trying to *talk sense to a recalcitrant world*," and that "he has to be reminded now of the war that he promised to fight,"[3] sound not only adulatory, but it is also not supported by the film text. Amitabh Bachchan is too great an actor to need such accolades.

Like any villain of the seventies, Teza of *Zanjeer*, for example, Kancha is accompanied by Shanti aka Laila, played by Archana Puram Singh. But unlike Teza, Kancha doesn't address his girl as Laila darling, showing any particular fondness for her. In keeping with our previous discussion on vamps, Laila is here only a woman, having no other identity. Kancha shares no secrets with this woman as Teza did. Kancha Cheena is different. He gets everything done by a mere flick of his finger. He's also unlike Dang, because he has no agenda to destabilize the country. He is only interested in having his *usul*, accumulating personal wealth. Nor is Kancha ever carried away by any vainglorious intention. He's a calculating villain, and, within the sociopolitical reality of the nineties, Kancha Cheena is an extension and improvement of Gabbar Singh.

Kancha warns Vijay not to trespass his path after arriving at Mandwa: "*Lekin ek baat yaad rakhna—mera raasta katne ki koshish maat karna.*" And, later, Kancha says, "*Apna usool kahta hai, har galati ke saaza maut hai, sirf maut.*" Danny Denzongpa, playing Kancha Cheena, gives a memorable performance and speaks in a particular accent and style, making pauses, as if he is weighing every speech before articulating it. This is a different Danny and his lips, as he says his words, are slightly held together. He doesn't rant. He will do so six years later, in *Ghatak*, for example, where he will be playing Katya, a tyrannical gangster. But, facing Vijay, who he knows is a veteran guy Kancha too uses restrained speech. Unfortunately, Kancha is trapped by Vijay's plan, possibly his hubris in this film. This is because he doesn't know Vijay's identity, the fact that he is the son of Dinanath, the teacher of Mandwa.

So, Kancha is taken by surprise to hear Vijay talk about Mandwa. He feels a bit amused also, but doesn't show it. Any other villain in his place might have laughed at the choice made by his adversary, rile at him, or break into huge peals of laughter. But, as said before, Kancha is different from others. One great feature of this villain is that Kancha hardly breaks into loud roars of laughter, like Mogambo, for example. That doesn't go with his plan and temperament. A calm sense of dignity never leaves Kancha. That's why Danny might have thought about his method of articulation in this film. He knew that Amitabh was a veteran guy, playing Vijay on many occasions before.

Kancha, on this occasion, makes an unforgettable delivery that will ring in the ears of many in future. Slightly amused, Kancha says, "*Mandwa mein kya milega tumhe?*" A simple, short query, asked with apparently avuncular concern. Vijay, remember, should have looked younger than Kancha, though he doesn't, unfortunately. That's, however, a different story. But, one point is true. Kancha is thoughtful about his speech in this meeting, no less than Vijay is. Minutes before this *friendly* prattle, Kancha had failed to kill Vijay by bombing the boat with the help Terelin, his henchman (Sharat Saxena). And, now, after signing the deal of friendship with Vijay, Kancha has Terelin killed by Bob Christo for failing in his mission ("*har galati ke saaza maut*"). But Kancha tells Vijay that Terelin's death is intended to be a *taufa* (gift) to Vijay, since the fool wanted to kill him. This is great piece of work and duplicity of the highest order, like Richard's wooing of Lady Anne in Shakespeare's famous play, *Richard III*.

As said before, great villains like Gabbar and Dang might have gone out of fashion during the late nineties when the dos and don'ts became blurred for the time being. But, that was actually a time when the villains from beyond the camera zone were watching with deep interest and an amused sense of pride how the heroes—those they'd fought with over the decades—were speaking their lines, and fighting their battles, though a little imperfectly and waywardly. After all, the villains are not especially suited to the task of making rollicking funs, like heroes. That's why they went underground for a while, though they surfaced occasionally to remind people that they weren't completely dead and could come back any time. This goes perfectly well with the scheme of nature in the planet we live in. So, Kancha Cheena is back again in 2012, in awesome height and dimension.

Notes

1. Bipan Chandra. *The Rise and Growth of Economic Nationalism in India* (New Delhi: Peoples' Publishers House, 1969), 469. This study, intended by Bipan

to be his PhD dissertation, was followed many years after by another excellent socio-politico-economic study *India after Independence*, published by Penguin Books India in 2000.

2. Susmita Dasgupta. 2006. *Amitabh: The Making of a Superstar* (New Delhi: Penguin Books India), 108. If it is true, as the rumor and belief then was, that Amitabh chose a different speech in *Agneepath*, having been inspired by Marlon Brando of *The Godfather* (1972) fame, who played the Don Vito Corleone in the film, then the fact is that it didn't work out. Brando in this film is the father of four children and an old man, contrasted to the Don's youngest son, Michael; now back from World War II when the film begins, and takes over the family business, shown elaborately in *The Godfather II* (1974). So, in Vijay's case in *Agneepath* (1990), this speech does hardly fit in, and cannot be empathized with even by Amitabh fans. For the interest of readers, it may be pointed out that *The Godfather III* was released in 1990. Marlon Brando didn't appear in the other two parts, although Al Pacino, playing Michael, appears in all the three parts. It is well-known that *Sarkar*, a film starring Amitabh and his son Abhishek Bachchan, is modeled for its narrative on *The Godfather*. Surprisingly, Susmita makes no mention to this film while discussing *Sarkar* in her book.

3. *Ibid.*, 108.

9

The End!

$\mathcal{H}$ad *Omkara* (2006) been made in Hollywood, it might have gone up to secure the nomination of prestigious awards. A film by Vishal Bhardwaj and intended to be an adaptation of Shakespeare's *Othello*, this film shows excellent technical expertise to claim attention. *Omkara* did, however, receive the attention of critics and others too, who care for good cinema, like Francis Ford Coppola, for example. Previously, Vishal had adopted Shakespeare's Macbeth in *Maqbool* (2003), composing the music of the film, a job done excellently by him in *Omkara* again. The photography of the film is a special treat to watch, and so is Saif Ali Khan's performance as Langda Tyagi, emulating the so-called "motiveless malignity" of Iago that expressed Shakespeare's commentary on the nature of evil on earth. Set in a village of Uttar Pradesh, the language of the film has a strong input of Khariboli dialect that causes difficulty for viewers belonging to the other regions of the country. Kareena Kapoor as Doli (Desdemona) and Ajay Devgan as Omi (Othello), a *baahubali*, actually a goon, helping Bhaisaab win the parliamentary election, give outstanding performances, supported by Vivek Oberoi, Konkona Sen Sharma, and others.

The character of Langda Tyagi, having been modeled on the wizard villain Iago, offers a strong commentary that villainy is ubiquitous, and can bounce back anytime. Vishal had the courage to end the film on a bleak note. The swing screeches along, carrying Dolly's dead innocence, while Omi lies dead on the floor. When the deception about the waistband's disappearance, a gift of Omi to Dolly, like the hanky motif in Shakespeare's play, is ferreted out, Langda gives an unforgettable helpless reaction without any sign of remorse. It is as if villainy runs so thick in the veins of Langda's blood that he can't help it. In the middle of the film, Langda openly confesses, "I'm a human after all, and a little perverted at that." This brings out the essence of Langda's villainy, making a commentary on the so-called muddle between the dos and don'ts noticed in films of the late nineties. The message is that villainy cannot be explained, like the puzzles of human nature. Omi hunts frantically after *saboot* (proof) for Doli's treachery, and Langda, wearing a plaster on the bridge of his nose, leads Omi on to a ditch of near total certainty. Both incidents form a series of effective and poignant frames that suddenly become arrested.

Indeed, it's difficult to read the human mind. It was equally difficult for Sahil (Bobby Deol) to read the mind of Isha (Kajol) in the film *Gupt*. He too, falsely implicated in a crime never committed by him and absconding from law, is after a hunt for the killer of his stepfather. Kajol, playing the role of a woman who has committed murder, bagged the Filmfare Award for playing a negative role. After the success of *Tridev* and *Mohra*, this was acclaimed to be the third blockbuster of director Rajiv Rai. Amrish Puri, playing the villain, a sexual maniac in *Koyla* that sent a reminder of *Pagal* (1940) and *Puja* of pre-Independence cinema, was a nominee for the award. Still, Puri couldn't beat Kajol. *Koyla* was produced and directed by Rakesh Roshan, who was going to make it big three years later in *Koi Mil Gaya* (2003) and *Krrish*. *Sarfarosh* treats Naseeruddin Shah as villain in the role of Gulfam Hassan, a gazal singer, trying to destabilize the country.

In fact, the list is endless, showing evil in different forms. Ashutosh Rana plays Gokul Pandit, a murderer by instinct; someone, who runs after girls in the film *Dushman* (1999). As a matter of fact, negative or villainous roles having different shades of evil in them continued to pour in the late nineties. The distinction between the dos and don'ts didn't get as much blurred as it was assumed. Sunil Shetty plays the bad man in *Dhadkan* (2000), intent on ruining the life of his previous girlfriend (Shilpa Shetty), now married. This clearly reminds one of the *Darr* motif. However, this film where Sunil plays Dev, the wounded lover, cannot shock as much, since Dev realizes his folly toward the end, and accepts another girl (Mahima Chaudhry) to finally settle with in life. But, this can also be interpreted as being a feature of the sixties when the villains returned to their folds. With the march of time, the nature and operation of villainy changed, retaining the human emotions like greed, passion, and envy unaffected. It might be that these permanent vices of human nature found some new roots to expand and engulf like an old banyan tree. So, in 2003, *Jism* came on the screen, showing Bipasha Basu in the role of a cruel woman. This film has already been discussed. Bipasha plays a strong vamp in this film, doing the job in absence of a strong villain.

After *Omkara*, we got frolicking professional show in *Om Shanti Om*, mentioned before. It is called the "red chillies" entertainment, and the film is directed by Farah Khan. Red chilli peppers were thrown before at the eyes of the villain Subedar (Naseeruddin Shah) by the women of the masala factory in *Mirch Masala* way back in 1985. The reason of mentioning this in the context of Shah Rukh's film is that the name "red chillies entertainment" could possibly suggest the promise of a different kind of entertainment where one has to expect both message and entertainment, moments of discomfiture as well as happiness. This is perfectly in tune with the Bollywood show.

Om Shanti Om doesn't offer cozy moments of respite as one would have expected. Once the new villain, Mukesh Mehra, an ambitious producer of films, enters the frame, things start looking ominous. We see Arjun Rampal, playing Mukesh in his new attire. He is soft-spoken, but arrogant, and is a hard guy. He's not ready to marry Shanti in spite of the fact that she bears his child. Later, Mukesh kills her and removes the dead body. Om, serving as a junior artist in films, cannot rescue the girl, and in the process he too is burnt to death.

Moments later, the hero is reborn to wealthy parents. He grows up to become a celebrated actor, sees Mehra, and remembers his past life. In this film, the hero is reincarnated to punish the hero. Later, he visits the same location to do a film on behalf of Mukesh Mehra. The location is charred and devastated. No one has visited it for 30 years.

Both *Madhumati* and *Karan Arjun* of the fifties and mid-nineties seem to have worked as the inspiration of *Om Shanti Om*. The villains in the previous films were Pran, Amrish Puri, and Ranjeet. Now, we have Arjun Rampal as Mukesh Mehra. Ugranarayan in *Madhumati* was a strong lascivious villain and was responsible for Madhu's death. Durjan and Saxena, aided by Durjan's wayward sons, look more menacing and atrocious (compared to *Madhumati*) in ruining the life of a woman and killing her sons mercilessly in *Karan Arjun*. Mukesh Mehra in *Om Shanti Om* destroys the dream of an actress and burns her to death. Mukesh is the new villain, operating in a completely different scenario where the villain can't be a raja (like Ugranarayan) or a thakur (like Durjan). He is, therefore, a film producer and a businessman, one who can go over to America in crisis situations. The age of computers, cellphones, and i-pods has gone into defining this new villain. He looks composed and relaxed (like the departed Ajit Khan), but doesn't confess his past crime even when he confronts Shanti's apparition. In *Madhumati*, on the other hand, Ugranarayan loses his cool, sweating heavily, and finally confesses his guilt. He is taken away by the police arriving on the spot. In *Om Shanti Om*, the hero is prevented from killing the villain by Shanti's apparition, which is a clever move of the ghost for saving Om from the gallows. This is how a modern variation of a well-known theme is shown in this film. The other implication is that Mukesh is Shanti's target and, therefore, he should meet his end by the same chandelier that played a role in her death. The chandelier is made to come down on Mukesh's head by the ghost's supernatural power. When the job is done, the ghost vanishes. The interesting point is that Sandy, a look-alike of Shanti Priya, arrives on the scene moments before the catastrophe occurs, enabling the hero to realize that the figure of Shanti Priya standing on the stairs is an apparition.

See how the villains are shown in these films, responding to the changed social scenario. They dress and appear differently and are punished in many different ways. In *Madhumati*, the villain doesn't die because it wasn't the convention of the time, while Durjan and Saxena both die in *Karan Arjun*. A rattled Durjan, after his son is killed, shoots Saxena, who cannot believe his eyes; Durjan is killed by the avenging brothers. However, both Durjan and Saxena didn't believe in the reincarnation story. To them, the brothers were just look-alikes. Similarly, in *Om Shanti Om*, Mukesh Mehra understands the game played by Om Kapoor, the lead actor of his film—the fact that Om is using a look-alike to trap him. It is only in the last moment when Shanti Priya's apparition narrates the story of how her dead body in the previous birth was removed by Mukesh that he becomes unnerved. These two instances show how the villains in the two later films have moved away from *Madhumati*.

The examples from the films of the fifties down to 2007 clearly show that there hasn't been any perceptive confusion between the dos and don'ts. Actually, we have never faltered very substantially and pathetically in distinguishing between the good and the bad. With changes in time, new people and actors (entirely new crew, in fact) arrived on the scene, wrote the scripts, and performed, judiciously avoiding in presenting the likes of Gabbar, Mogambo, and Dang. Underworld dons and criminal activities that became the trend of films in the seventies are still shown even in an otherwise romantic action film like Siddique's *Bodyguard* (2011), but in a new form. Girls are locked inside a large factory to be smuggled out of the country. That needs a bodyguard, doing wonders, as if in a fantasy. This film has, of course, not much to do with villains. But, there are people in the film to wreck the happiness of Sartaz Rana and his daughter, and that brings Lovely Singh, the bodyguard on the scene. In *Dabangg* (2010), much of the action revolves round the political rivalry between Chedi Singh and Dayal Babu. Sonu Sood as Chedi Singh, a goon, is the new villain. Interestingly, they belong to a regional party like Lok Manch, indicating how things are going on currently. This change in approach toward villains and criminal activities are best shown in *Agneepath* (2012) since it is a reworked version of the old *Agneepath* of 1990.

Let's hear Karan Johar, son of Yash Johar, the producer of the old *Agneepath*, about what the plan was and how he decided to approach the old film:

> We are adopting the film from the original but ours would be a *new age version* that would fit in well with today's time. We really hope that we are able to do justice to the original and make the remake exciting for today's generation.[1]

In another interview to the *Times of India*, Karan lamented saying that although the old *Agneepath* garnered plenty of critical acclaim, Yash Johar was disillusioned with its commercial success and wanted always to remake it. "*Agneepath* broke my father's heart," the news ran with this caption.[2]

It is reported that the old *Agneepath*, after its release, was a failure both at the box-office and among the critics, some of whom thought that the dialogs often veered to melodrama and that the audience didn't accept the change made by Amitabh in his voice, inspired by Marlon Brando's *Godfather*. This has already been discussed. Somehow, as time rolled on, the merit of the film was appreciated in some corners, often acclaiming it as a classic. Looking back sometimes does a world of good, enabling one to see the subtleties unnoticed before.

In spite of this, Karan's confession reveals two points that can be mentioned in passing here. One major source of trouble with the old *Agneepath* might have been that it was focused on Amitabh Bachchan, the thematic source being a line from his father's poetry. It was intended to bring back his superstar image which, at least during the time, was on decline. Films like *Shahenshah*, *Ganga Jamuna Saraswati*, both 1988 films, and *Main Azad Hoon*, *Toofan*, and *Jadugaar*, all 1989 experiments, couldn't be said to have done anything very spectacular at the box-office. *Agneepath* followed these five weak efforts of the previous two years, riding on the superstar image of Amitabh Bachchan of the seventies in the changed environment of the nineties. This was in spite of the fact that new heroes and villains were by this time found around the scene.

With this exaggerated focus on Vijay Dinanath Chauhan, Kancha Cheena and the essentially blood-chilling violence of the theme was forgotten. The much-celebrated role of Krishnan Iyer M. A., perfomed so well by Mithun Chakraborty, gained an importance and attention that moved, ironically enough, well over the roles of both Vijay and Kancha. Iyer's comic extravaganza, however brilliantly done, didn't fit in well with the theme. Added to this, Amitabh was aging, and his makeshift romance with Madhavi further killed the possibility of box-office response. Amitabh had to fight with some stumbling blocks, apart from his adversary Kancha Cheena—Krishan Iyer, Madhavi, and his new articulation. Had the focus been on the villain and the fundamentally gory subject of the film, making it relevant to the nineties, then the box-office response could have been different.

Look at the remake now. Karan Johar said in an interview with *Filmfare* that he wanted the protagonist to be "more of an underdog," and the antagonist "more flamboyant and menacing" than the older version. This changed the entire perspective, making the role of Iyer look convincingly dispensable. Priyanka Chopra, playing the heroine with the Bollywood hunk Hrithik Roshan, and dying in the film, is a further throw-up on the excessively pumped-up revenge and violence story. Look at a minor addition made by Karan Malhotra. Banwarilal Taneja, playing Kancha's father in the new version, is a fabulous invention to highlight Kancha's villainy because he pushes the old man violently down the stairs. Many wouldn't notice it, taking into consideration the glossy fringe-lines of this film—its score by Ajay Gogavale and Atul Gogavale, and the brilliant edit by Akiv

Ali, shown especially in the fight scenes, and the "Chikni Chameli" dance carnival. But, this musical bonanza too has been integrated into the theme. During the dance sequence, Kancha asks Vijay, "Want to sell the right of Mumbai. Must be asking something in exchange." "Mandwa," says Vijay, unperturbed. Again, "Seeing you I remember something, though don't know exactly," Kancha says, groping down the memory lane. This is good work.

Look now at the major addition, noticed by all—that of Rauf Lala. Rishi Kapoor, initially surprised when he was offered the role, makes most of it, giving a mega performance. The result of all these is that on the opening day, the new version of *Agneepath* ended fetching in ₹217.6 million, breaking the record of what looked like a Mount Everest collection of *Bodyguard* on day one of its release. The fact may be that the old *Agneepath*, directed by Mukul Anand, had in it the elements of a classic, some latent, and others bouncing out occasionally on to the surface. The only thing is that the perspective was a little confused, and not worked out well to become a strong full-fledged narrative. The story was written by Santosh Saroj, who is scarcely mentioned now.

The *Agneepath* of 2012 is all about villainy, carried out on a staggeringly breathless pace, shooting Sanjay Dutt to the top of the charts. It was amazing to see Sanjay often clapped by the audience in the theater, justifying the relevance of a strong villain for box-office crack in the present sociopolitical scenario. Kancha of Mandwa brings back successfully the unforgotten image of Gabbar Singh of Ramgad village. Like Gabbar, Kancha too operates from Mandwa. Hrithik Roshan, playing Vijay Dinanath Chauhan, was the calling card of Karan Malhotra but as an underdog, mind you. And, as an underdog, Vijay is more a part of a large community in Mumbai where he lives as Rauf Lala's henchman, though with more sense of honor and pride than are usually given to a villain's henchman. As a necessary part of this design, the character of nurse Mary Matthew, played by Madhavi in the old film, has been done away with, replaced by Kaali Gawde (Priyanka Chopra), a girl who gabbles all the time, reminding one of Basanti in *Sholay*. This community of people welcomes Shiksha, Vijay's sister, when she goes to meet her brother. The new-age hero looks like an ordinary guy, belonging to his community. Hrithik has eked out what at this moment seems to be a lifetime achievement in his career even when one remembers his previous feats. The bouts of acting before